BALANCED
APOLOGETICS

BALANCED APOLOGETICS

*Using Evidences
and Presuppositions
in Defense of the Faith*

Ronald B.
MAYERS

kregel
PUBLICATIONS

Grand Rapids, MI 49501

Balanced Apologetics: Using Evidences and Presuppositions in Defense of the Faith

Copyright © 1984 by Ronald B. Mayers

Published by Kregel Publications, a division of Kregel, Inc., P.O. Box 2607, Grand Rapids, MI 49501. Kregel Publications provides trusted, biblical publications for Christian growth and service. Your comments and suggestions are valued.

Cover design: Alan G. Hartman

Library of Congress Cataloging-in-Publication Data
Mayers, Ronald B.
    [Both/and: a balanced apologetic]
    Balanced apologetics / by Ronald B. Mayers.
    Originally published: Chicago, Ill.: Moody Press, 1984.
    Includes bibliographical references and index.
        p.   cm.
    1. Apologetics I. Title.
BT1102.M39   1996   239—dc20   95-50964
                                                              CIP

ISBN 0-8254-3265-0

        1 2 3 4 5 printing / year 00 99 98 97 96

Printed in the United States of America

This book is presented to my past students who have helpfully instructed me, and my future students who will doubtless guide me into additional insights.

CONTENTS

FOREWORD

The end of the twentieth century finds Christian apologetics at a low ebb. At best it has fought bravely and well over isolated issues, to shore them up against devastating attacks from modern unbelief. At worst it has degenerated into haggling over secondary or tertiary issues not of crucial importance for orthodox and biblical faith. At times it has wandered off into false issues of its own making. No apologist of the stature of James Orr, Abraham Kuyper, or Benjamin B. Warfield has appeared at the end of the twentieth century.

Christian apologetics has, indeed, suffered severe blows at the hands of avowed opponents of evangelical Christian faith. Hume and Kant led the way. Contemporary naturalistic thought has all but pushed any biblical apologetics out of serious consideration by the intelligentsia. Among defenders of the Christian faith, not a few capitulated to the antiapologetic trend of the times and argued for a fideism that could stand independent of rational supports.

The greatest of these modern fideists was the Swiss theologian, Karl Barth. Drawing his earliest insights from Sören Kierkegaard, Barth employed logic and his brilliant reasoning powers to show that faith needed no support from reason. And he almost won the day. Even many evangelicals, who at many points retained serious reservations about Barth's theology, accepted his basic fideism.

In the face of this double onslaught from outright unbelief and fideism, evangelical apologetics failed to unite before the common enemy. It drifted into a continual skirmish between "presuppositionalists" and "evidentialists" (some rationalist, some empirical, and some eclectic). No dominant school of apologetics rose to withstand the enemy of faith. The best minds among evangelical apologists seemed to be consumed with this internecine struggle within their own ranks. No time or energy was left to engage the real enemy, modern unbelief.

In this volume, Ronald B. Mayers seeks to present a contemporary apologetic that encompasses the best of both contending parties. He calls his apologetics *Both/And*, because he sees the valid insights of both positions. He seeks to set forth a system that he hopes will satisfy many in both camps and provide evangelicals with a stronger, more vigorous, and more biblical apologetic than it has seen in many a day.

In achieving his goal, Professor Mayers displays a mastery of the history of apologetic thought. As a modern eclectic, he draws freely from every tradition. Throughout he hews rigorously to the biblical data.

We believe he has done an excellent job. Whether contemporary "presuppositionalists" or "evidentialists" will agree that he has bridged the gulf between them, we leave to them to say.

We commend Professor Mayers for his serious endeavor to present a biblically-grounded and rationally coherent defense of Christian faith.

Kenneth Kantzer

PREFACE

For at least the past fifty years, the evangelical world has been torn between two apologetic approaches: evidentialism and presuppositionalism. This book is an attempt to bring both methodologies under one roof, as uncomfortable as this may be to the purist of either school. The defense of the truth of Christianity cannot be adequately accomplished by half-a-loaf. Both creation and historic revelation demand an a priori presuppositionalism due to the priority of God and His initiatives of creation and special revelation in the midst of history, but they also demand an a posteriori evidentialism to properly acknowledge the existence of man, made in God's image, as well as the objective factuality of God's activity in history. This attempt to emphasize both approaches results in a dialectical third option: Both/And, A Balanced Apologetic.

This book has been brewing for a number of years, and special thanks must be extended to the trustees of the Grand Rapids Baptist College and Seminary for the semester sabbatical that provided the opportunity to write. My thanks too to the only typist who could have deciphered my handwritten manuscript — my beloved wife, Charlotte.

1

WHAT IS APOLOGETICS?

"King Agrippa, I consider myself fortunate to stand before you today as I make my defense [*apologeisthai*] against all the accusations of the Jews" (Acts 26:2). This was not Paul's first defense (apology). He had made an emotional and personal apology (*apologias*) in the Aramaic language to the Jews of Jerusalem from the steps of the Roman barracks (Acts 22:1). Additional public defenses of the charges against him, as well as an argued presentation of the truth of the Christian sect within Judaism, had been accomplished before the Roman procurators, Felix and Festus (Acts 24:10; 25:8). Paul now stood before Agrippa at the request of Festus, who needed expert Jewish counsel as to the charges against Paul so that he might forward such charges to the Emperor. As Festus stated, "I think it is unreasonable to send on a prisoner without specifying the charges against him" (Acts 25:27). That passage will be examined in chapter 6 in terms of its overall significance for New Testament apologetics.

My purpose here is simply to note the biblical precedent of an argued, rational *apology* of the truth of Christianity. These

celebrated apologies before Felix, Festus, and Agrippa, similar
to Socrates' apologies 450 years previously, were new to Paul in
their personal and legal import, but they were not new in style
and methodology. In Thessalonica (Acts 17:2), Athens (Acts
17:17), Corinth (Acts 18:4), and Ephesus (Acts 19:8), Paul had
reasoned with and persuaded (*dialegomenos*) men in Jewish
synagogues of the fulfillment of the Scriptures and the reality
of the kingdom of God as seen in the life of Jesus, the Christ.
Dialegomenos, "to argue," was used of Greek logicians and philosophers who practiced dialectic—a give-and-take that
attempted to elicit conclusions by discussion. Luke uses the
additional word *peithō* for Paul's activity at Corinth (Acts 18:4)
and Ephesus (19:8), thus emphasizing Paul's attempt to persuade his listeners of the truth of his reasoning. It is interesting
to note that the same type of reasoning (*peithomenou*) failed
when used by Paul's friends to try to dissuade him from going
to Jerusalem (21:14).[1] Though evangelism, or even apologetics,
is not merely argument, these passages point out that rational,
logical, and factual preaching is not an illegitimate enterprise,
but a biblical mandate reinforced by New Testament example.
When obstinate minds would not be persuaded, and in fact
spoke maliciously of "the Way," Paul spoke daily for two years
in the lecture hall of Tyrannus (19:9).[2] Such an endeavor
required, as Michael Green notes, "the full range of intellectual
equipment." Green points out that it was not as if "Paul or anyone else in the early Christian mission thought that argument
alone could bring anyone into the kingdom of God. But they
knew that it could break down barriers which obstructed men's
vision of the moral and existential choice which faced them, of
whether to respond to Christ or not."[3]

1. Henry George Liddell and Robert Scott, *A Greek-English Lexicon*, pp. 400, 1353.
2. Whether Tyrannus was a living philosopher in Ephesus, or a school that continued after his death like the Academy of Plato or the Lyceum of Aristotle,
   we do not know. Ramsay notes that Paul's lectures were probably held "after
   business hours," which in Ionian cities was after the fifth hour (11:00 A.M.),
   so for two years Paul continued such teaching with the result that many in
   the Roman province of Asia heard the gospel. (William M. Ramsay, *St. Paul,
   The Traveler and Roman Citizen*, p. 271).
3. Michael Green, *Evangelism in the Early Church*, p. 206.

Proclamation and defense (apology) of the good news of the gospel go hand-in-hand. Though Paul may have had only a few occasions when he offered a formal apology before a court, the Greek word from which *apologetics* is derived is found frequently in the New Testament. *Apologia* originally referred to a defendant's reply to the speech of the prosecution, as in Plato's record of Socrates' *Apology*. Though we need not be particularly concerned with its noun or verbal usage, it is worthwhile to see how the word was used by Jesus, by Paul, and by Peter. In Luke 12:11-12 (and similarly in 21:14) Jesus says, "Do not worry about how you will defend yourselves or what you will say, for the Holy Spirit will teach you at that time what you should say."

Paul experienced that first-hand, especially before the Jerusalem mob that had been—just prior to his rescue by soldiers—trying to kill him (Acts 21:31–22:29). Paul had the words to say to give a rational (if not premeditated) verbal defense as promised by Jesus to His disciples. Paul may also have been meditating on Jesus' words when he wrote the Philippian letter, provided that Luke's gospel was written this early.[4] Whatever the case, Paul is thankful for the active partnership of the Philippian Christians in his work (1:7) of defending (*apologia*) and establishing (*bebaiōsis*) the good news (*euaggeliou*). Even though there are some who preach Christ but are envious of and even rivals of Paul, Paul rejoices that others preach in love, recognizing that his imprisonment is due to his defense of the gospel (1:16). Elsewhere Paul uses this same word to defend his apostleship (1 Cor. 9:3; 2 Cor. 12:19; see also Acts 19:33; 25:16; 26:1, 24; 2 Tim. 4:16 for related usages of this word).

Two somewhat different and more personal, but insightful, uses of this key word are found in Romans 2:15 and 2 Corinthians 7:11. In the latter passage Paul pictures the eager attempt by the Corinthians to clear (*apologian*) themselves of their sins through repentance. Similarly, the indictment of the Gentiles by the law written on their conscience either accuses or excuses

4. In 1 Timothy 5:18, Paul claims the Scriptures say "The worker deserves his wages." This is found only in Luke 10:7. It is possible that Luke was written in the interim between the Philippian prison experience and the subsequent pastorals—perhaps from Rome.

(defends/*apologoumenōn*) them. The law written on man's heart is thus both prosecutor and defense attorney. The suggestion of the latter, though it may be more personal rationalization than an actual declaration of innocence, might quite properly be translated "excusing" (KJV) rather than "defending" (NIV). Although the idea of being released or excused from a wrongful accusation is legitimate, the more popular connotation of an apology's being an admission of error or discourtesy accompanied by expressions of regret can be seen in this passage. This is not, however, the primary meaning of *apologia* in the Greek culture, its almost exclusive New Testament usage, or its explicit meaning as a theological discipline—all of these being centered on the more basic meaning of "defense" as pointed out above.

One final verse must be noted. Although apologetics is an academic discipline for those called particularly to the gospel ministry, it is *not exclusively a professional concern*. The ability to give an answer is necessary for every Christian. Peter writes,

> But in your hearts set apart Christ as Lord. Always be prepared to give an answer to everyone who asks you to give the reason for the hope that you have. But do this with gentleness and respect. (1 Pet. 3:15)

This is perhaps the single most important verse for apologetics. The Greek word for "answer" is *apologia*. But this answer is not a formal one in a court of law. It is the convinced answer of a true believer, not a task reserved only for apostle or prophet. Green states that the evangelism of the first two hundred years of Christianity was a spontaneous lay activity.[5] Fred Howe is wrong in contending that "a clear distinction between biblical *witness* and biblical *defense* must be made and maintained."[6] Rather, Cornelius Van Til is correct in asserting that there is no "sharp distinction between witnessing to and defending the Christian faith" since "we do not really witness to Christ adequately unless we set forth the significance of his person and

5. Green, pp. 207-26, 274.
6. Frederic Howe, "Kerygma and Apologia," in *Jerusalem and Athens*, ed. E. R. Greehan, pp. 446-47.

work *for all men and for the whole of their culture.*"[7] This is what is expected of all who obey the imperative to sanctify (set apart) Christ as Lord. It is necessary that *every* believer be able and prepared to answer all who make inquiry of his faith.

This text does more than provide a universal assignment for all Christians. It also notes the prerequisite for carrying out the assignment and the attitude the Christian must have to do so successfully. An egotistic and immature Christian is bound to fail as he will not meet the prerequisite of putting one's self-hood (heart) under the lordship of Christ by taking "captive every thought to make it obedient to Christ" (2 Cor. 10:5). This is not an intellectual and/or voluntaristic exercise. It is a spiritual discipleship. For there to be lordship, there must also be servanthood. *Servant* translates into loving obedience as the expression of biblical faith. *Loving obedience* presents an attractive and magnetic life-style. Such a life-style provokes questions to answer and opportunities to witness. This answering witness must be both kind and respectful. Kindness or "gentleness" (1 Pet. 3:15) is part of the fruit of the Spirit (Gal. 5:22-23). It connotes a humble attitude that is tactful and does not demean the humanity of the questioner. *Phobos,* translated "respect," is also translated "fear" (KJV) and is the source of our English word *phobia* (Matt. 14:26; 28:4; Luke 1:12, 65; 2:9; Rom. 3:18). Though "respect" is doubtless a possible translation given both the context and the subject under discussion, "fear" may be more appropriate as one's realization of the awesomeness of the responsibility of an adequate answer comes home. This is no classroom examination where the difference between an *A* and a *C* has no absolute or eternal significance. This is a life-and-death matter. Paul sees a close relationship between the ideas of fearing God and persuading men, since knowing "what it is to fear the Lord, we try to persuade men" (2 Cor. 5:11).

Evangelistic work in the early centuries was based upon the church's feeling of responsibility and concern for others, as well as a very real sense of gratitude toward God.[8] Of course, our sense of responsibility must be mitigated by the knowledge that

---

7. Ibid., p. 452.
8. Green, pp. 236-55.

our answers to the questions of others are not the only factors in their response toward salvation. But at the same time the Holy Spirit does use our testimony and apology as evidence in which to ground His conviction. Our answers must provide credible evidence in an intelligent fashion so that the question-er can make a meaningful response to the conviction of sin, righteousness, and judgment by the Holy Spirit (John 16:9-11). As Clark Pinnock writes: "We are instruments in the Spirit's grasp. Without His skill no lasting results ensue. Yet, paradoxi-cally, without the preacher and apologist the Spirit is silent (Rom. 10:14-17). The inner event originates with us. We are commanded to perform *our* task, not His, and this task includes Christian apologetics."[9]

PHILOSOPHICAL TASK

Apologetics is often identified with theological prolegomena and/or philosophy of religion. It is neither. Prolegomena deals with the presuppositions and philosophical methodology of various theological systems.[10] It is the manner in which the the-ologian takes the data of revelation and systematically presents it to his contemporary world. Thus the framework and vocabu-lary of a twentieth century Paul Tillich is vastly different from that of the nineteenth century theologian Charles Hodge. Phi-losophy of religion is also not identical with apologetics, since the latter attempts to demonstrate the truthfulness of the reli-gion it deals with, but philosophy of religion is usually accom-plished oblivious to the theological claims of the world's great religions. Nevertheless, philosophical concepts and orientations will greatly determine one's apologetic framework. This is espe-cially true for orthodox Christians who fervently believe in the truthfulness of their theological assertions and structure their apologetic frameworks around the dictates of their theological statements regarding God and fallen man's rational possibility of knowing God.

What then is the relationship of Christian theology to apolo-getics? Here there is little agreement. Roman Catholicism, con-

---

9. Clark Pinnock, *Set Forth Your Case*, p. 17.
10. A very helpful book dealing with prolegomena issues is Winfried Corduan, *Handmaid to Theology*

trary to the above, identifies apologetics as prolegomena through the arguments for God's existence. This is usually called natural theology as its formulations are made by man's reason observing the reality and design of the natural world. Catholicism contends, following Thomas Aquinas, that although the doctrine of creation is known only by biblical revelation, natural theology logically proves the existence of God by arguments that are ultimately intelligible only on the basis of the fact of creation. Thus for Catholicism natural theology proves the existence of God by logical arguments that are supposedly independent of special revelation though rooted in a doctrine of creation. In this manner an a posteriori natural theology goes far beyond the intuitive or innate musings of an a priori natural revelation that is concomitant with the actuality of creation. Philosophical argumentation, labeled apologetics, becomes the foundation and thus the necessary prolegomena for systematic theology. Knowledge of God's existence is seen as a task for reason, not the gracious and loving historical initiative of the personal and living God.

Many Protestants have followed that approach, including some evangelicals. The approach predominanted until David Hume and Immanuel Kant raised serious objections in the eighteenth century. If such reasoning from effect to cause, particular to universal, man to God, is not logically compelling, then seemingly the purpose of apologetics is not to *prove* God's existence, nor build a philosophical foundation for systematic theology. Rather theology must begin with the revelation of God per se, assuming God as Scripture does. The theologian's task is then to systematize this revelation, providing a Christian understanding of reality that is interrelated with data from all avenues of life. The Christian theologian assumes the truth of the Christian faith. Theological prolegomena does not attempt to verify this world view, rather, its job is to clarify the underlying assumptions of the theologian in regard to both epistemology and metaphysics and to delineate any indications of favoritism for one philosophical school over another, for example, Berkeleyian idealism or Kierkegaardian existentialism.

Apologetics, therefore, is here understood to be the attempt to demonstrate the *truthfulness* of Christianity and the viability of the theologian's assumptions. Apologetics is comprehensive. It is more than simply Christian evidences of fulfilled prophecy or scientific evidence for creationism. As this book will demonstrate, it is a philosophical, theological, and historical demonstration of the truthfulness of Christianity. Christian apologetics is never independent of Christian theology. Theology is primary. Theology must shape and mold the intellectual framework and the practical methodology of the apologist. However, in apologetics, theology is not presented prior to any demonstration of the truthfulness of that theology to the unbeliever. The non-Christian is obviously not a Christian theologian. He must not be expected to interpret data of history, psychology, and morality—let alone revelation and miracle—as does the Christian. But *he must be given such data as the Christian interprets it*, or he is not being witnessed to by a Christian. This is the dilemma of Christian witness and apologetics. The Christian can never agree for a moment to a non-theistic interpretation of reality, and the naturalistic unbeliever of our generation finds it intellectually impossible to comprehend the supernatural and transcendent dimension of reality.[11] This hermeneutical gap will most likely grow wider, and thus the apologetic link will have to be more intimate and personal. Francis Schaeffer calls this link pre-evangelism, and it will have to be chronologically longer and more painstaking than in previous generations when a Christian mentality was pervasive and even non-Christians believed in the realities of God and personal immortality. But as Paul concluded with Agrippa "short time or long—I pray God that not only you but all who are listening to me today may become what I am" (Acts 26:29).

Apologetics, as it deals with historical, philosophical, and theological constructs and data, has numerous functions. Its primary responsibility, as previously stated, is to demonstrate the truth claims of Christianity. The practices and rites of any religion are meaningful and significant only if the supporting world view behind those practices is true. Of course, all religions claim such truth, though truth itself may be differently

---

11. See Ronald Mayers, *Religious Ministry in a Trancendentless Culture* for an analysis and critique of the three primary intellectual determinants of this culture.

understood between the East and West. Truth in the East is One and must be understood as transcontradiction rather than noncontradiction as in Western thought. Though Christianity is in one sense originally Eastern, or at least mideastern, it in no manner or form makes reality ultimately "one," which would make truth ultimately one. For Christianity, creation demands dialectic, and therefore noncontradiction must be the criterion of truthfulness. (This will be fully developed and clarified in chapter 3—"Epistemological Determinations.") This concern with truth and the establishment of such through both deductive and inductive logic demands that Christian apologetics rub shoulders with philosophy. The men who have most concerned themselves with theories of truth and the rigors of logic are philosophers. Christianity cannot appeal to empirical data of what has been seen and heard (e.g., 1 John 1:1-4) without struggling with the philosophical problems of knowledge inherent in all sensation-based theories of knowledge. Likewise, apologists who argue more deductively from the given of revelation cannot violate the rules of logic first delineated and clarified by Aristotle. This is not to turn Christianity over to human judgment, or apologetics over to philosophy. It is to recognize that the Christian apologist *must* enter the domains of philosophy if he is to seriously and honestly face the question of truth.

Christian apologetics also strives for "wholism," meaning that Christianity has a distinctive perspective on all facets of reality. Christianity is concerned not only with eternity, but with time; not only with evangelism, but with ethics; and not only with proper worship, but with vocational choices as well. This is what the German philosophers call a *Weltanschauung*. It is what Christian colleges describe in their school catalogs as a Christian world-and-life view. It is not the task of the apologist alone. It is a task that demands that every Christian bring his expertise and insights to bear on particular issues and problems in a distinctively Christian way. It is the task of the theologian to so interpret the doctrines of Scripture that they provide overarching parameters to contemporary Christian thought and penetrating insights to detailed specifics. It means that the Christian doctrine of man's dignity and depravity throws more light on the totality of man than any humanistic philosophy or biologized psychology. It means that the normative ethical standards of holy Scripture cannot be dismissed as easily as secularism asserts. Rather, these standards provide the only alternative to man's preying on man, since man is no longer seen as impersonal nature but as a divine creation made in the distinct image of a holy and infinite God who is cognizant of man's treatment of man. It is the apologist's task to attempt to correlate these contributions and show Christianity's power of interpretation to both her followers and her gainsayers.

Lastly, Christian apologetics is also polemics. Though this is not the prime function of this book, it is nevertheless an important function of apologetics. Irenaeus wrote his vast tome *Against Heresies* to refute Gnosticism. Origen squared off with his pagan counterpart Celsus on numerous occasions. Perhaps Paul's most frequent exhortation in the Pastorals is for Timothy and Titus not only to differentiate between truth and error, but to refute the latter tactfully but directly (1 Tim. 6:20-21; 2 Tim. 2:24-26; Titus 1:9-11). This cannot be done without some knowledge of the teachings of those opposed to sound doctrine, including theoretical and practical implications of the philosophies to be refuted. Paul obviously practiced what he preached as seen by his experience on Mars Hill and the two years lecturing in the school of Tyrannus. But if this is the case—and it is—what can be said of the usual evangelical tirade against philosophy based on Paul's statement:

> See to it that no one takes you captive through hollow and deceptive philosophy, which depends on human tradition and the basic principles of this world rather than on Christ. (Col. 2:8; cf. 1 Cor. 1:18-25)

Perhaps no other verse is more popular to the anti-intellectual vein of evangelical Christianity. However, it must be understood in the context of Paul's polemic against a Gnostic-like movement within the church at Colosse (note Col. 2:16-23). Paul is warning the Colossians against a specific heresy that threatened to carry them off "as so much booty."[12] Philosophy is not absolutely condemned, though it is certainly disparaged

12. J. B. Lightfoot, *Saint Paul's Epistles to the Colossians and to Philemon*, p. 178.

in its Colossian manifestation and in its inherent tendency to be humanistic and cosmological rather than Christocentric and theological. Philosophy that begins only with temporal horizons and self-deduced wisdom can never know the eternal and infinite God (1 Cor. 1:21). In regard to assumptions and content, Christianity is anti-philosophy as this verse makes abundantly clear. However, there is a Christian philosophy, an outlook upon life as well as a way to live. This outlook is not discovered by man but given to man. It is God-initiated through historical and propositional revelation, culminating in the revelation or uncovering of God Himself in Jesus Christ.

That is the very point of 1 Corinthians 1:18-25. The center of the Christian "philosophy" is Christ and His cross, a stumbling block to Jews and outright foolishness to Greeks. (The issue of the stumbling block will be taken up in chapter 6.) Why the gospel is "foolishness" to the Greek mind can be better understood by looking at the dominant philosophies of the first century (note the philosophers with Paul on Mars Hill in Acts 17:18). Epicureanism was not atheistic, but it was ardently naturalistic. This paradoxical arrangement came about because Epicurus (341-270 B.C.) believed that man's primary problem was the double fear of the gods and of punishment after death. His solution was simple: deny the interest of the Greek gods in the affairs of men and adopt an atomistic metaphysics that denies any possibility of human immortality. The atoms naturally dissipate at death, leaving no possibility of consciousness, and thus the fear of punishment after death is absolutely irrational. Obviously, resurrection would not be a possibility.

Stoics were nearly as adamant about the infeasibility of resurrection in their world view. First of all, they were ultimately pantheistic, and thus man was one with God be He dead or alive. More important, Stoicism was deterministic, even fatalistic, and the very concept of resurrection seemed to deny the finality of death. Thus either world view made a doctrine of resurrection not only untenable, but moronic—which is what the Greek word for foolishness in the text of 1 Corinthians literally means. When the continuing influence of the Platonic Academy, denying the very reality of the body, is added to the Epicurean and Stoic philosophies, it is considerably easier to understand why the Greek mind found the gospel to be unintelligible and "foolish." Nevertheless, some Greeks, like some Jews who previously stumbled, believed and experienced the power of God in salvation.

The rejection of Gnostic philosophy by Paul in the letter to the Colossians, the rejection of the gospel by Greek philosophers at Athens, and the statement to that effect in 1 Corinthians, raises a perennial question for the Christian apologist. Since we have already argued that because Christianity makes truth-claims the apologist for Christianity cannot avoid philosophic issues and inquiries, what then is to be the relationship between Christianity and philosophy? The early church was as divided as we are today over this issue. Tertullian's (c. 160-220) famous statement that "Jerusalem has nothing to do with Athens" reflects the feelings of one extreme, that philosophy is the source of all heresy and must be rejected out-of-hand. Justin Martyr (100-165), Clement of Alexandria (c. 150-203), and Origen (c. 185-254) echo the opposite extreme, whereby philosophy was seen as preparatory for Christian teaching, especially through the *logos* doctrine. Some even saw Socrates and Plato as Christians. Obviously, neither extreme is correct and the issue must be resolved by a mediating stance. Tertullian is correct in that the *Weltanschauung* of the two cities is mutually exclusive—revelation will never be the same as human wisdom. Nevertheless, as Justin, Clement, and Origen realized, explication of biblical revelation must use the same linguistic structures and logical categories as the philosophers. The content and starting point are different. The reasoning process, possibilities of language, and logical principles are actually gifts to man from the God whose image man expresses by these very gifts. Content and form, then, are two different things. Christian apologists must use the same forms as all thinkers. But they must be constantly alert to the tendency to adopt any philosophical framework in which the gospel is made to fit and reside (e.g. Bultmannian existentialism). Lightfoot properly grasped the tension that must be maintained between the philosophic extremes when he stated that "St. Paul's speech at Athens, on the only occasion when he is known to have been brought into direct personal contact with Greek philosophers (Acts 17:18), shows that his sympathies would have been at least as much with Clement's representations as with Tertullian's."[13]

This question concerning the proper role of philosophy in theology and apologetics is the first of seven salient questions with which all Christian apologists must struggle. Some of these questions are philosophical in nature. Others are historical or theological, though usually with philosophical implications. Perhaps the most important question is simply a facet of the philosophy/Christianity problem: what are the respective roles of, and extent of interdependence between, reason and faith? Closely connected with this question are questions relating to the intellectual and volitional affects of sin, the viability of the theistic arguments, and the very difficult issue as to the plausibility of any type of communication between the believer and unbeliever. Two final questions relate to the place of probability and historical evidences in Christian argumentation and the degree of objective and subjective certainty one may personally have of the truth of Christianity. The actual questions that will be discussed throughout this book are as follows:

- What is the role of philosophy in Christian theology and apologetics?
- How are faith and reason related?
- Of what significance is the doctrine of sin for Christian apologetics?
- Do the theistic proofs have any worth for convincing the unbeliever?
- To what extent may a believer and unbeliever form a shared point of contact on common ground?
- Are historical Christian evidences important, or even possible, as evidence for the unbeliever?
- What degree of certainty is there in the truthfulness of Christianity?

Each of these seven questions will be dealt with at some length in regard to the possible apologetic systems discussed in chapter 5. But first attention must be turned to the ontological,

13. Ibid., p. 179.

epistemological, and biblical theological constructs that determine the foundations for any apologetic superstructure.

2

Ontological Foundations

Ontology is a word made up of two words in Greek: *on*, meaning "being" or "is-ness," and *logos*, meaning "word" or "study of." Therefore, ontology is the study of being or of what is. There is no more fundamental study. Ontology is basic, bottom line. What does it mean to say that something is or exists? Why does existence exist? Or expressed classically, Why is there something rather than nothing?

These questions have attracted Western philosophers for at least the past 2,500 years. Probably the best-known sentence in this regard is by Parmenides (515-440 B.C.), "Being is, non-Being is not." One cannot say that "nothing is." Only that which is, is. For Parmenides this meant that Being is static and therefore all possibility of change is denied. Permanence was reality and reality was permanent.

But surely things do change! Heraclitus (530-470 B.C.), with whom Parmenides was arguing, had stated the extreme opposite, "all is flux" (*panta rhei*). Heraclitus had anchored his judgments in sense experience contrary to Parmenides' use of logic. One of Heraclitus's disciples, Cratylus, a supposed teacher of Plato, took an absolute vow of silence because truth was impossible to express in language as the reality changed even in the time it took to verbalize a description or interpretation.

These ancient extremes are alive today. The Platonic tradition, kept alive in various idealisms down through the centuries, emphasizes that the *real*, the truly permanent, is nonempirical. The things of this world are temporal and not ultimately real or truly knowable. The reality of this world may appear to be irrefutably real, but it is actually only the appearance of that which is the truly real; the truly real being "the Good" or "the Absolute." It is interesting to note that the ultimate is always assumed *to be*. For instance, Plato writes of the Good: "the objects of knowledge not only derive from the good the gift of being known, but are further endowed by it with a real and essential existence; though the good, far from being identical with real existence, actually transcends it in dignity and power."[1] Though Platonism may be thought of as dualistic, most idealisms are monistic, similar to Eastern thought, in emphasizing that physical aspects of this world are actually only manifestations of *Being itself*—the Absolute or One. On the bottom line everything is as it always has been. Permanence reigns!

There is another track, of course, in Western philosophy. Aristotle brought the transempirical ideas (forms) of Plato "down" to this world. Philosophic reason, stripped of sensation, was no longer the path to knowledge. The real was no longer ideal but natural. Thus man's empirical and scientific investigation of this world was the path to both reality and truth. There was no transcendent reality. Actualities of forms (ideas) and possibilities of matter were one. Reality was inherently change as the chain of being made clear. Only the natural was real.

Here then are the two primary philosophic perspectives and schools: Rationalistic Idealisms and Empirical Naturalisms. Idealisms stress the unity and permanence of truth at the expense of the real diversity and change of the parts, or in philosophic jargon, the particulars. Naturalisms rightly stress the diversity and development of these particulars but always at the expense of unified knowability and thus inherently breed skepticism. It is the perennial philosophic problem of Being

1. T. V. Smith, ed., *From Thales to Plato*, p. 258.

versus Becoming, or from a slightly different perspective, the One versus the Many. These are *not* artificial or idle problems. Philosophers have not been needlessly chasing their tails as many believe. Obviously reality is unified and permanent, and at the same time diverse and changing. The difference between the two philosophic traditions is simply an emphasis in direction, that is, what one chooses to look at and emphasize. But we cannot choose between these emphases. Both are correct! Reality is avowedly *both* permanent *and* changing, *both* eternal Being *and* temporal becoming. Reality is *both* the inherently self-existing and absolute spirit Being of God *and* the acquired existence and relative natural being of creation. Reality, then, is not monistic for the Christian, be it a nonmaterial, spiritualistic idealism or a materialistic naturalism. Either orientation has a truncated view of reality. Both perspectives are reductionist, i.e., they reduce reality either to ideas or nature, spirit or body. To have either to the exclusion of the other is to have only half a loaf. Reality as we now (postcreation) know it is *both* Spirit *and* Nature. Philosophers know this dualistic dialectic intimately as *man alone is spirit/nature.* An "extrovertive" philosopher sees nature enveloping and conditioning him until the point of final change—death. The "introvertive" philosopher sees himself as more than nature—as spirit, idea, and mind—and thus has inklings of that which transcends nature and is therefore permanent. Both are correct! Man alone partakes of both dimensions. He is changing nature and in light of nature's present condition is doomed to natural death. He is dependent but permanent spirit and is thus made to have a relationship with the independent and permanent Spirit. But before we proceed with man, the acme of terrestrial being, we must begin with the acme of celestial Being: God.

GOD: INTRINSIC BEING

Note the preceding difference in speaking of God as *Being* and man as *being.* This is not a spelling or typographical error. Christianity recognizes two dimensions of that which now is: God who is independent and absolute, having necessary existence, and who therefore *is* Being, or *the* ontological foundation; and created reality that is dependent and relative having

only *contingent* being, but nevertheless an ontological foundation. Philosophy has usually stressed one of these dimensions,
but not both. Thus no idealism or naturalism is ever satisfactory. Although either may be internally self-consistent, one is still
conscious that "there is more" and that real adequacy and true
satisfaction are missing. Christianity affirms both. Thus no
Christian apologetic framework can—in practice—forget that
there is *both* God *and* creation.

God and creation solve more than the intellectual problems
of permanence and change. Obviously, God alone is permanent
and this is what is meant when God is defined theologically as
immutable. Infinite perfection cannot change. Such immutabil-
ity, however, does not suggest a static God who cannot relate to
His creatures. It simply affirms the unchanging perfection of
His character and essence. But such infinite perfection does
demand eternal existence, for God can be neither unlimited nor
immutable if once He did not exist. If once there *was* nothing,
nothing there will always *be* since *ex nihilo nihil fit* ("out of
nothing, nothing comes"). (Parmenides did correctly note the
limitations of language.) God thus must be and is "intrinsic
Being."

How do we think, let alone speak, of "intrinsic Being"? Everything we know from a this-worldly perspective can either
exist or not exist and thus being is extrinsic and not intrinsic.
The Bible itself nowhere directly confronts this issue but simply
assumes the existence of God. Moses asked for identification
and was matter of factly met with "I am who I am. This is what
you are to say to the Israelites: 'I AM has sent me to you' " (Ex.
3:14). But to use the identical words "I am" of myself is not to
express the same meaning. There is, as Kierkegaard was fond
of saying, "an infinite qualitative difference" between God and
man. My existence is contingent. There was a time I was not.
My existence is given. My being is acquired. It is extrinsic to my
very nature or essence. God, however, cannot not exist. It is His
very nature to exist. We cannot speak the word *God* without
inferring His actual existence.

It was this absolutely unique existence of God that inspired
Anselm's famous argument. Anselm (1033-1109) was supposedly charged by his superior with the task of constructing an irrefutable theistic argument. He accomplished the task, for no

argument has been more baffling and few have been more influential. Contemporary philosophy's greatest minds are divided over the argument, reflecting the history of philosophy itself; Kant refuted it, but Spinoza and Hegel virtually built their systems upon it.

While not choosing sides in the debate on the validity of Anselm's argument, we can see that the argument makes some points that are worth looking at. Its force is based on the conceptualization of the word *God*. As noted above, we cannot speak the word God without inferring His existence. Anselm's statement and subsequent commentary in chapter 4 of the *Proslogium* is sufficient for our purposes:

Statement: How the fool has said in his heart what cannot be conceived.—A thing may be conceived in two ways: (1) when the word signifying it is conceived; (2) when the thing itself is understood. As far as the word goes, God can be conceived not to exist; in reality he cannot.

Commentary: But how has the fool said in his heart what he could not conceive; or how is it that he could not conceive what he said in his heart? since it is the same to say in the heart, and to conceive. . . . For, in one sense, an object is conceived, when the word signifying it is conceived; and in another, when the very entity, which the object is, is understood. In the former sense, then, God can be conceived not to exist; but in the latter, not at all. For no one who understands what water and fire are can conceive fire to be water, in accordance with the nature of the facts themselves, although this is possible according to the words. So, then, no one who understands what God is can conceive that God does not exist; although he says these words in his heart, either without any, or with some foreign, signification. For, God is that than which a greater cannot he conceived. And he who thoroughly understands this, assuredly understands that this being so truly exists, that not even in concept can it be non-existent. Therefore, he who understands that God so exists, cannot conceive that he does not exist.[2]

The intriguing attraction of this argument over the centuries

2. Alvin Plantinga, *The Ontological Argument*, pp. 5-6.

is not its form, which the philosophers have argued over, but its content and subject of argumentation—God. Certainly the form leaves something to be desired on the basis of ordinary standards of argumentation. If contemporary philosophers are correct (which is questionable) in their analysis that Anselm was attempting to deduce *factual* necessity from *logical* necessity, the argument is *most likely* invalid. However, the entire history of philosophy has probably mistaken Anselm's argument as rationalistic in nature. It is very important to realize that the entire argument is within the context of a prayer and thus Anselm *already knows* God as existing. He writes in chapter 1 of the *Proslogium*, which could be rendered *Prayer*: "I do not endeavor, O Lord, to penetrate thy sublimity, for in no wise do I compare my understanding with that; but I long to understand in some degree thy truth, which my heart believes and loves. For I do not seek to understand that I may believe, but I believe in order to understand. For this also I believe,—that unless I believe, I should not understand."[3]

Aquinas contended that to argue for God's existence on the basis of His nature is to put the cart before the horse. However, this is Anselm's very point—*God is not the usual subject of ordinary argumentation*. God alone has intrinsic Being. Since this is the case, one cannot separate God's nature from His existence as does Aquinas, though they must be separated for every other existing being. Likewise, because God's nature and existence are one, God may be the one exception to the existential fallacy, i.e., deducing factual or existential existence from logical necessity. Stated logically, this is the confusion of truth with validity. All one can claim on the basis of Scripture, however, is that God is an existential and factual necessity—"I am"—and not a logical necessity. But if logical and factual necessity can ever be equated, God will be the single subject. Until such time, the validity of the ontological argument must be left open, thus continuing the debate.

There is one additional facet of Christian theism that must be taken into ontological consideration. Christianity is trinitarian. The Father, the Son Jesus Christ, and the Holy Spirit each equally, distinctively, and personally share in the one essence of

3. Ibid., p. 3.

God. Biblical evidence is conclusive and cannot be extensively dealt with here (see Gen. 1:26-27; 3:22; 11:7; Deut. 6:4; Isa. 48:16; 61:1; 63:9-10; John 1:1, 18; 6:27; Acts 5:3-4; 2 Cor. 13:14; Titus 2:13; 1 Pet. 1:2.) One verse, however (Deut. 6:4), is believed by many to be absolutely antithetical to the plurality of personhood in the Godhead, but is actually one of the strongest biblical statements in support of the triunity of God. The passage reads:

> Hear, O Israel: The LORD our God, the LORD is one.

This verse has some ambiguity as to English word order and meaning. The NIV notes three possible alternatives:

- The Lord our God is one Lord.
- The Lord is our God, the Lord is one.
- The Lord is our God, the Lord alone.

However, the most important consideration here is the meaning of the word translated "one" (Hebrew, *'eḥad*). A second Hebrew word for "one" is *yāḥîd*, which connotes absolute singularity as seen in reference to Abraham's *one* son of promise in Genesis 22:2, 12, 16. Similarly, Jephthah came home in Judges 11:34 and was met by his *only* child (see also Psalm 22:20; Jer. 6:26; Amos 8:10; and Zech. 12:10). The word used in Deuteronomy (*'eḥad*) signifies unity and oneness in plurality. Perhaps the clearest such use is Genesis 2:24 where Adam and Eve are instructed to be "one flesh." Another very graphic use of this word is found in Numbers 13:23, which records the Hebrew spies returning with a "single cluster" of grapes (see also Ezra 6:24; Jer. 32:38-39). Obviously *'eḥad* means oneness in plurality. In light of this, it is very interesting that Moses selected *'eḥad* rather than *yāḥîd* in Deuteronomy 6:4. Though trinity cannot be proved by the use of this word, it certainly allows for unified plurality and implicitly is supportive of the biblical doctrine of the Trinity.

The reality of the Trinity is very important ontologically. A passing reference was made to the problem of unity and diversity, or the one and the many, above. Our previous emphasis was on the other philosophic problem of Being and Becoming—

no change only permanence, or all is change and thus no permanence. This was not an artificial problem of the early Greek philosophers, but simply the conceived and perceived necessities. The Christian position solves this problem by understanding that there is intrinsic Being that is permanent, and extrinsic being (to which we shall soon turn) that constantly experiences growth and decay. In a very similar manner, Christian theism is the only answer to how reality is both one and many, unified but diverse; for Christian theism teaches just that! The ultimate Reality, God, is three-in-one and one-in-three. Philosophers have not been on a "wild goose chase" while attempting to solve this problem. Nor have they created a problem and then tried to solve it. But as the Council of Nicaea (325) concluded, Christ is the eternal and internal generation from the very essence of the Father. Fatherhood is as inherent in God's Being as omniscience. Were it not for the Son, He would not be the Father. Likewise the eternal procession of the Holy Spirit from the Father and Son was theologically defined at Constantinople in 381. Living in God's universe, then, philosophers have rightly deciphered two of the prime questions of ontology: the questions of Being/Becoming and of Unity/Diversity. Their problem was that they were unable to come up with the correct answers. Revelation was necessary. As Francis Schaeffer testifies:

> Every once in a while in my discussions someone asks how I can believe in the Trinity. My answer is always the same. I would still be an agnostic if there were no Trinity, because there would be no answers. Without the high order of personal unity and diversity as given in the Trinity, *there are no answers*.[4]

Christian thought is not theology only. As indispensable as revelation, incarnation, and redemption are for man's spiritual needs, a full-orbed Christian thought is equally indispensable for man's present intellectual needs. Christianity is not simply the best answer a la Schleirermacher and others of the nineteenth-century liberal tradition; it is the *only* answer. Christianity is intellectually honest. One need not hide for fear of academic intimidation. Though more precise ontological technical

4. Francis Schaeffer, *He Is There and He Is Not Silent*, p. 14.

detail is possible elsewhere,[5] enough has been said to indicate that Christianity can answer the perennial question "Why is there something rather than nothing?" even if the question "Why is there God rather than no God?" can only be met by "I am who I am."

CREATION: EXTRINSIC BEING

"In the beginning God created the heavens and the earth" (Gen. 1:1). Creation was neither a logical nor factual necessity. God did not need to create. God was not only self-existing, but self-fulfilling. Creation was not necessitated by any lack of fullness on God's part. God needed neither angels nor man to be able to love or communicate. Only infinite person can fully communicate with infinite person. The persons of the Trinity are alone inherently worthy of love in their respective holiness. In short, God does not need the particulars of creation, be they personal or impersonal, as they need Him.

God thus exists in no necessary relation to finite things. He is absolutely free in His own right. This does not mean that the relationship between God and creation is arbitrary or variable. God's Word is final. Laws of nature as well as laws of reasoning are neither ambivalent nor unreliable. If they were, all knowledge, including the most elemental physical science, would be impossible. Silence would reign. Not only interpersonal communication but intrapersonal thoughts would be incongruous and senseless.

God's self-imposed limitation in relation to man is most poignantly illustrated in Exodus 32:9-14:

> "I have seen these people," the LORD said to Moses, "and they are a stiff-necked people. Now leave me alone so that my anger may burn against them and that I may destroy them. Then I will make you into a great nation."

> But Moses sought the favor of the LORD his God. "O LORD," he said, "why should your anger burn against your people, whom you brought out of Egypt with great power and a mighty hand? Why

---

5. See Herman Dooyeweerd, *New Critique of Theoretical Thought*; J. M. Spier, *An Introduction to Christian Philosophy*; and L. Kalsbeek, *Contours of a Christian Philosophy*.

should the Egyptians say, 'It was with evil intent that he brought them out, to kill them in the mountains and to wipe them off the face of the earth'? Turn from your fierce anger; relent and do not bring disaster on your people. Remember your servants Abraham, Isaac and Israel, to whom you swore by your own self: 'I will make your descendants as numerous as the stars in the sky and I will give your descendants all this land I promised them, and it will be their inheritance forever.' " Then the Lord relented and did not bring on his people the disaster he had threatened.

This incident cannot be fully comprehended. It is certain, nevertheless, that God *could* have brought about the threatened destruction but did not. Why? Because God had sworn by His own Self and "it is impossible for God to lie" (Heb. 6:18). (The context in Hebrews 6 is also the Abrahamic Covenant.) In other words, God was "limited" by His holy nature, absolute will, and truthful word. Nothing outside of God limits Him. He has no extrinsic limitations, only intrinsic ones. God is independent and unconditioned—*free*. This episode demonstrates, however, that although *God can do all that He wills, He will not do all that He can*. Final judgment, for instance, is possible tonight, but it will not be actual until all the preceding predictions of God's Word are accomplished. Thus, though there is no logical necessary relationship between God and creation, *there is a factual necessary relationship*. A straight line is the shortest distance between two spacial points such as Galilee and Jerusalem even for our incarnate Master. Scripture contains no logical contradictions or the very possibility of propositional revelation is denied—to say nothing of the claims to inerrancy of verbal plenary inspiration. This can be easily seen by the Hebrews 6 reference that "it is impossible for God to lie." If contradiction is permitted to God Himself, then God could lie. If contradiction is permitted to God in His revelation because of either His infinite Being or our finite capacities, then the statement itself becomes unintelligible and all possibility of truly knowing God via propositional revelation is lost.

The fact of creation means that God freely chose out of grace and love to have something else exist in its own right. Extrinsic being is created to be itself and to be of interest and value in its own right. God has, so to speak, renounced being the only existent. Nevertheless, though creation has a definite and nonarbitrary existence, it is never independent of God. Psalm 104:19-29 captures the totality of this dependence of all creation—inanimate, animate, and even man—on God:

> The moon marks off the seasons,
>   and the sun knows when to go down.
>
> You bring darkness, it becomes night,
>   and all the beasts of the forest prowl.
>
> The lions roar for their prey
>   and seek their food from God.
>
> The sun rises, and they steal away;
>   they return and lie down in their dens.
>
> Then man goes out to his work,
>   to his labor until evening.
>
> How many are your works, O LORD!
>   In wisdom you made them all;
>   the earth is full of your creatures
>
> There is the sea, vast and spacious,
>   teeming with creatures beyond number—
>   living things both large and small
>
> There the ships go to and fro,
>   and the leviathan, which you formed to frolic there.
>
> These all look to you
>   to give them their food at the proper time.
>
> When you give it to them,
>   they gather it up;
> when you open your hand,
>   they are satisfied with good things.
>
> When you hide your face,
>   they are terrified;
> when you take away their breath,
>   they die and return to the dust.[6]

Little can be added to this all-encompassing perspective. Sun

6. Cf. Isaiah 40:12-26.

and moon, earth and sea, king of beast and man himself are all depicted as totally dependent on the grace and providence of God. Due to the regular and nonarbitrary relationship of God and created nature, nature can be studied, understood, and even greatly controlled and enhanced by man. Chemistry and biology, physics and physiology, along with innumerable other disciplines that are concerned with nature can be investigated by the scientist because there is this inherent regularity. Colossians 1:16-17 pictures man and the entire physical world in which the human community exists as oriented toward and sustained by Christ. It was these foundational doctrines of creation and providence that gave the early scientists like Bacon, Kepler, Galileo, Pascal, Boyle, and Newton the surety that the world was experimentally knowable.[7] This scientific realism and epistemological assurance is lost in the nominalistic and ultimately skeptical attitude that pervades much of the contemporary philosophy of science.

Christian apologetics can neglect the ontological status of created nature only at its own peril. This does not mean the apologist must develop a natural theology. The impossibility of a purely inductive natural theology will be subsequently demonstrated. But it does mean that *the foundation of a Christian apologetic must be firmly based on the Christian understanding of ontology.* Given creation, the Christian apologist/theologian can no more speak adequately of God in total neglect of His creation than the secular humanist/naturalist can speak adequately of man and nature in total neglect of God. Intrinsic Being and extrinsic being must be constantly juxtaposed one with the other. This is the very foundation of a Both/And apologetic. It means, as will be demonstrated, that God and revelation cannot be presuppositionally emphasized apart from creation and history, and contrariwise, creation and/or history cannot be emphasized through natural theology or evidentialism apart from the distinct word of God.

Before we go on, however, a few words must be directed to the acme of terrestial creation—man. Genesis 1:26-27 states:

7. See R. Hooykaas, *Religion and the Rise of Modern Science*; and Alfred North Whitehead, *Science and the Modern World.*

Then God said, "Let us make man in our image, in our likeness, and let them rule over the fish of the sea and the birds of the air, over the livestock, over all the earth, and over all the creatures that move along the ground."

> So God created man in his own image,
> in the image of God he created him;
> male and female he created them.

Probably only the doctrine of the fall of man has had as much discussion in theological anthropology as the meaning of the phrase "God created man in his own image." Before discussing what the content of the image may be, the exact significance must be pinpointed. In Genesis 5:1 we read that "when God created man, he made him in the likeness of God." What does it mean for man to be like God? Since God is infinite and man is finite, does this mean that there is no similarity whatever between God and man? Though a few theologians have denied any *real* ontological likeness between God and man, John Calvin wrote that "as for myself, before I define the image of God, I would deny that it differs from his likeness,"[8] Keil and Delitzsch note that the two words for "image" and "likeness" in Genesis 1:26 are synonymous and are merely combined to add intensity to the thought: " 'an image which is like Us' (Luther)."[9] With both Calvin and Luther understanding the text to imply a real likeness between God and man, we are seemingly on safe ground with no need of extended exegetical argument for our apologetic purposes. To be made in the "image of God" means that man has an essential likeness and/or similarity in a finite, relative manner to the infinite, self-existing God.

8. John Calvin *Calvin's Commentaries, The Pentateuch*, 1:10.
9. C. F. Keil and F. Delitzsch, *Commentary on the Old Testament*, 1:63. It must be noted that the words they are directly commenting on are the Greek words *eikōn* and *homoiōsis* in the Septuagint text, though they conclude the same for the Hebrew words *ṣelēm* and *demûṯ* also. It is of at least passing interest to note that *eikōn* is not only used of man in God's image in the Septuagint, but that Paul uses it of Christ in God's image in Colossians 1:15. Hermann Kleinknecht ("The Greek Use of *eikōn*," *TDNT*, 2:389) comments on its use in Colossians 1:15 that must have some bearing on its use in the Septuagint thusly: "It has a share in the reality. Indeed, it is the reality. Thus *eikōn* does not imply a weakening or a feeble copy of something. It implies the illumination of its inner core and essence."

Some have claimed that man is only "similar" to God but does not have God's "likeness." However, "similar" is defined by Webster as "1. like; resembling; having a general resemblance but not exactly the same. 2. homogeneous; of like structure or character throughout." So man is "like" God; this is further confirmed when it is noted that *homoiōsis* is used for both man "made in God's likeness" in James 3:9 and Christ "made in human likeness" in Philippians 2:7. There can be no double standard.

This ontological resemblance between God and man is of extreme importance for the epistemological concerns of the following chapter. First, however, we must turn our attention briefly to the content of this image. There is little direct evidence in the Old Testament to help us, though it is natural that the transcendence and ineffability of God should draw a veil around the divine likeness in man. The immediate context of Genesis 1:28 seems to connect man's unique creation with his being steward of God's world. He is God's vice-regent. Adam and his descendants delineate our unique relation to God by our unique direction and responsible care of the earth, from which man himself was taken. Man is to will God's will as God's steward. We see this in Adam's naming of the animals, whereas God named man, demonstrating both his responsibility and Godlikeness. Such naming also reveals his Godlike logical and verbal abilities. It is these abilities and conscious use of such that make his dominion over the rest of creation possible and, in some measure, uncover the content of God's image in man.

The naming of the animals illustrates two facets of God's image in man: reasoning intelligence and intuitive creativity. Naming always demonstrates verbal acumen and creative discernment, and especially so in this particular task in light of the vastness of the responsibility and the introductory nature of the event. Although it is not a substantial creation (out of nothing), it is a verbal creation *ex nihilo*. This ability to create on a finite level is a very clear mirroring of the divine image. Creativity, every bit as much as logical/symbolic communication skills, delineates man uniquely from the rest of the animate creation. Painting, music, sculpture, architecture, engineering, and even writing, are all creations where there was nothing before. Animals do not create in this manner. Man does because of the distinctive and distinguishing gift of God's image.

The pinnacle of man's creativity, however, is not artistic, scientific, or symbolic, as great as these are, but physical. Male and female, who are equally created in God's image (Gen. 1:26-27), together transmit God's image through their own images in their progeny. Genesis 5:2-3 states: "He created them male and female; at the time they were created, he blessed them and called them 'man.' When Adam had lived 130 years, he had a son in his own likeness, in his own image; and he named him Seth." The same Hebrew words ($ṣelēm$ and $demût$) are used of Seth being in the likeness and image of his father, Adam, as were used of man being made in the likeness and image of God (Gen. 1:26-27). This doubtless reinforces the above argument of the essential resemblance between God and man, but it is not our main point here. Rather we find here that Adam and Eve necessarily transmit God's image to their children as they transmit their own physical likeness. Animals transmit physical likeness also and this simply illustrates man's continuity with nature. But man *also* transmits God's unique image to his offspring through sexual union. Man is more than physical nature and man and woman together create this "moreness" in eternal, finite beings just as the trinity "cooperated" in creating in the first place. This is creativity par excellence. But even more important, as Gerhard von Rad notes, "it ensures the theological actuality for all generations of the witness to the divine likeness."[10] This very image of God is obviously in all men (though we must yet explore the consequences of the Fall) since Genesis 9:6 institutes capital punishment for murder *because* man is made in God's image. Also James 3:9 elucidates the contradiction in praising God with the same tongue by which "we curse men, who have been made in God's likeness."

God's image is not exhausted by man's reasoning and various creativities. The command of Genesis 2:16-17 can serve to illustrate two additional facets of this image: "And the LORD God commanded the man, 'You are free to eat from any tree in the garden; but you must not eat from the tree of the knowledge of

10. Gerhard von Rad, "The Divine Likeness in the OT," *TDNT*, 2:390.

good and evil, for when you eat of it you will surely die.' "
Although this command certainly anticipates man's logical and
verbal capabilities for it to be received and assimilated, it most
definitely assumes a moral consciousness and sensitivity as
well. The most compelling of the theistic arguments (as even
Immanuel Kant asserted) is based on the reality of this moral
inclination in man and thus the necessity of an absolute lawgiver. C. S. Lewis developed this argument in a most telling way in
the *Abolition of Man*. But our interest is not in the moral argument for God, except as it illustrates the dynamic and inherent
moral dimension in man that gives the argument the degree of
feasibility it has. Man's likeness to God demands relationship
with God. An infinite/finite relationship is one of dependence
and obedience for the finite. However, the history of the
divine/human relationship might be titled "the conflict of
wills." From Adam to you and me, the battle has been one of
autonomy, literally self-law versus God's law. In short, man
desired to be "like" God absolutely instead of finitely and relatively. Man aspired to independence rather than dependence.
Man's failure was the incorrect use of his God-given and Godlike will in the very same way another dependent creature
failed in Isaiah 14:12-14.

Conscience is another aspect of this moral nature of man.
The Genesis account of the fall of man records man's immediate recognition of wrongdoing and ensuing guilt (Gen. 3:7-8).
All subsequent history and our own personal experiences reveal
the same thing. Though there is much self or group-imposed
guilt that is artificial, there is abundant evidence of the truth
and reality of moral guilt before a holy God. Paul recognized
the limitations of culture-conditioned, sin-conditioned conscience in Ephesians 4:17-20 and 1 Timothy 4:2. Nevertheless,
he also recognized the validity of the conscience bearing witness to the moral law being written on the heart, the center and
essence of man, in Romans 2:15.

The final facet of God's image in man is the sum total of his
rational, ethical, and spiritual nature—righteous personality.
Personality for man transcends animality though based upon it.
God formed Adam's body as directly as He gave him life (Gen.
2:7) to indicate his differentiation from and continuity with the
rest of creation. Delitzsch writes:

> The earth does not bring forth his body, but God Himself put His
> hand to the work and forms him; nor does the life already
> imparted to the world by the Spirit of God individualize itself in
> him, but God breathes directly into the nostrils of the one man, in
> the whole fulness of His personality, the breath of life, that in a
> manner corresponding to the personality of God he may become a
> living soul. This was the foundation of the pre-eminence of man,
> of his likeness to God and his immortality.[11]

Man's personality corresponds to God's personality in pro-
portional recognition of God's umlimitedness and our very
clear boundaries as delineated by the imperative of Genesis
2:17. But nevertheless man is still personal if not infinite Person. This is illustrated by God's communion with man both
before (Gen. 1:29, 30; 2:15-23) and after the Fall (Gen. 3:8-9).
This resemblance of man and God in personality is indispensable for both epistemological and soteriological concerns. Only
on the basis of this ontological similarity can there be the reality of a natural revelation of God *in* man; the feasibility of a
propositional revelation where words can have univocal meaning and thus provide a true disclosure of God's Person and will;
and lastly, the possibility of an incarnation that is not inherently contradictory.

Man was not only personal at creation, but *righteous* person.
His innocence and righteous character were as much a gift of
God, and the reflection of God's image, as were his rational and
creative abilities. Man lost this righteousness, if not his personality, in willful disobedience. Man is thus alienated from God
and but dimly reflects His likeness by an image shorn of essential righteousness. Man thus inherently misuses the rational and
creative dimensions of this image by a perverted will in autonomous separation from God, the very source of his being. Salvation, by providing justification through faith in Christ, restores
man's righteous personhood. Like creation, then, recreation (2
Cor. 5:17) demonstrates that righteous character is the gift of a
holy and loving God, not the acquired achievement of the creature (Rom. 1:17; 3:24; 5:1; 1 Cor. 1:30).

Psalm 8:3-9 (NASB) perfectly summarizes the argument of

---

11. Keil and Delitzsch, 1:80.

man's ontological uniqueness without allowing us to forget the holy and infinite distinctiveness of God:

> When I consider Thy heavens, the work of Thy fingers,
> The moon and the stars, which Thou hast ordained;
> What is man, that Thou dost take thought of him?
> And the son of man, that Thou dost care for him?
> Yet Thou hast made him a little lower than God,
> And dost crown him with glory and majesty.
> Thou dost make him to rule over the works of Thy hands;
> Thou hast put all things under his feet,
> All sheep and oxen,
> And also the beasts of the field,
> The birds of the heavens, and the fish of the sea,
> Whatever passes through the paths of the sea.
>
> O LORD, our Lord,
> How majestic is Thy name in all the earth!

Two things must be singled out here in conclusion. First, the NASB is seemingly correct when it says of man that he was made a "little lower than God." The word in the Hebrew text is *Elohim*. Though there is some debate as to the meaning of this word here as perhaps referring to angels (KJV) in light of Hebrews 2:7, Calvin prefers to understand this as "God" because it is more "natural, and as it is almost universally adopted by the Jewish interpreters."[12] Certainly this understanding seems appropriate as it reinforces the fact that though man is similar to God through being made in His image and likeness, he is far from identical as he is always conditioned, dependent, and finite and thus "a little lower." "Man's being, though linked with the divine, is itself essentially not divine, but created, and thus dependent on God, and of a different order from His own being, though akin to it."[13] Second, but more briefly, glory in the Old Testament "belongs supremely to Yahweh" but is used here to refer to man who is distinctively seen as God's steward and vice regent over all earthly aspects of the created order.[14] Man's status and dignity is great. But he is still of the created order and under the curse brought on that

12. John Calvin *Calvin's Commentaries, Joshua and the Psalms*, 2:167.
13. David Cairns, *The Image of God in Man*, p. 56.
14. von Rad, 2:390.

order by man in his rebellion against his creaturely status. As similar as he may be to God, his ontology is still infinitely different. His being is not intrinsic, but like all of the created reality, extrinsic. Man is not a factual necessity like God. Man is contingent. He can *not* exist. There will be a time that physically he will not be, though he spiritually shares in God's immortality in eternity future. Psalm 103:13-16 succinctly reminds us that the acme of God's creation still has only extrinsic being:

> As a father has compassion on his children,
>   so the LORD has compassion on those who fear him;
> for he knows how we are formed,
>   he remembers that we are dust.
> As for man, his days are like grass,
>   he flourishes like a flower of the field;
> the wind blows over it and it is gone,
>   and its place remembers it no more.

3

EPISTEMOLOGICAL DETERMINATIONS

Epistemology (how we know that we know) must be, and always is, determined by the nature of reality. In one sense, epistemology and ontology have a chicken-and-egg relationship. Which comes first? How can we "know" the existing reality without first "knowing how we know" that particular reality? But we cannot determine our epistemological parameters prior to our actual experience of reality. Many in the history of philosophy have done just that. Idealists usually eliminate the value of sense data—if not sensation itself—by assuming that reality is totally nonempirical, regardless of their everyday experience. Naturalists do the opposite and thus frequently reduce reality only to that which can be known by sense data. Although the nineteenth century generally practiced the former, and the twentieth century has most frequently followed the latter, culminating in positivism, *we can do neither!* Nor may we reject both and speak of an "apprehension of *an ultimate nonsensuous unity in all things*, a oneness or a One to which neither the senses nor the reason can penetrate."[1]

1. Walter T. Stace, "The Nature of Mysticism" in *Philosophy of Religions: Selected Readings*, ed. William L. Rowe and William J. Wainwright, p. 269.

If the three above alternatives (rationalism, empiricism, mysticism) are individually set aside when segregated from the other two, it does not mean we totally reject them when seen in conjunction with one another. Reason or logic, sensation or empiricism, intuition or innateness are all legitimate ways of knowing particular subjects. Thus while I cannot intuitively know of *your* existence, I can intuitively know I exist through my own innate self-consciousness. Likewise, though I may not know empirically the contents of *A*, *B*, and *C*, I know logically that if "all *A* is *B*," and "all *B* is *C*," then "all *A* is *C*."

This eclectic epistemology is not dictated by the results and epistemological turmoil of the past three hundred years of philosophy. Rather it is the necessary consequence of the Christian understanding of reality. Reality is *both* infinite, intrinsic Being and finite, extrinsic being; or *both* God *and* creation. Man is the only true *knowing subject* of the natural order. Man's means of knowing are determined by his own ontological structure as well as the ontological nature of that which is external to him: God, and everything else that, like himself, is created. The *process* of knowing is itself very complicated and is not the purpose of this chapter. However, that *we do know*, regardless of all the intellectual subterfuge and philosophical quibbles, *we know*. It is the purpose of this chapter to demonstrate that man's ontological being made in God's image and living in God's created order demands that man can and does know logically, empirically, and intuitively; *and* that all three means of knowing are not only viable but vital to Christian apologetics. We turn, then, to each of these three ontologically determined means of knowing in God's created universe.

LOGICAL KNOWLEDGE

> "For my thoughts are not your thoughts,
>   neither are your ways my way," declares the
>   LORD.
> As the heavens are higher than the earth,
>   so are my ways higher than your ways.
>   and my thoughts than your thoughts.
>   (Isaiah 55:8-9)

This passage of Scripture is frequently quoted and interpreted by well-meaning but mistaken Christians to mean that God's reasoning or logic is different in kind from our reasoning and logic. It is most readily referred to in regard to logical difficulties relating to the problem of evil, the divine prerogative, the incarnation, and the doctrine of biblical inspiration. However, the context of Isaiah 55 will not permit such an interpretation. In fact, the exact opposite is the case: God is desirous that the wicked would forsake his way and the evil man his thoughts for the way and thought of God Himself.

> Seek the LORD while he may be found;
>   call on him while he is near.
> Let the wicked forsake his way
>   and the evil man his thoughts.
> Let him turn to the LORD, and he will
>   have mercy on him,
> and to our God, for he will freely pardon.
>
> As the rain and the snow
>   come down from heaven,
> and do not return to it
>   without watering the earth
> and making it bud and flourish,
>   so that it yields seed for the sower
>   and bread for the eater,
> so is my word that goes out from my mouth:
>   It will not return to me empty,
> but will accomplish what I desire
>   and achieve the purpose for which I sent it.
>   (Isaiah 55:6-7, 10-11)

These two preceding and subsequent verses inform us of two very important facts. First, verses 10-11 assure us that revelation by means of language will accomplish God's purpose and thus adequately communicate *His* thoughts to *us*. If this is not the case, then God's Word would not provide the seed of new birth or the bread of eternal life. But the very point of the analogy is that it does not go forth void any more than snow and rain can avoid watering the earth so that the earth produces essential seed and life-sustaining bread. Second, and even more forcefully, verses 6-7 invite man to turn to God's ways and thoughts by turning from their own "wicked" ways and "evil" thoughts. In New Testament terms, it is Paul's instruction that whatever we do, "whether in word or deed, do it all in the name of the Lord Jesus, giving thanks to God the Father through him" (Col. 3:17). It is the biblical injunction to "be holy, because I am holy" (Lev. 11:44, 45; 19:2; 20:7; 1 Pet. 1:16). Man's ways and thoughts can be both obedient and pure. Isaiah 55:6-11 is thus speaking of the *ethical* difference between man and God, and *not a logical difference.*[2] Calvin points out that this passage "draws a distinction between God's disposition and man's disposition."[3] By this Calvin means that God is not harsh and irreconcilable to men as men often are to one another after a personal affront or injury. The ethical difference is what causes man's deeds and thoughts to be disobedient to God and therefore impure. Isaiah is calling for national repentance so that Judah might return to the ways and thoughts of God and find His pardon instead of His judgment in defeat and captivity (cf. Isa. 1:16-20).

The reason it is possible for man to obey God in deed and word is because man is uniquely made in God's image. As seen in the previous chapter (p. 28), our ability to think rationally and to communicate verbally and logically is because God's image is in us. God, not man, is the source of logic. Logic is not something beyond God to which He is responsible, therefore making God less than the ultimate reference point. *Logic is not God. Logic is God-thinking.* Logic is in us because we are reflections of God ontologically. Logic is the bridge whereby it is possible for God to communicate to us and for us to communicate with our Creator. Logic is the epistemological prerequisite for the very possibility of revelation and Scripture. The declarative sentences of the Bible assume the rules of logic to convey cognitive propositional revelation as truth. Logic is ultimately rooted in God and is derivatively rooted in man by the act of the gracious Creator-God. Thus to use logic in the apologetic enterprise is not to use mere "human" criteria to judge special revelation. Rather it is to apply God-given principles to the world as He created it. Being created in God's image means we are created rational beings and thus the very use of reason is

2. Joseph Addison Alexander, *Commentary on the Prophecies of Isaiah*, 2:331.
3. John Calvin *Calvin's Commentaries, Isaiah* 3:751.

legitimate not only in regard to created nature, but also in regard to special revelation when God discloses Himself to us. Logic is therefore an acceptable and necessary tool for the assimilation of propositional revelation. If it were not for logic, God's revelation could not differentiate between meaning *this* and not *that*. Even worse, we could not distinguish between the voice of God and the voice of the devil without logic. If contradiction is eliminated, then good may be evil and evil good. As Mark M. Hanna succinctly writes:

> Logicians recognize that if contradiction is allowed, any proposition can be inferred; the affirmation and denial of every proposition—even the principle of noncontradiction itself—becomes possible. Hence, no absurdity can be more fundamental than the denial of the principle of noncontradiction.[4]

What then is logic? What are these basic principles and rules of thought previously alluded to? Why is the law of noncontradiction so fundamental?

Logic, as has been implied if not explicitly stated, was discovered and elucidated by Aristotle, not invented. Aristotle made into an explicit science the tacit working of man's logical mind. He enumerated three basic laws:

- Law of Identity—if any statement is true, then it is true.
- Law of Noncontradiction—no statement can be both true and false.
- Law of Excluded Middle—any statement is either true or false.

These three certainly do not exhaust the possibilities of a logic course, but all courses do begin here, and these are adequate to succinctly outline the universal logical structure of man's mind as mirroring God's mind. To say that "I am Ronald Mayers" is a true statement illustrating that $A = A$. To say that "I am Ronald Reagan" is to utter a false statement because I have violated the law of noncontradiction by saying $A = B$ when A and B are two mutually exclusive subjects. Similarly, to know

---

4. Mark M. Hanna, *Crucial Questions in Apologetics*, p. 48.

that the Son of God was always the eternally generated Son, and not the Holy Spirit, means one could never write a sentence that would contradict this by identifying the Son as the Holy Spirit. Such a sentence would be false and never true regardless of who uttered the sentence—God or man! This is what the Bible necessarily relies on when it says, "God cannot lie." If the statement is true, then God not only does not but cannot lie. If the statement is false, then either God can lie even if He does not, or else He does actually lie. But the statement cannot be both true and false, that is, it cannot be true that God cannot lie and nevertheless true that He does lie. It is one way or the other. In this case, it is either/or, *not* both/and!

Logic is thus God's universal endowment for all men. The law of noncontradiction is never set aside in practice even if a particular individual is unaware of it as formally stated, or if one's philosophy or religion denies it. The philosophical or religious devotee still constantly uses this law to differentiate truth from error, fact from fantasy, in everyday life. Logic is an a priori necessity for sense experience since a thing is not really empirically known as a thing until *this* is distinguished from *that*. Likewise, speech is made possible only by the innate realization that words must stand for *something* and not for *anything* or *everything*. The law of noncontradiction, therefore, is so basic to meaningful thought and intelligible conversation that it cannot be demonstrated. The only proof would be the silence that would reign because nothing would be meaningful without the law being presupposed. It is self-authenticating as the very attempt to deny its priority assumes it.

The reference to speech brings us back to the epistemological problems relating to human language and divine revelation. Isaiah 55:10-11, quoted above, assure us that God's Word accomplishes God's desire and purpose. Though we have seen that logic is a prerequisite to all speech communication between God and man as well as man and man, this does not solve the problem of man having "true truth" (to borrow Francis Schaeffer's phrase) of the Infinite-Personal God. Obviously, since we are men and not God, we do not have a complete and perfect integration of everything as does God, the source and infinite reference point of the totality of finite reality. But we, nevertheless, know such things truly if not exhaustively.

Though man is not cognizant of *all* the processes of an organ as involved and complicated as the human liver, we do have "true truth" about some dimensions of the liver's processes. This incapability of exhaustive knowledge for man can be said for everything and anything, not just the far reaches of astronomy, mathematics, nuclear physics, and, perhaps the most unlimited of all finite dimensions, the human mind. But if this is true of the finite, what of knowledge of the infinite? Can man have true, or univocal, knowledge of God? God Himself asks in Isaiah 46:5: "To whom will you compare me or count me equal? To whom will you liken me that we may be compared?" Though we obviously cannot have exhaustive truth of the Infinite if we are incapable of such for the finite, are we absolutely precluded from any literal, true truth, of God? Does the Infinite/finite barrier eliminate even God from providing us literal truth of Himself?

The answer to the last two questions must be a resounding no! Carl F. H. Henry, recognized by friend and foe as evangelicalism's most distinctive living theologian, writes that "the alternative to univocal knowledge of God is equivocation and skepticism."[5] There is no middle ground between *equivocal* (two or more meanings) and *univocal* (one meaning only). Neither Thomistic nor Calvinistic advocates of analogy who deny any degree of univocacy to words used of God and man can escape equivocation and the resulting theological skepticism. Without univocacy, we cannot lay claim to an absolute revelation or uncovering of God in the Bible.

The normal use of language is always to lead one to the unknown by means of something already known. Is God so ontologically different from everything else that nothing is an adequate analogy to give us even inklings of Him as He really is?

Another resounding no if we take the biblical conception of creation seriously. There man is the "pointer," or theological reference point, to God. *Because* man is made in God's image, man will not only try to understand God in reference to himself, but, more important, God reveals Himself in terms that are also attributable to man in some degree. When a word like *wisdom*

5. Carl F. H. Henry, *God, Revelation and Authority*, 3:364.

is used of both God and man it is implied that there is a relation existing between the wisdom of man and the wisdom of God. Similarly, *existence* is predicated of both God and man, though for God existence is eternal and independent of everything else as He is self-existent; man, on the other hand, is very dependent on others and his environment and is obviously not the cause of his own existence. But we still know in a literal way that God exists, as we exist, even if differently. But God is not uncovered if when the Bible says, "God so loves the world," *love* has a meaning *totally different* from "Ron loves Charlotte." Without doubt there is certainly a difference in the scope of the two loves, and a difference in the ability to love in those doing the loving, but these are differences of degree and not kind. Man understands something very definite about the Infinite-Personal God: He is a loving God. The same must be said of all the other ways in which Scripture reveals the Personal God to us. There is *no knowledge of God whatsoever* if when the Bible says God loves, hates, knows, seeks, judges, is angry, jealous, righteous, or powerful those words do not mean the same for Him, though in some accomodated manner, as they do when used of man. What sense, for instance, does the primary biblical command "be holy as I am holy" make if we do not have the slightest idea what "holy" means in reference to God? "Holy" like "love" must mean something similar on our finite scale as it does on God's infinite dimension, or we are left with *three horrible evils* — no knowledge of the nature of God; no divine, inerrant revelation; and no moral/ethical guidelines for the fulfillment of man's dependent being.

Man made in God's image is the ontological foundation for God's univocal use of revelatory analogies (see pp. 27-31). Man's univocacy or ontological similarity to God Himself in a finite and relative manner through God's image makes an epistemological univocacy possible. Because man is personal and can love, was made righteous initially and can be declared such again through the new birth, exercises power, can become personally angry, makes decisions of judgment, can distinguish between things that differ, makes moral decisions, and so on, he has an inherent grounding in and innate insight into the being of God. It is this prior ontological foundation that provides an intelligible framework in which man can cognitively know and finitely comprehend the person of God when He freely chooses to reveal Himself.

This ontological similarity is unquestionably a necessity for man to understand God's revelation of Himself. The rest of creation does not cognitively comprehend God's uncovering of Himself. It cannot! God communicates verbally only to man, not to a stone or a tree. But communication also requires a *means* of communicating univocally in language, not just an ontological foundation as prerequisite to language univocacy. As already hinted, analogy is our linguistic tool. But *there is no analogy if there is no univocal element in the analogy*. Epistemological univocacy is only possible through God-chosen, univocally-faceted analogies. Ontological similarities must truly exist or there can be no analogic statement. But these analogic propositions must be God-initiated to actually fit the structured reality of the God/man relationship. This is no more than to say that "men spoke from God as they were carried along by the Holy Spirit" (2 Pet. 1:21). To quote Henry again, "Only univocal assertions protect us from equivocacy; only univocal knowledge is, therefore, genuine and authentic knowledge."[6]

Both analogy of attribution and analogy of proportionality can provide us with such univocal knowledge of God and thus save us from equivocation and theological skepticism. In analogies of attribution the predicate *loves* (in "God loves") belongs absolutely or properly to God, who is the source of finite being, and only relatively or derivatively to us. Thus we are claiming that God's ability to love is necessary if His creatures are to be capable of love. Since we are capable of such, our love, though only relative on our finite scale of being, is yet univocal in kind to God who gave us this capacity. Analogy of proportionality is even more helpful to religious and revelatory language. An analogy of proportionality means that the analogue or term under discussion is found in each of the subjects in a mode that is determined by the respective subjects themselves.[7] Thus power and knowledge are known in God as omnipotence and omniscience, but as Hodge noted long ago, they are still power

---

6. Ibid.
7. Two very helpful books for analogy and religious language are Austin Farrer, *Finite and Infinite*, and E. L. Mascall, *Existence and Analogy*.

and knowledge.[8] Henry is undoubtedly correct when he concludes:

> In the biblical view, God's self-revelation to man, created in the divine image for the knowledge and service of his Maker, vouchsafes valid knowledge of God. Knowledge that is literally true of God has its basis not in abstractions from human experience and relationships projected upon the infinite in a superlative way, but in God's own initiative and intelligible disclosure. In answering the question of authentic knowledge of God, evangelical theology appeals not simply to an a priori ontology. It notes the scriptural emphasis that as a creature of God, man has revelational knowledge of God as he truly is, and stresses also the logical consistency and superiority of the biblical views against alternatives prone to skepticism.[9]

There is yet one final problem. If all men are made in God's image, and all men have the same logic, why do not all men accept the reality of God and His definitive revelation? Here is the crux of the epistemological problem for Christian apologetics. *To claim that all men have the same logic does not mean that all men have the same reasoning process.* Man *should* reason with God as his ultimate reference point, but beginning with Adam man makes himself the final and ultimate reference point. The very heart of the initial temptation was that man might "be like God" (Gen. 3:5). Man, consciously or unconsciously, waves the fist of independence in God's face. Isaiah pictures men as sheep who have gone astray, each turning to his own way. Man was initially made to have a relationship with God; to obey the Creator in a theonomously guided pathway. Man, however, is now born (Rom. 5:12) on his own autonomous path in complete alienation and estrangement from God. Ephesians 2:1 portrays man as dead in his transgressions and sin. Man, in theological language, is totally depraved. He is consciously godless and wicked, suppressing the innate truth of God's reality that lies within his person. His inherent religiosity is "like filthy rags" (Isa. 64:6) before a totally holy and righteous God. In short, "all have sinned and fall short of the glory of

8. Charles Hodge, *Systematic Theology*, 1:338.
9. Henry, 3:365-66.

God" (Rom. 3:23), and thus "the wages of sin is death [spiritual and eternal separation from God], but the gift of God is eternal life through Christ Jesus our Lord" (Rom. 6:23).

Total depravity, therefore, affects the reasoning process if not the very ability to reason by the men for whom Christ died, that is, wayward, lost, and unbelieving men in need of new birth. All men have the same logic. There is not a believing and unbelieving, pagan and Christian, logic. Lost men are still men made in God's image with the gifts of rationality, language, creativity, personality, and moral—albeit selfish—inclinations. But because of the Fall, man will not use his abilities for the purposes of God's will and glory. He will not will God's will in the universe naturally. He is in an abnormal, fallen state in comparison with his original splendor. Therefore his will is "bent" away from God to self-rule. He believes himself to be independent. In contemporary jargon, he lives "to do his own thing," not, as was intended for Adam and us, God's "thing" or will. Therefore, his logic may be the same, but the actual content of his reasoning *begins* with man's will and reason, not God's will and Word. It is not that man's logic functions improperly, but that it now functions apart from, and therefore really against, God. This autonomous framework means that man does not interpret this world as a God-ordained and thus God-interpreted world. Facts are ontologically objective but either are not perceived with sufficient clarity due to the Fall, and/or are given subjective meaning. For instance, pragmatic naturalists interpret the same facts as existentialists but see them optimistically since man is understood as the controller of his environment through applying the scientific method to his social problems (John Dewey, 1859-1948), rather than pessimistically where man is seen as caught in the meaningless web of existence by the accident of a particular month (Jean Paul Sartre, 1905-1980) or a pawn of his own technology (Herbert Marcuse, 1898-1980). Actually, the facts do point to both optimistic and pessimistic conclusions—man is both great and highly capable by being made in God's image, and wretched and trapped by the depravity of his own autonomy. Instead of seeing both sides of man and the provision for such by God in Christ, fallen man attempts to maintain his independence by interpreting himself and the surrounding universe in his own metaphysical framework, be it pragmatic, existential, or materialistic naturalisms, an evolutionary processive philosophy, or countless other perspectives. Man's continuous drive for ultimate autonomy demands that whenever he thinks of origins, death, and other ultimate issues, his self-produced presuppositions must reinterpret God's universe in an agnostic or atheistic manner. Francis Schaeffer put this well in one of his early books when commenting on Romans 1:18-32:

> Paul is saying men—because they refuse to bow to the God who is there and because they hold their presuppositions as an implicit faith—hold some of the truth about themselves and about the universe, but they do not carry these things to their logical conclusions because they contradict their presuppositions.
>
> Men who refuse to bow before God take the facts concerning the universe and man, push these facts through their own presuppositional grid, fail to carrying their thinking to a reasonable conclusion, and so are faced with an overwhelming lie.[10]

Thus the Fall and the resultant total depravity affects all facets of man's being—intellectual, moral, and emotional. Man is in constant revolt against God and His revelation, both general and special. Man will not read general revelation in nature and himself correctly. He cannot, for the recognition of an omnipotent, omniscient, and holy Creator would demand the surrender of his autonomy to a gracious, loving, and resurrected Redeemer. This he cannot do without the convicting and regenerating work of the Holy Spirit. But that no ethically redemptive act of the will is possible for unsaved man does not mean that the unregenerate man cannot use the laws of inductive inference or the rules of deductive syllogisms correctly. The noetic, or intellectual, effect of sin is seen by the premises and presuppositions man adopts in his spiritual and ethical alienation from God and *not* by the structure of logic and mental activity itself. Sin certainly affects man's psychological activity, hindering his ability to think correctly, but not the universal laws of logic themselves provided by God in creation. Gordon Clark, the most helpful contemporary apologist in differentiating logic

10. Francis Schaeffer, *Death in the City*, pp. 101, 106.

from the actual reasoning process, writes that "logic, the law of contradiction, is not affected by sin. Even if everyone constantly violated the laws of logic, they would not be less true than if everyone constantly observed them."[11]

The Fall of man does not destroy man's rational powers. The Bible holds man responsible for the light that he has (John 1:4-9; Rom. 1:20). If man's rational abilities were destroyed at the Fall, there would be no intelligible argument possible to the unbeliever. All preaching, especially evangelistic preaching, presumes that unsaved man can intellectually comprehend the cognitive content and moral obligation of the gospel. The Bible is eliminated if the revelation therein cannot be intelligibly appropriated. The divine image in man was effaced and misdirected, but not destroyed. Even after the Fall *man is still God's unique creature*, and this precipitates God's entrance into His created order by donning this very image as the Last Adam.

EMPIRICAL KNOWLEDGE

Empiricism, as we are using it here, is not to be understood in the technical philosophic sense that all knowledge must begin in sense data, or that the sense data we must begin with is not the object itself but merely its mental or phenomenal respresentative. Rather, we are simply asserting that we do gain real knowledge of the created order by observation and sense experience. Many philosophical difficulties relate to pure empiricism of a Lockean type or even the hybrid empiricism of Kant. Since we do not share their assumptions, we do not inherit their philosophical problems and thus there is no need to deal with the usual questions related to pure or hybrid empiricism. However, because a number of evangelical apologists play down the role of historical evidences due to their uneasiness with empirical knowability, it appears necessary to note the biblical affirmation of this knowability. As it will become obvious in the following chapter, a Both/And apologetic insists that the revelatory events of the past were empirically knowable by both the first-hand witness (John) and the second-

---

11. Gordon Clark, "The Axiom of Revelation," in *The Philosophy of Gordon H. Clark*, ed. Ronald H. Nash, p. 75. See also Gordon H. Clark, *Religion, Reason and Revelation*.

hand witness (Luke). Therefore, if revelatory events provide real and true knowledge of God's reality and nature manifested through His relationship with His people, something must be knowable by sensation for the Bible to assert such knowledge through historical events. If knowledge by sense experience is impossible, then the Bible is in error to assert otherwise.

Our purpose here is simply to demonstrate that knowledge acquisition through the means of sensation of either mundane or even revelatory events is assumed to be possible, if not necessary, by the Bible. This is enough to demonstrate the viability of Christian evidences for contemporary apologetics, if not enough to answer all the scientific and philosophical questions relating to *how* physical sense data is converted to mental knowledge, or to answer in detail the question of the relationship of subject and object. The *why* of such questions is answerable for a Christian, however, since the physical objects and events of the created realm are made by God to be knowable, just as sensate beings fashioned in God's image are made such as to be able to know in this way.

It would seem, then, that the Bible presupposes that the acquisition of knowledge is possible and significant through sense experience. Proverbs 20:12 assumes the Lord has made both "ears that hear and eyes that see." There is no explanation as to *how* this happens, or *how* such sense experience contributes to the knowledge enterprise, but both are surely expected. In opposite fashion, Moses is answered when he claims he is not fluent of speech by the Lord's statement that He makes both those who speak and those who cannot, as well as those who see and hear and those who are blind or deaf (Ex. 4:11). The implication is that there is a *real difference* between seeing and blindness, hearing and deafness. This would not be the case if hearing and sight have no role in the acquisition of knowledge.

The New Testament is replete with direct reference to the acquisition of knowledge through seeing, hearing, and touching. Jesus points John's disciples to His true identity by telling them to "go back and report to John what you hear and see" (His messianic miracles, Matt. 11:4-5). Jesus encouraged His disciples to be assured of His postresurrection identity by asking them to "look at my hands and my feet. It is I myself!

Touch me and see; a ghost does not have flesh and bones, as you see I have" (Luke 24:39). The offer of empirical evidence to doubting Thomas is well known (John 20:27). Peter guarantees his readers by *historical testimony based on empirical knowledge* that their faith is not a myth but literal historical fact. He himself was one of the "eyewitnesses of his majesty" on the Mount of Transfiguration (2 Pet. 1:16). Even more startling, but also more substantial as original empirical knowledge and now transmittable historical evidence, is that he "heard this voice that came from heaven when we were with him on the sacred mountain" (2 Pet. 1:18). Peter's biblical record of such a unique revelatory experience, given to only three men and then offered by one of them to a subsequent generation as historical evidence to the reality and truthfulness of the Christian message, absolutely refutes those who deny either empirical knowability or any apologetic significance to traditional Christian evidences based on original empirical perception and historiographical testimony.

We need not review in this section the great amount of historical evidences that elucidate and support the truth of Christianity. Many books do that, centering usually on the irrefutable evidence of fulfilled prophecy and the life and climactic resurrection of Jesus Christ.[12] We intend only to look at the most important and remembered events in the Old Testament to indicate that the Bible supports *both* the fact that revelatory events are knowable or understandable by at least the indispensable aid of empirical knowledge *and* that such events can be recorded and historically remembered as the pinnacle of God's manifestation of His sovereignty, providence, and power in Jewish history. These Old Testament events are the plagues in Egypt, culminating in the Passover—the center of Jewish history.

The purpose of the plagues is given by God to Moses in Exodus 7:3-5:

---

12. The most comprehensive book in this regard if not the most readable is the compilation of historical evidences in Josh McDowell, *Evidence That Demands a Verdict.* An interesting book is Frank Morison's *Who Moved the Stone?* The author intended to write a book refuting the resurrection but could not due to "the very stubbornness of the facts themselves," p. 5.

> But I will harden Pharaoh's heart, and though I multiply my miraculous signs and wonders in Egypt, he will not listen to you. Then I will lay my hand on Egypt and with mighty acts of judgment I will bring out my divisions, my people the Israelites. And the *Egyptians will know* that I am the LORD when I stretch out my hand against Egypt and bring the Israelites out of it (italics added).

Two things are to be noted here. First, though God performed "miraculous signs and wonders" it was not necessary that Pharaoh acquiesce to the knowledge that is possible through such deeds. However, it is possible for unbelievers to at least intellectually know by hearing and seeing these signs, wonders, and acts that the living God is present. This was exactly what Moses claimed was possible to Pharaoh when he predicted the frogs would withdraw to the Nile on the very next day so that Pharaoh "may know there is no one like the Lord our God" (Ex. 8:10).

Pharaoh, however, was stubborn, and the Lord confirmed him in hardness of heart. This was not the case for either his magicians or his court officials. They *knew* that the plagues were the work of *the* living and true God. The magicians clearly told Pharaoh that the continuing plagues were "the finger of God" (Ex. 8:19). The officials, becoming impatient after additional plagues, cried out: "How long will this man be a snare to us? Let the people go, so that they may worship the LORD their God. Do you not yet realize that Egypt is ruined?" (Ex. 10:7).

We can conclude this brief analysis of the possibility of the knowledge of God through supernatural historical events by noting the words addressed to the believing Jews and about the Egyptians in regard to the crossing of the Red Sea. To the Israelites Moses said, "Do not be afraid. Stand firm and you will *see* the deliverance the LORD will bring you today" (Ex. 14:13, italics added). To Moses, but on behalf of the Egyptians, God said, "The Egyptians will *know* that I am the LORD when I gain glory through Pharaoh, his chariots and his horsemen" (Ex. 14:18, italics added). For the Israelites empirical acquisition of knowledge was quite evident as they would "see" the Lord's deliverance. The pagan Egyptians would even be able to infer from this same event the evidence that Yahweh was truly the Lord.

Our conclusion is not only that empirically based knowledge is possible, but that revelatory historical events can be correctly comprehended intellectually, if not personally and existentially, by unbelievers. Immediate and empirical Christian evidence presented to first-hand witnesses cannot therefore be denied.

But we are not immediate witnesses to such evidence. Is there any biblical indication that men of subsequent generations can know of previous revelatory actions and supernatural events in a legitimate and satisfactory manner? There most certainly is! Through most of Moses' final speech to Israel prior to their entrance into the land, he reminded them of what God had done for their parents and ancestors, even themselves as young people under twenty years of age, in bringing them out of Egypt:

> Only be careful, and watch yourselves closely so that you do not forget the things your eyes have seen or let them slip from your heart as long as you live .... Has any god ever tried to take for himself one nation out of another nation, by testings, by miraculous signs and wonders, by war, by a mighty hand and an outstretched arm, or by great and awesome deeds, like all the things the LORD your God did for you in Egypt before your very eyes? (Deut. 4:9, 34)

Similar verses in Deuteronomy emphasize both the past empirical knowability of God through historical deeds, and the possibility of communicating this knowledge based on history (see 6:22; 7:19; 10:21; 11:2-7). The same appeal to God's past activity as evidence of His ultimacy was made by Joshua at the completion of the conquest of the land (Josh. 24:2-18) and by Gideon (Judg. 6:8-10, 13). The ability to verbally communicate historical events as empirical evidence—either as items to remember for those who had experienced them or for subsequent generations—is clearly affirmed in these verses. Rahab illustrates that those of the same generation, but with only hearsay or second-hand evidence, can intellectually know that "the LORD your God is God in heaven above and in the earth below" (Josh. 2:11; see also Josh. 4:20—5:1). Even more telling is God's promise that these revelatory historical events were being done for the very purpose of definitive evidence of His existence and sovereignty to later generations:

> Then the LORD said to Moses, "Go to Pharaoh, for I have hardened his heart and the hearts of his officials so that I may perform these miraculous signs of mine among them *so that you may tell your children and grandchildren how I dealt harshly with the Egyptians and how I performed my signs among them, and that you may know that I am the LORD*". (Ex. 10:1-2, italics added)

It does not seem that there could be any more definitive endorsement of historical evidences for apologetics than that. Those signs point beyond the event to the divine purpose and intention of the events in question. On the basis of those sign acts or revelatory events not only could the then current generation know that Yahweh was Lord, but also their children and grandchildren, and by extension, people of the twentieth century can similarly know that Yahweh is Lord. We see this principle of extension in practice throughout the Old Testament. The Psalms, used in worship by later generations of Israel, constantly remind us *both* of God's supernatural deeds and revelatory acts that were empirically known *and* of the possibility of oral or written transmission of this evidence. The most definitive statements are Psalms 78 and 105. Asaph's introduction to Psalm 78 is sufficient for our purposes:

> O my people, hear my teaching;
>   listen to the words of my mouth.
> I will open my mouth in parables,
>   I will utter things hidden from of old—
> things we have heard and known,
>   things our fathers have told us.
>   (Psalm 78:1-3)

The Scriptures and the practice in Israel confirm the role historical evidences must play in our apologetic framework. This does not endorse all evidential approaches in contemporary apologetics that seemingly forget that the unbeliever *cannot*, because he will not, *apply* these facts of Jewish/Christian history as they must be personally applied. But it does mean that the Christian apologist *cannot* forsake historical evidence for scriptural presuppositions supposedly free of the ambiguity of history and its interpretation, because biblical revelation is *both* history as event *and* word as divine interpretation of these events. In other words, the evidentialist cannot appeal to Christian evidences without bringing with him the Christian understanding of those evidences and thus Christian presuppositions, and the presuppositionalist cannot bring the Word of God to bear on the heart of twentieth-century man without bringing with him the record of God's past revelatory and redemptive activity in history and therefore evidences. It is not simply a matter of emphasis or starting point, for event and word, evidence and scriptural presuppositions, can never be separated. *One can neither exclusively start with nor emphasize either historical evidence or theological presuppositions as these are never apart in Scripture.* Biblical revelation is *both* the recorded evidence *and* having the correct interpretation and meaning of that evidence. These cannot be separated. Our apologetic epistemology must follow, not bifurcate, God's revelation.

INTUITIVE KNOWLEDGE

Our final way of knowing what is vital to Christian apologetics is intuition. To quickly dispel any misconceptions of what is intended here by specifying intuition as a way of knowing, we shall define the term from Webster: "the immediate knowing or learning of something without the conscious use of reasoning; instantaneous apprehension."

Intuitionism usually has two emphases in philosophy: the doctrine that the reality of perceived objects is known by intuition; and the doctrine that absolute ethical principles are known by intuition. Both of these teachings are seemingly correct, especially the latter as man has inherent moral consciousness through being made in God's image. Paul speaks of Gentiles doing by nature the things required by the revealed law, thus demonstrating that "the requirements of the law are written on their hearts, their consciences also bearing witness, and their thoughts now accusing, now even defending them" (Rom. 2:15). It is that *inherent apprehension* we are concerned with here. Not, however, the inherent apprehension that sense objects are real regardless of the problems of substantiating such epistemologically, nor the self-authenticating and thus really intuitive aware-

ness of the universal applicability of the law of noncontradiction. Rather we are concerned with the innate knowledge of God
in every person, regardless of the extent of a person's consciousness of or suppression of that knowledge. The most definitive
passage for general/natural revelation is Romans 1:18-32. Verses
18-20 are especially important:

> The wrath of God is being revealed from heaven against all the
> godlessness and wickedness of men who suppress the truth by
> their wickedness, since what may be known about God is plain
> [in] them, because God has made it plain to them. For since the
> creation of the world God's invisible qualities—his eternal power
> and divine nature—have been clearly seen, being understood
> from what has been made, so that men are without excuse.

The word translated by the NIV "to them" in verse 19 is *en*,
usually in the locative ("in") or instrumental ("by") case rather
than the dative ("for" or "to"). The second phrase seems to
repeat the first phrase if *en* is translated as dative. Therefore
the locative case ("in them") is preferred, as per the KJV and
the NASB. Verse 20 clearly affirms that what we call the general
or natural revelation of God is inherent in and simultaneous
with the act of creation. What is true of creation in general is of
course true of man in particular, since man has been made in
the very image of God with the intent and purpose of having
fellowship with Him. As conscious beings made to relate to
God, and with His image stamped upon our being, we not only
can empirically see the visible things that necessarily point to
the reality of the eternal and omnipotent God, but we can know
with "instantaneous apprehension" the reality and presence of
God within us without the conscious use of either inductive or
deductive reasoning. Calvin wrote "there exists in the human
mind, and indeed by natural instinct, some sense of Deity, we
hold to be beyond despute, since God himself . . . has endued
all men with some idea of his Godhead."[13] This sense of deity is
"indelibly engraven on the human heart."[14]

Man can never escape this fact of his nature. Individual men
may claim to be atheistic, and intellectually and consciously they

13. John Calvin *Institutes of the Christian Religion* 1.3. 1.
14. Ibid., 1.3.3.

honestly are. Nevertheless, they still have the stamp and "inspection ticket" of being God's product. The Fall of man did not eradicate this intuitive knowledge of God. Fallen man is still God-created man, and thus, though the knowledge of God is blurred because of the effacement of God's image, the image is still resident within man and so, therefore, is the knowledge of God. Man has lost neither his rational competency and creativity given by God nor his ethical accountability to God. Man looking within himself cannot totally erase this intuitive knowledge. He tries mightily to explain himself by a plethora of psychological and sociological theories, in much the same way that he attempts to explain the general revelation of God external to himself by various evolutionary hypotheses. Man, however, cannot suppress the knowledge he holds within his being.

Verse 18 is frequently translated men "hold the truth" (KJV), or men "suppress the truth" (RSV, NASB, NIV), or "are stifling the truth" (NEB). The word in the Greek text is *katechontōn* from *katechō* meaning "to hold, retain, hinder, restrain, to hold fast, to hold back."[15] The contextual usage normally has to determine its positive or negative connotation. For instance, in 1 Corinthians 7:30 and 2 Corinthians 6:10 *katechō* is used positively as a participle meaning presently possessing, whereas in Luke 4:42 and Philemon 13 it has the idea of detaining or keeping one from going on his intended or rightful way. The problem with Romans 1:18 is that the context does not absolutely demand a positive or negative meaning to Paul's use of this word. I believe this was intentional on Paul's part. Paul realized that man *both* holds the revelation of God within himself by the creation fiat *and* universally hinders or holds down this revelation subsequent to his separation from God in rebellion. Thus because of his wickedness and desire to remain independent of *the* God, man continues to dream the humanistically inspired dream of himself as an autonomous god and necessarily suppresses the truth of his own dependence and ethical accountability.

This autonomous rebellion of man frequently hits low ebbs historically, and revival occurs to bring at least a greater portion of mankind to a renewed relationship with God through forgiveness of sins by the substitutionary atonement of Christ and the regeneration (new birth) of the very essence of man's

---

15. Henry George Liddell and Robert Scott, *A Greek-English Lexicon*, p. 926.

being. Without such revival, civilizations eventually become more and more wayward and die a social death because of the degree of abnormality of personal and social relationships from what God intended for man. Our day may be such a day. Dreadful godlessness and wickedness seem to surround us on every side, and the wrath of God hangs over fallen man like a guillotine. Man senses little purpose or meaning in his existence. Novels and plays depict the horror of nuclear war, economic catastrophe, and senseless and hideous crimes against the person. Meaninglessness plagues us, and we are nauseated by our own existence and a stranger even to ourselves—let alone to others—believing there to be no exit other than drugs or suicide. Man's plight really never changes. During his twenties Augustine felt the same way as he exchanged women and philosophies as easily as he changed clothes, but he eventually turned by God's grace from such a life-style and realized that the reason for the change was that "thou hast formed us for Thyself, and our hearts are restless till they find rest in Thee."[16]

As it will be emphasized in the final segment of this chapter, the Christian apologist must not shy away from this fact of man's inherent restlessness without the divine relationship. Forgiveness and freedom from more than self-imposed or group-induced guilt is needed by every man cut adrift of his ultimate meaning and purpose, as all psychiatrists either in frustration admit or themselves consciously suppress. Christian apologists must always be cognizant that secular world views are innately incapable of fulfilling man's transcendent needs. Only the transcendent God fulfills man's longings for ultimate love and therefore provides a rationale for personal love between human subjects. God also quells the questions of intuitive fear before the threat of nonbeing, and provides absolute guidelines and moral enablement for ethical accountability.[17] Because these needs are a part of man's nature, however much he denies and suppresses

16. Augustine _Confessions_ 1. 1. 1.
17. It must be realized that although we are writing of an intuitive knowledge of God based on the ontological makeup of man in God's image, God and man are absolutely two different realities and thus a monistic mysticism is impossible. However, because God is reflected in man's being, though certainly not identical with man, there is a semblance of truth in introvertive mysticisms that attempt to find God at the "bottom" of the human personality.

them either consciously or unconsiously, we know the gospel of Christ has an innate appeal to man's essence. We therefore need not always argue on a strictly rational basis of facts that may be true but will not be rightly understood due to the individual's intellectual framework; rather, we may sometimes reach the unconverted "heart" by appealing to the nature of man's being, because as Christian apologists we know that knowledge of God is engraven indelibly on that heart.

DISTINGUISHING WORLD VIEWS

There is yet one apologetic task for an ontologically determined epistemology. If there are numerous world views, how are we to distinguish between the true and the false, or, put apologetically, between Christian theism and the host of philosophical and theological "isms?" That would require a book in its own right if it were attempted for individual systems. Subsequent chapters, especially 4 and 6, will point out the theological necessities of positive historical evidence and the manner and tactics of the apostles. Here is offered only a general orientation to the subject of tests for truth. There are four tests: systematic consistency, empirical adequacy, experiential sufficiency, and pragmatic reliability. These tests can never be divided or separated. The latter three are really subdivisions of the first, systematic consistency. It might be pictured thus:

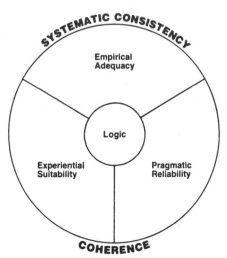

Systematic consistency is more than observance of the law of noncontradiction, but it is not less. The absence of logical consistency is a sure test for the absence of truth. That is why hypocrisy is so damaging to Christian apologetics. The individual who says he is a Christian, but does not live like a Christian, actually gives the lie to his own testimony. Unfortunately, unbelievers interpret this contradiction as an indication of the absence of truth in the claims of Christianity.

Logical consistency is not sufficient in its own right to establish truth. Syllogisms may be consistent and valid but not true. The content of the premises that make up a syllogism is all-important, because truth is not the same as logical validity. For instance, *all Christian apologists are philosophers; all philosophers are Communists; therefore, all Christian apologists are Communists!* The syllogism is valid as it meets all the rules of deductive validity, but it is patently untrue. The problem is with the second statement, which is false: "All philosophers are Communists." Therefore the conclusion does not match reality and is also false. This is why the outer circle of the above diagram is labeled *coherence* as well as *systematic consistency.* *Coherence* involves more than deductive correctness; it also includes empirical adequacy and experiential sufficiency, and pragmatic reliability. Truth matches what is and at the same time meets personal needs; in short, it can be tested and found to work. Each of these subsidiary tests is as inadequate separately as logical (systematic) consistency alone was shown to be in the syllogistic illustration above. Truth is *both* formal (valid or consistent) *and* also material, that is, whatever exists and is brought into our experience in a meaningful, fruitful way must be systematically comprehended. This is exactly what is done for revelatory data in biblical theology, and the goal of systematic theology is simply more all-encompassing.

Systematic consistency is thus a combination of formal and material truth. As *consistency* it is formal, as *systematic* it is material in that it attempts to make all the data—objective, subjective, and practical—fit together in one coherent wholistic perspective. This is the *Both/And* of facts and logic, induction and deduction, content and form. Or in Kantian terms, formal validity without material facts is empty; material facts without the formal direction of logic are blind.

The three facets (empirical adequacy, experiential sufficiency, and pragmatic reliability) that provide the data for systematic consistency must be looked at more closely. First, it must be reiterated that none of these taken separately is a sufficient test of truth. Each is important only as it provides the facts that individually and corporately relate in a coherent manner within the circle of systematic consistency. They are the realities of the space-time universe relating in a noncontradictory fashion.

Empirical realities are the ordinary data of the academic disciplines and all fields of knowledge as well as the extraordinary data of revelation and miracle. Coherence relates, then, to all the physical and social sciences as well as the supernatural elements of Christianity, including those things usually labeled Christian evidences that are considered irrational by other world views, that is, fulfilled prophecy, the Person of Jesus Christ, His resurrection, and the testimonies of millions of transformed lives. It is our contention that Christian theism is the only perspective that coherently relates all the data, natural as well as supernatural, by means of an empirical adequacy that is both personally appropriate and practically workable. Two additional circles visualize these universal and particular constructs:

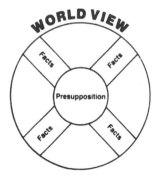

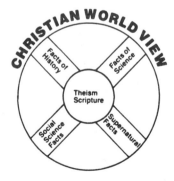

Distinguishing among world views is not totally a matter of systematic consistency or coherence. Coherence, in one respect at least, is a matter of perspective. If two people are looking at the facts of paleontology through evolutionary and creationist glasses respectively, they are not really looking at the same facts. They both believe that their respective beliefs are coherent. However, the Christian apologist "knows" that the facts are *pure* facts to God alone. The honest Christian apologist does not naively attempt to identify his understanding of particular facts with God's. God's undistorted and unlimited perspective of all facts is the sole objective interpretation of the "facts." Nevertheless, the Christian does realize that the objective facts are not as the naturalist or evolutionary scientist interprets them, even if he realizes that his own understanding is also incomplete, if not totally erroneous as theirs is. The world, be it facts of hard or soft sciences or history, questions of origins or destiny, meaning or purpose, is always a God-interpreted world. The divine parameter, which does not necessarily provide all the details, is the circumference of God's Word—holy Scripture. Scripture is and must be the final criterion of ordering, grouping, and interpreting the facts.

This does not mean the Christian is constantly quoting the Bible to the unbeliever. It does, however, mean that the world view he presents is not Christian if it contradicts the clear instruction of the Bible. It also means that his entire witness and perspective is implicitly molded by the Bible at all times and all points, even if this is not continuously made explicit to the unbeliever. This was Paul's practice on the Areopagus. Therefore, the apologist must continue to "drive home" the objective, God-created, God-interpreted facts that do not "fit" in a truly objective manner with nontheistic assumptions. In the case of paleontology, the Christian apologist must, for example, repeatedly question whether the presence of the footprints of huge reptiles in the same geological strata as man's is more conducive to evolutionary or creationist understanding. The well-known incompatibility of the Second Law of Thermodynamics (law of energy decay) with an evolutionary model must be emphasized, especially in light of the creation model virtually *predicting* it. The evidence of a world-wide flood must be cogently presented as more comprehensively explaining many of the facts for which uniformitarian geology requires millions, and according to some scientists, billions of years to explain.

Such God-interpreted facts as these will not break down the barriers of ethical alienation and sinful estrangement between God and man. As apologists we must remember that the unbelieving perspectives taken are programmed and conditioned by man's fallen nature as well as one's particular family, education, social and cultural environment, and a host of other temporal factors. Nevertheless, an honest scientist, or truly searching person, will *know*—perhaps even better, *feel*— by means of his God-given logic that data similar to the above point to a Creator, not a "big bang." Since God made man's mind, and wishes to convey true knowledge of Himself to man's mind, God will not rescue the individual from himself and his own sinfulness, bringing him to Himself through the blood of Christ, *without appealing to truth.*

Because each unbeliever is an individual made in God's image, he deserves our total respect as a person and therefore must be witnessed to and dealt with in a very personal and individual way. Paul instructs us: "Be wise in the way you act toward outsiders; make the most of every opportunity. Let your conversation be always full of grace, seasoned with salt, so that you may know how to answer [each] one" (Col. 4:5-6). It should be noted that the Greek construction *eni ekastō* would seem to comprehend every person individually, therefore "each one" rather than "everyone" (NIV) is preferable. This means we try to meet people individually "where they are." For our philosophic or scientific friends who believe they "have it all together" that will probably mean providing them facts, as in the previous paragraph, that are incompatible with their naturalistic or evolutionary viewpoints. For others, who admittedly do not have it all together, this may simply mean presenting the biblical understanding of reality as well as answering their philosophical, psychological, and other questions to aid them in seeing their own and the universe's meaning. For both types, personal testimony and a clear presentation of man's need and God's provision in Christ must never be attenuated or downplayed.

That mention of man's need cannot be apologetically overlooked. Though the objective evidence (whether received negatively because of atheistic presuppositions or positively because of traditional Christian presuppositions) is indispensable, it may still not be the most important factor. Man is God's creature whether individual men recognize this or not. Many of man's emotional and psychological problems are caused by his unconscious suppression of his God-consciousness discussed above. We must make the unbeliever as conscious as possible of this intuitive knowledge of God. In denying God he separates himself not only from the personal source of being, but also from his own personhood because he consciously cannot reconcile his personality with his assumed evolutionary origins. He, therefore, has sociological problems because, if he denies his unique status as made in God's image, he naturally perceives others in the same way and thus inherently cannot treat them as they personally expect and as he likewise for _some reason_ expects himself to be treated. _No other world view explains the source, desires, destiny, and transcendent longings of man's personhood:_ not the philosophic idealisms of Plato, Spinoza, or Hegel; not the impersonal naturalisms of Aristotle, Epicurus, Heidegger, or Whitehead; not the personality denying religions of Buddhism and Hinduism. We fail miserably as Christian apologists and theologians if we fail at this point. Man is personal! God is personal! Christ manifests the congruent personality of both in one Person! A glimpse of this personal emphasis can be seen in Paul's argument from the personal nature of the Athenians to the absurdity of believing the ultimate is impersonal: "Therefore since we are God's offspring, we should not think that the divine being is like gold or silver or stone—an image made by man's design and skill" (Acts 17:29).

Enough has been said above and in the two previous sections of this chapter about empiricism and intuition to indicate the basic thrust of empirical adequacy and experiential suitability. But what of pragmatic reliability? While remembering this is not a separate test for truth, what is meant by such a test? Some apologists go out of their way to critique it (Carnell),[18] and other Christian apologists are labeled in a rather pejorative way as pragmatic (Schaeffer).[19] By pragmatic reliability we are not thinking of the extremes of William James (1842-1910) when he writes that "truth _happens_ to an idea. It _becomes_ true, is _made_ true by events."[20] More agreeable is Charles Sanders Peirce's (1839-1914) famous statement that "the essence of

18. Edward J. Carnell, _An Introduction to Christian Apologetics_, pp. 50-55.
19. Norman Geisler, _Christian Apologetics_, p. 110.
20. William James, _Pragmatism_, p. 133.

belief is the establishment of a habit, and different beliefs are distinguished by the different modes of action to which they give rise."[21] Peirce's pragmatism was not really a test for truth but a theory of meaning. Certainly different actions should become habitual for the Christian. Actions and habits should indicate the change of the new birth. Prayer replaces cursing. Love now transcends selfishness. Self-discipline becomes habitual rather than debauchery.

In this sense, pragmatic reliability is to be understood as explaining the great testimonies of transformed lives and the continued reliable transformations that indicate the truth of Christianity. Be it Paul or Augustine, Christianity demonstrates its truth by the workability of its message in producing "new creations" (2 Cor. 5:17) in Christ.[22] Jesus prayed that His disciples might be sanctified, separated, "by the truth; your word is truth" (John 17:17). This sanctification process shows the practical and truth-attesting workability of Christian faith. Twice in the Sermon on the Mount Jesus distinguished false from true prophets by their fruits (Matt. 7:16-20). In the Upper Room Discourse Christ used the analogy of the vine and the branches to illustrate the change in a true believer's life. Paul prayed that the Colossians might be fruitful in every good work (Col. 1:10) and that the Philippians might be "filled with the fruit of righteousness" (Phil. 1:11). He listed such fruit production in Galatians 5:22-23. Peter pungently testified to the evangelistic import of a transformed life when he instructed believing wives to win over their unbelieving husbands "without talk by [their] behavior" (1 Pet. 3:1; see also v. 2). Christianity's most telling apologetic is the steady and pragmatic reliability of the Christ-like life so that, as Christ prayed, "the world may believe that you have sent me" (John 17:21). Contemporary believers are the ongoing Christian evidence in every generation. We, by word and deed, are His witnesses. *The transformed life is an ultimately irrefutable apologetic, if not a complete and self-authenticating one.*

21. Charles Sanders Peirce, "How to Make Our Ideas Clear," *Philosophical Writings of Peirce,* p. 29.
22. See Josh McDowell, *Evidence That Demands a Verdict,* The final chapter of this book is devoted to relating numerous testimonies of the Christian experience.

4

BIBLICAL THEOLOGICAL NECESSITIES

An apologetic framework is not only molded by the ontological structure and its epistemological determinations, but also by the theological characteristics of Christianity itself. Apologetic construction must take into account, and remain within the parameters of, the nature of Christianity. These might be labeled the biblical theological necessities of our apologetic methodology. For example, if Christianity is inherently historical, in fact making claims for history that no other religion claims, then the resultant apology of Christianity must be greatly determined by historical emphases. Similarly, if Christianity is also inherently supernatural and authoritative, to look at two other facets, then the defense of its truthfulness cannot be tentative as to the reality of miracles and the absolute authority of the Word of the absolute God.

This chapter need not be as lengthy as one might think. This is not because theology takes a backseat to philosophy, but because a few of these biblical theological dimensions have been dealt with at least indirectly to illustrate the roles of reason, sensation, and intuitive knowledge. Nothing more need be said, for instance, on general revelation. The sections on special revelation and the historical nature of Christianity can be briefer than otherwise in light of the previous statements about these in chapter 3. We begin with the historical nature of Christianity.[1]

The first three theological necessities cannot really be separated as they are essentially identical ontologically; Christianity is historical, revelatory, and supernatural. The historicity of Christianity will be looked at first in order to emphasize both the "checkability" of Christianity and how Christianity differs from other religions. Christianity is not deism—God *is* involved in the affairs of men. Daniel is able to interpret the prophetic dream because "there is a God in heaven who reveals mysteries. He has shown King Nebuchadnezzar what will happen in days to come" (Dan. 2:28). Whether prophecy is given directly to God's people, or indirectly as when given first to Nebuchadnezzar, its fulfillment demonstrates God's sovereignty over the affairs of either nations or individual men. In Nebuchadnezzar's case, it was both national and individual (cf. Dan. 2:37-38; 4:25-37).

Daniel is not unique among the prophets of Israel. They all insist that God controls history. Idols are spiritless and powerless, but Yahweh, the living God, has both spirit and life and discloses Himself in both the ordinary course of affairs and the extraordinary, as in the clash of Elijah with the prophets of Baal. The circumstances of this contest are remote to modern minds: two offerings and the waiting for fire. But the results are as real as the providential directing, healing, and supplying that God in Christ has always provided for His children. Whereas the prophets of Baal had "no response, no one answered, no one paid attention" (1 Kings 18:29), the response to Elijah's prayer was that "the fire of the LORD fell and burned up the sacrifice, the wood, the stones and the soil, and also licked up the water in the trench" (18:38). Verse 39 continues: "When all the people saw this, they fell prostrate and cried, 'The LORD— he is God! The LORD—he is God.' " Such is the differentiation

---

1. I owe my initial insights on these enumerated characteristics to Dr. Victor Matthews's book *Growth in Grace*.

of the false god from the true God. It is always the same. Historical deed and historically fulfilled prediction distinguish the dead from the living, the false from the true, the idol from the self-revealing, sovereign God. Pharaoh knew both deed and fulfilled prediction, as was seen previously.

History is not only past events. History is also the written record of the past. Quotations from 1 Kings provide the written record of Elijah's past deed. Many cast skeptical aspersions on the possibilities of historiography—the writing of history. Doubtless it is never an easy task, but that does not mean that it is a hopeless task.[2] It is important for our purposes, however, to note the New Testament affirmation of the possibility of communicating accurate knowledge by means of historical writing, be the historian an eyewitness or a second-hand witness.

As an eyewitness, the apostle John obviously believed that he could convey accurate knowledge of past events, to people either one or two generations later than the Christ-event, by a written record:

> That which was from the beginning, which we have heard, which we have seen with our eyes, which we have looked at and our hands have touched—this we proclaim concerning the Word of life. The life appeared; we have seen it and testify to it, and we proclaim to you the eternal life, which was with the Father and has appeared to us. We proclaim to you what we have seen and heard, so that you also may have fellowship with us. And our fellowship is with the Father and with his Son, Jesus Christ. We write this to make [your] joy complete. (1 John 1:1-4)[3]

This verse could have been easily appealed to above in support of the possibility and reliability of empirical knowledge. It seems impossible to deny all empirical knowledge, as one leading evangelical apologist does, in light of John's assertions here. Nevertheless, that is not our primary concern. This is historical

2. Three valuable books on historiography are: Harry Elmer Barnes, *A History of Historical Writing*; Louis Gottschalk, *Understanding History*; Wood Gray et. al., *Historian's Handbook*.
3. Recent English translations read "our joy," but numerous ancient manuscripts, including Alexandrinus and most minuscules, read "your" (*humōn*). "Your" would appear to be the natural reading.

writing by an eyewitness. This is the kind of sworn testimony that judge and jury desire in court. Not what you have heard rumored, or second-hand evidence, but the kind of empirical evidence that indicates an immediate witness to the events in question. Thus John is giving to his original readers a definitive record of the incarnation of Him who was from the beginning of beginnings (*archē*). This record is equally valid for the reader of today since the reliability of the testimony does not depend on the historical proximity of the reader to the original document.

John, then, is like and unlike all other historians. Like all other historians, John is reliable to us to the same degree he was reliable to his original readers. Unlike all nonbiblical historians, John had the Holy Spirit of God to superintend and direct his selection of data, his recording of that data, and his interpretation of the historiographical account so that his product is 100 percent accurate. This is not an inductive historical conclusion, however, but is known a priori by the biblical and theological doctrine of divine inspiration of Scripture. In the final analysis, biblical accounts are different from all other historical records as they are the joint product of God and the human historian. Thus John can write near the conclusion of his gospel that "Jesus did many other miraculous signs in the presence of his disciples, which are not recorded in this book. But these are written that you may believe that Jesus is the Christ, the Son of God, and that by believing you may have life in his name" (John 20:30-31).

Obviously, the same must be said of Luke, except there is one major distinction: Luke, like ourselves, is a second-hand witness. He opens his two-volume history thusly:

> Many have undertaken to draw up an account of the things that have been fulfilled among us, just as they were handed down to us by those who from the first were eyewitnesses and servants of the word. Therefore, since I myself have carefully investigated everything from the beginning, it seemed good also to me to write an orderly account for you, most excellent Theophilus, so that you may know the certainty of the things you have been taught. (Luke 1:1-4)

Historical research was conductible and capable of giving Theophilus an account that would provide objective evidence of the things concerning Jesus of Nazareth in whom he had already been taught and apparently believed. Inspired or not, Luke did very careful historical research. He drew on previous records and eyewitness testimony. His careful investigation permitted him to compile his own account of the recent revelatory (fulfilled events) history. Theophilus could then read that account and gain additional knowledge of the saving history.

The epistemological and apologetic importance of Luke's introductory paragraph is often overlooked by people in a hurry to get to the "real" beginning. That paragraph provides the Bible-centered Christian with the assurance that truth can be conveyed by means of historical documents. Though the history book is not *the history*, it nevertheless can transmit an accurate record and at least partial interpretation of the particular history the historian is interested in. Also of crucial importance (given the neo-orthodox differentiation of secular history and revelatory-salvation history as two species of a different kind, *Historie* and *Geschichte*), Luke believed he could record the events of revelatory-salvation history like all other history. Luke made a very special effort to show that the Christ-event is embedded in the history of the first century (Luke 1:5; 2:1-3; 3:1-2; Acts 13:7; 18:12; 24:1-2, 27; 25:13-15).[4] For Luke historical information was essential for one to accept and believe an historical revelation and thus have an historical faith. However, this does not give full warrant to the usual evidential approach in Christian apologetics. True revelatory history is as historical as any other history. *But*, it cannot be interpreted like all other history. All other history may be and is understandable within the horizontal flow of cause and effect in the domain of created nature. Luke's historical subject cannot be so understood. This does not make it any less history, though it must eliminate the historicistic orientation of the historian. As historically oriented as Luke is, the first three chapters make a historicistic orientation impossible. Virgin births do not occur among humans;

---

4. Two books that delineate Luke's historiographical ability and accuracy are I. Howard Marshall, *Luke: Historian and Theologian*; and A. N. Sherwin-White, *Roman Society and Roman Law in the New Testament*.

only a supernatural frame of reference is possible. We cannot separate Luke's historical data from its Holy Spirit guided and interpreted Word. There is no naturalistic or historicistic common ground between Luke and his fellow historians of the first century, like Tacitus and perhaps even Josephus. Christian revelatory history can never be presented in the same evidential manner as other historical events. There is an absolute and therefore normative interpretation, while at the same time it is historical fact and may not be lightly dismissed by the unbeliever. Christian historical evidences, rightly interpreted, are indispensable to every Christian apology.

CHRISTIANITY IS REVELATORY

The difference between ordinary historical events and extraordinary historical events is the latter's supernatural character and revelatory function. Although every event recorded in the Bible is definitely not miraculous and supernatural, many events are. It is these events that are the most directly revelatory of God's person and will, although the entire biblical record gives evidence of God's providence and sovereignty over man's history in general, and the people of God in particular.

Special revelation is not coincidental with creation and is thus not logically necessary as is general revelation. Special revelation is the prerogative of divine grace and love; post-Fall, it is primarily redemptive in intent. It is the story of God's provision and is therefore *both* the event *and* written record of God's redemptive activity on behalf of His fallen creation. Special revelation may thus be defined as the demonstration and sharing by God of His person, will, and redemptive activity. By being both historical event and interpretive word, special revelation is neither solely propositional nor solely existential (personal), but Both/And.

Special revelation is a projection of God into history that makes a difference. From Abraham on, the nation of Israel was the recipient of God's revelatory/redemptive activity that distinguished her from among the nations. Thus from the Passover experience, through the crossing of the Red Sea to the institution of the sacrificial system, Yahweh was progressively revealing (uncovering) and continuously reminding Israel of both His person and will through His redemptive program (see Deut. 7:18-19; Josh. 24:17).

Special revelation as historical event, however, is in need of revelation as Word, and vice versa. Historical events are open to diverse interpretations as even a cursory reading of the New Testament illustrates concerning the culmination of God's progressive revelation in the person of Jesus Christ of Nazareth. The incident recorded of the Pharisees' confusion as to the source of His power in exorcism is a case in point (Matt. 12:24-28). There are many others. Therefore, God provides His revelation in history with an interpretive word. Event and word must be nearly one or the event itself will be misinterpreted or, even worse, meaningless. Inspiration is thus inseparable from and indispensable to revelation since *both* event *and* word together are biblical revelation. The Scripture is the Word of God, inerrant in its propositional interpretation of God's person, will, and redemptive activity.[5] Frequently, the Word comes prior to the event as in prophecy (e.g., Christ's second coming), but usually the events transpire prior to the interpretive Word (e.g., the cross and empty tomb are interpreted throughout the New Testament).

The passing reference to Christ demands a few more comments. Jesus Christ is *both* the supreme event of revelation *and* the definitive Word of God's speaking (Heb. 1:1-2). He is the *final expression* of revelation both as historical event and divine Word as God Himself took on flesh and entered into the flow of history. His deeds and words are one, and we cannot choose between them (John 10:37-38). Nothing more can be uncovered of God as God has manifested Himself in person. Jesus Christ is the epitome of the revelation of God's person and will as well as the culmination of redemption. As such, He is the center of both history and revelation and thus subject to preinterpretation (Old Testament) and postinterpretation (New Testament). Nothing can be added to the historical revelation of God in Jesus, the Christ (Rev. 22:18-19; note also John 1:1-2, 14; 14:6;

---

5. It may be appropriate to note that methodologically ontology is prior to epistemology as chapters 2 and 3 demonstrate. Thus, in one sense, we should not say that something is true because the Bible says it, but rather the Bible records it because it is true.

17:14). The *only* Christ is the Christ disclosed to us in holy Scripture. The written witness of the life of Christ is the extension of His spoken Word. One cannot accept the authority of Christ's spoken Word, or understand His message, without understanding and accepting the authority of the New Testament.

This intertwining of scriptural revelation as *both* event *and* word makes the two most common apologetic frameworks and methodologies *logically impossible*. One cannot appeal to revelatory events and the historical words of Jesus without appealing to the Bible itself. The inspired character of the Bible cannot be argued by appeal to Jesus' testimony and attitude toward the Old Testament without basically assuming what you are trying to prove by quoting the New Testament. There is no truly "neutral" appeal to the facts in some forensic and legal manner as the facts are already previously given definitive interpretation in Scripture. This rules out the approach of those who feel there is an analogy between neutral jurors and autonomous and alienated unbelievers who analyze, evaluate, and decide for or against a supernatural and authoritative revelation of the Creator's person and will. Such interpretive common ground simply does not and cannot exist between the believer and unbeliever. Pure common-ground evidentialism is impossible for Christian apologetics. The Christian apologist is not a defense lawyer approaching a neutral and undecided jury. Rather, he faces a self-determined and God-rejecting enemy of Christ in need of divine reconciliation.

This assessment does not indirectly endorse the usual methodology of presuppositionalists who in rightly rejecting man's autonomy deny man any cognitive powers to inductively scrutinize historical evidence. This functionally dichotomizes revelation as event and word, leaving one with an authoritative fideism of word only. Their problem is not really an overstressing of the sovereignty of God—though they frequently forget or overlook God's self-limitation in recognizing man as a personal being created ontologically in God's image. Rather, it is the delimitation of fallen man as less than true man. Fallen man still has cognitive powers to intellectually perceive the intent of revelatory events, if not a spiritual capacity to either personally "know" or voluntarily surrender his autonomy to Him who is behind those events. This must be the case or, as previously noted, the reaction of some of the Egyptians to the plagues is incomprehensible, to say nothing of Jesus' action in the raising of Lazarus (John 11:42, 45-46), or Peter at Pentecost claiming that "Jesus of Nazareth was a man accredited by God to you by miracles, wonders and signs, which God did among you through him, *as you yourselves know*" (Acts 2:22, italics added). Man made and still remaining in God's image has an ontological if not personal right to cognitive evidence of God's historical and thus revelatory activity. He must be confronted with the former before he will be Spirit-induced to accept the latter. As Paul remarks, "How, then, can they call on the one they have not believed in? And how can they believe in the one they have not heard? And how can they hear without someone preaching to them?" (Rom. 10:14). To divorce word from event and refuse historical evidence to the unbeliever on the grounds that to provide such plays to his autonomy is to misunderstand the biblical doctrine of man made in God's image, post-Fall as well as pre-Fall. Such is done not on the basis of biblical considerations, but for the sake of a theological system. It is little wonder that the extreme logical extension of this system sends "no preachers so that men may hear," since men supposedly no longer can cognitively hear the Word of God.

CHRISTIANITY IS SUPERNATURAL

In light of the previous two divisions of this chapter, one cannot deny, nor is extended argument needed to demonstrate, that Christianity is supernatural. This is necessarily the case whenever history and revelation are tangential to one another. The Bible is full of events where history and God's supernatural disclosure are identical. Some miracles are inherently unverifiable (e.g., the virgin birth). Others have great circumstantial as well as first-hand evidence of their facticity (e.g., the resurrection). Archaeology has not only provided great assistance in understanding biblical history and customs, but it has also provided direct evidence of the historicity of many biblical miracles. For instance, the discoveries of John Garstang and others at Jericho agree totally with Joshua 6:20 that the walls of the city fell outward and not inward. Garstang writes: "As to the main fact, then there remains no doubt: the walls fell outwards so completely that the attackers would be able to clamber up and over their ruins into the city."[6]

One additional biblically recorded event that is confirmed by archaeology is the confrontation between Sennacherib and Hezekiah (Isa. 36:1—37:38). The Bible and Sennacherib's own records agree. In the latter, Sennacherib notes that "as for Hezekiah the Jew, who did not submit to my yoke, 46 of his strong walled cities, as well as the small cities in their neighborhood, which were without number . . . I beseiged and took." He continues: "Himself, like a caged bird, I shut up in Jerusalem, his royal city."[7] Nowhere does Sennacherib ever record the capture of Jerusalem and the defeat of Hezekiah as he does all other cities. His western campaign of 701 B.C. ended in the disaster recorded in 2 Kings 19:35 and Isaiah 37:36. This miracle of God's judgment on Assyria and providential protection of Judah might have had a natural basis in plague or pestilence.[8] Though this is unknown, it still would not detract from the supernatural source of the miracle. To reject a miracle on the basis of the probability of that miracle's occurring within an absolute uniformity of nature, per David Hume (1711-1776), is to deny beforehand the very thing in question. Whether God caused something "new" to happen or whether He caused a naturally occurring plague to happen at *that time*, the death of Sennacherib as Isaiah portrays it is a fact confirmed by inscriptions left by his son Esarhaddon and grandson Ashurbanipal.[9] Concerning this and other miracles recorded in the Bible, it may be said that "the excessive skepticism of many liberal theologians stems not from a careful evaluation of the available data, but from an enormous predisposition against the supernatural."[10]

Miracle, then, is inherent in the doctrine of Christian theism, which affirms both God's transcendence and immanence. If God is only transcendent as in deism, miracle does not exist because God is not involved with His creation. This was the

---

6. John Garstang, *Joshua Judges*, p. 146.
7. Merrill F. Unger, *Archaeology and the Old Testment*, p. 267.
8. See Jack Finegan, *Light From the Ancient Past*, pp. 178f.
9. Unger, p. 270.
10. Robert H. Mounce, "Is the New Testament Historically Accurate?" in *Can I Trust The Bible?* ed. Howard F. Vos, p. 176.

outlook of Thomas Jefferson in his infamous edition of the Bible. If God is only immanent as in various pantheisms and idealisms, there is only one order, and thus the very concept of special revelation is eliminated and with it the very possibility of the supernatural itself, let alone miracle. But whenever God is understood as transcendent as well as immanent, miracle is not only possible, *but probable*. In Christianity, where miracle is not simply probable but factual, the apologist must never tacitly downplay such. He must shape his apology to fit his faith and never shape his religion by the necessities of contemporary apology.[11]

CHRISTIANITY IS AUTHORITATIVE

> I have given them your word and the world has hated them, for they are not of the world any more than I am of the world. My prayer is not that you take them out of the world but that you protect them from the evil one. They are not of the world, even as I am not of it. Sanctify them by the truth; your word is truth. (John 17:14-17)

Is there an appeal against truth? If truth is truly true, can it be anything less than authoritative? The answer to these questions is no! Therefore Christianity is authoritative. This does not mean the apologist or preacher is authoritative. Neither does it mean that the Hebrew scholar or the New Testament exegete is the fount of authority. It does mean that God and the expression of Himself in His Word is authoritative. This is the expressed meaning of the many occurrences of "Thus said the Lord" in the Old Testament. This is the obvious meaning of Jesus' words in His prayer, "Your word is truth."

Why then is God's Word so blatantly rejected? Why is it that Jesus says "I have given them your word and the world has hated them"? The hatred directed toward His disciples is not because of their temperaments, personalities, or life-styles— but because they are recipients and transmitters of God's Word of truth. Jesus asked the Jewish populace and Pharisees

---

11. For an extended and excellent treatment of the supernatural and miracle itself in the context of contemporary apologetics see C. S. Lewis, *Miracles*.

a question similar to the above: "If I am telling the truth, why don't you believe me?" (John 8:46). He actually answers His own question in the following verse when He says, "He who belongs to God hears what God says. The reason you do not hear is that you do not belong to God" (8:47). Previously he told them, "You belong to your father, the devil, and you want to carry out your father's desire. He was a murderer from the beginning, not holding to the truth, for there is no truth in him. When he lies, he speaks his native language, for he is a liar and the father of lies" (8:44). This is why the world hates those who are sanctified by the Word of truth. They are no longer under the dominion of the "father of lies." They are set apart to a new Master; the truth has "set [them] free" (8:32) from Satan's activity of blinding "the minds of unbelievers, so that they cannot see the light of the gospel of the glory of Christ, who is the image of God" (2 Cor. 4:4). These blinded men will continue to reject the truths of God's Spirit as foolishness since they "cannot understand them, because they are spiritually discerned" (1 Cor. 2:14).

Truth rejected is truth still! Authority rejected is authority still. Though presumably most Poles would reject their present military government, it is still the authority. Though most men deny that the Bible is the inscripturated absolute Word of God, that does not deny its true reality; only their recognition of and immediate and complete obedience to its dictates are denied. The recognition of the Bible for *what it is* makes it *subjective* authoritative revelation to an individual in his practiced life-style after the scales of spiritual blindness are removed. But that is only because it is the *objective* Word of and from God and therefore both absolute truth and absolute authority. The Christian apologist can never argue independently of this authoritative Word. To do so is to make him a slave to his own opinions and perspectives, leaving him with an orientation no more objective than that of the one to whom he supposedly bears witness. To do so is to lose his theistically-interpreted world, and thus all realities, into an epistemological grab-bag. To do so is to forfeit the very truthfulness of Christianity that apologetics is presumed to be defending.

CHRISTIANITY IS PERSONAL

Paul's request, which should be every Christian's prayer, is: "I want to know Christ and the power of his resurrection and the fellowship of sharing in his sufferings, becoming like him in his death" (Phil. 3:10). Man was originally made, and still is, a personal being able to have personal relationships with God and his fellow men. As a physical and social being, Adam was given Eve to complement his individual reality. Man is intrinsically gregarious.

Man is also *homo religiosus*. Augustine said, "Thou hast formed us for Thyself, and our hearts are restless till they find rest in Thee" (*Confession* 1.1.1.). An atheist is as abnormal as a hermit. As personality degenerates without personal encounter, so too man's spirit shrivels without confrontation with God. Man's personal and ontological essence in God's likeness is not totally fulfilled by finite personhood. Augustine rightly expresses man's pre-Fall experience and post-Fall longings. Paul argues for the necessity of a personal *God* rather than an impersonal *god* of stone or precious metal to adequately explain man's personhood as God's offspring (Acts 17:29). Calvin succinctly notes that "though in old times there were some, and in the present day not a few are found who deny the being of a God, yet, whether they will or not, they occasionally feel the truth which they are desirous not to know" (*Institutes* 1.3.2.).

This innate knowledge and longing by humankind cannot be neglected by the Christian apologist. Though not identical with general revelation, which is an intuitive awareness of the being of God arising from the ontological substructure, this unfulfilled yearning for the infinite springs from this same substratum. It might be possible to visualize this twin phenomena as man *looking inward* to find the ultimate source of his personhood, and *looking outward* to find the ultimate fulfillment of his personal being. Although distinct from mysticism in its usual denial of personhood and attachment to monism, it nevertheless is similar to both the introvertive and extrovertive paths of the mystic way.

Because every man is made in the image of God, we as Christian apologists know who man essentially is, and because of our fallen state alienated from the source of our own being, we know who man actually is. Jesus Christ is the only man whose essential and actual being are one as He was "tempted in every way, just as we are—yet was without sin" (Heb. 4:15). This is the reason Paul keeps asking "that the God of our Lord Jesus Christ, the glorious Father, may give you the Spirit of wisdom and revelation, so that you may know him better" (Eph. 1:17). This is prerequisite for the Christian apologist. He cannot expect to introduce an unbeliever to one who is a stranger to himself in terms of daily relationship. Neither can he expect to be a viable witness if his personal life reflects a tension and alienation between his spiritual reality and his historical actuality. Christ prays that the individual Christian might be one in actuality and essence "so that the world may believe that you have sent me" (John 17:21). Psychiatrists testify that the differentiation between what man perceives himself to be and what he is is frequently the cause of serious mental breakdowns. Our facades wear out. Autonomous fallen man desires to see himself as ultimate—Satan's perpetual temptation—but cannot rid himself of his consciousness of the reality of God. The believer frequently portrays himself as a spiritual giant when in truth he is a defeated Christian pygmy. In other generations when testimony and reality were not identical it was labeled hypocrisy. It still is, if less frequently so labeled.

Christ knows that the world can only know of His reality if His disciples are truly one in deed and word. As the Father and Christ are one in external appearance and inward essence— "Anyone who has seen me has seen the Father" (John 14:9)— so Christ prays that the world might see true personal oneness of the outer and inner man in His disciples and thus be introduced to the One who made such possible. This is life-style apologetics. It is indispensable if believers are really "set apart in truth." For truth is always one. The spoken external word is identical with the reality to which it refers. This is the goal of the Christian life—conformity to the image of His Son. It must not be totally unexperienced in this life. If so, one has never been "set apart in truth."

CHRISTIANITY IS REDEMPTIVE

> There is no difference, for all have sinned and fall short of the glory of God, and are justified freely by his grace through the redemption that came by Christ Jesus. God presented Him as a sacrifice of atonement, through faith in his blood. He did this to demonstrate his justice, because in his forbearance he had left the sins committed beforehand unpunished—he did it to demonstrate his justice at the present time, so as to be just and the one who justifies the man who has faith in Jesus. (Rom. 3:22-26)

The Christian apologist has no message if he overlooks the very heart of the gospel—redemption. The personal relationship intended between God and man was broken by the latter, resulting in spiritual, physical, and eternal death. Death in the Bible is separation—separation from God in personal relationship (spiritual), separation of the life from the body (physical), and separation from God for eternity (eternal). Sin is the sting of death.

Redemption is the very essence of special revelation. From the *protevangelium* of Genesis 3:5 through the call of Abraham, the promise of a Messiah-King to David, and on to the birth of Jesus in Bethlehem, God's purposes have been primarily redemptive—the providing of a means to buy back His created beings by paying the penalty of sin: death! The old theological term *propitiation* (*hilasmos*; NIV, "sacrifice of atonement") conveys the idea of satisfaction by means of a covering. This term referred to the blood sprinkled on the doorpost as a protective covering from the death angel and to the activities of the high priest on the Day of Atonement for the covering of Israel's sin. Christ is our Passover Lamb, our sacrifice of atonement, to cover us from the judgment of God by literally being made "sin for us who knew no sin" (2 Cor. 5:21*a*, KJV). Christ as the final high priest is also the final sacrifice and complete covering for sin, completely satisfying God's righteousness with God's righteousness so that we might be declared justified and thus "become the righteousness of God" (5:21*b*). "Therefore, there is now no condemnation for those who are in Christ Jesus" (Rom. 8:1). Or, put positively, "since we have been justified through faith, we have peace with God through our Lord Jesus Christ" (Rom. 5:1).

Christianity is a "bloody" religion. Redemption is procured only by "faith in his blood" (death) according to our primary text (Rom. 3:25). "We have now been justified by his blood, how much more shall we be saved from God's wrath through him!" (Rom. 5:9). We now "have confidence on the day of judgment, because in this world we are like him" (1 John 4:17). Judgment is a thing of the past. It was accomplished on our behalf by God Himself for even "while we were still sinners, Christ died for us" (Rom. 5:8). Christ's substitutionary death provides forgiveness for moral guilt, cleansing for man's total depravity, reconciliation from our previous alienation, life in place of death, and reunion with God instead of eternal separation. These cannot be subjects only for the preacher or theologian. These are the fruits of Christ's work. They are the good news of the heralds of the new covenant. Apologetics loses its *raison d'être* if either these fruits or redemption itself is left out of the picture. Apologetics, in light of redemption, is no intellectual game. Evangelism is urgent if men are really alienated from God, in bondage to their own depravity, and under the eternal sentence of death: separation from the source of one's being. Apologetics frequently must do battle with intellectual issues and genuine questions. For many in our day, such pre-evangelism is critical. But apologetics must never stop here. It has soteriological concerns. These must not be sidetracked if we are truly "to give an answer to everyone who asks you to give the reason for the hope that you have" (1 Pet. 3:15).

CHRISTIANITY IS COVENANTAL

> For this reason Christ is the mediator of a new covenant, that those who are called may receive the promised eternal inheritance—now that he has died as a ransom to set them free from the sins committed under the first covenant. (Heb. 9:15)

This new relationship is based on the finished work of redemption. According to Paul, "if, when we were God's enemies, we were reconciled to him through the death of his Son, how much more, having been reconciled, shall we be saved through his life!" (Rom. 5:10). This new covenant still only partially fulfills the covenant announced by Jeremiah (Jer. 31:31-34; Heb. 8:6-13). These are the last (post-Messiah) days from the Old Testament perspective (Acts 2:16-17, 33; 1 John 2:18). The new covenant has been instituted and is commemorated every time we participate in the Lord's Supper (Luke 22:20; 1 Cor. 11:25).

John 17 enumerates the various facets of this new relationship between Christ and His disciples (v. 20). They are given a new life principle (vv. 2-3; cf. 2 Cor. 5:17), a new name (v. 6; eventually Christians, Acts 11:26), a new word (v. 8), a new purpose (v. 18), a new master (v. 23), a new love (v. 26), and lastly a new means of communication (vv. 1-26; cf. Matt. 21:22; Luke 11:9; 1 Tim. 2:5; 1 John 2:1). The most substantial of these are the new word and new life. These are the foundations of the other facets of this new covenantal relationship. It is the Word of good news that announces the arrival of a real covering for our sin and actually makes possible the realities of new birth; the sins under the first covenant are finally adequately punished and totally obliterated (Rom. 3:25-26; Heb. 9:15). This word based on God's provision in Christ brings about the switch in allegiance from the temporary "prince of this world" (John 12:31) to the "name that is above every name" (Phil. 2:9).

This new covenantal relationship has life-style implications for apologetics. Apologists are not Christian secessionists. Christ prays for us in John 17 because we are to be left in the world after He has left (v. 11). We are not left to be idle and theologize about the last days (2 Thess. 2:1-2; 3:6-15). Rather, we are sent into the world even as Christ was sent into the world (John 17:18). The comparison is breathtaking. We are indispensable, because of Christ's prior incarnation, death, and resurrection, for the salvation of the world. Heralds there must be! Therefore apologetics is not an enterprise to be carried on between the brethren. It is an enterprise to be taken to the enemy in the midst of the world. We defend in Satan's domain under the headship of our new and victorious Master. It is ultimately His war, and He has already won the decisive battle. We are simply extending the beachhead. We are sent into the world with the enablement of the Holy Spirit *only after* Christ's successful entrance into and exit from this world and ascension into heaven. We are ambassadors of heaven (2 Cor. 5:18-20). We go with the new *agape* love (John 17:26) and with the imperative to "love one another" because "all men will know that you are my disciples if you love one another" (John 13:34-35). Certainly a new covenantal relationship with God in Christ should bear fruit individually and collectively so that the world may know and believe that the covenant-maker has been sent (John 17:21, 23).

CHRISTIANITY IS EXCLUSIVE

In light of the new covenantal relationship provided by God-given redemption, Christianity is absolutely exclusive, for there is only one way to God—Jesus Christ (John 14:6). "He who has the Son has life; he who does not have the Son of God does not have life" (1 John 5:12). There is no personal new creation and restored fellowship with God without the acceptance of the finished work of God in the person of Jesus Christ, God's unique Son. Jesus' high priestly prayer clearly draws this demarcation as He prays for His disciples, not for the world (John 17:9).

Christianity is exclusive because it is God's self-disclosure of His person, absolute will, and redemptive activity. Although there are elements of truth in most religions due to the universality of general revelation, it is this very revelation that also leaves man "without excuse" (Romans 1:18-32). Christianity is not simply the peak of man's religious quest. Christianity is more than the best among many. *It is the only.* "Whoever believes in the Son has eternal life, but whoever rejects the Son will not see life, for God's wrath remains on him" (John 3:36).

As with our conclusion to the section above on redemption, which is the prime factor in Christianity's exclusiveness, apologetics is urgent, urgent, urgent! True, many questions arise in our minds because of this exclusivity. Contemporary theologians resurrect the doctrine of universalism to eradicate the seemingly arbitrary and unjust aspects that they believe they perceive in this teaching. Does God accept those who honestly live up to the law "written on their hearts" as some surmise from Romans 2:14-15? Is there a universal application of Christ's universal provision based on such actualization of

God's law (Rom. 5:18-19)? The "exclusive" passages quoted above do not appear to permit an affirmative answer. Paul shames the Corinthians with the fact that many are ignorant of the truth of God (1 Cor. 15:34). He encourages the Romans to send preachers so that men might hear this truth (Rom. 10:9-15). He explains to the Thessalonians that in the endtime there will be an accentuation of Satan's continued deception of "those who are perishing" (2 Thess. 2:9-12). Thus our prayer, as instructed by Jesus, must be to "ask the Lord of the harvest, therefore, to send out workers [evangelistic apologists] into his harvest field" (Matt. 9:38).

CHRISTIANITY IS DEMANDING

Christianity not only separates men into unbelievers and believers, lost and saved, but it is totally demanding of those who are labeled as His disciples. This demand is not legalistic. It is wholistic. If God has redeemed me from the slave market of sin it is not for the purpose of merely acquiring my talent, time, or money. God has purchased me! My personhood now stands afresh, reconciled, before the Creator. "I am His and He is mine" as the hymn writer put it. When Peter rightly identifies Jesus for who He is, Christ answers: "If anyone would come after me, he must deny himself and take up his cross daily and follow me. For whoever wants to save his life will lose it, but whoever loses his life for me will save it" (Luke 9:23-24).

This is not the place for a Keswick-like sermon. Nevertheless, the Christian apologist must not mislead by "selling" Christianity as the religious panacea. It *is* the cure for man's basic problem—sin and the resultant estrangement between himself and God. It is not the immediate cure for academic, financial, marital, personal, or physical difficulties. And it is demanding! Christianity is not an easy-believism or a fire escape from hell. One cannot initially accept Christ as Savior without accepting Him as Lord. Paul realized this immediately when on the Damascus road he answered, "Who are you, Lord?" (Acts 9:5). Salvation is the reinstitution of the proper Creator-creature relationship. It means I can meet the demands of the first and greatest commandment to "Love the Lord [my] God with all [my] heart, with all [my] soul and with all [my] mind" (Matt.

22:37; see Deut. 6:5). "Heart" in the Jewish perspective means the whole being. My creaturely personhood is no longer attempting to be the center of my personal universe; autonomy has been replaced by theonomy. I now "participate in the divine nature" through the Second Adam (2 Pet. 1:4). The famous Christian philosopher Herman Dooyeweerd writes:

> It is only in Jesus Christ, the incarnate Word and Redeemer, that the image of God has been restored in the religious center of human nature. The redemption by Jesus Christ in its radical biblical sense, means the rebirth of our *heart* and must reveal itself in the whole of our temporal life. Consequently, there now can be no real self-knowledge apart from Jesus Christ. And this biblical self-knowledge implies that our whole world-and-life view must be reformed in a Christo-centric sense.[12]

This is the ongoing experience of the absolute lordship of Christ. This is what Paul means when he says that "I have been crucified with Christ and I no longer live, but Christ lives in me" (Gal. 2:20). This is the Christian "new man" of Ephesians and Colossians (Eph. 2:15; 4:22-24; Col. 3:9-10). Therefore, in Christ and through this continual expression of His lordship, the expectation of God for a creation in His image is met, as is the imperative of Peter based on Leviticus: "Be holy, because I am holy" (1 Pet. 1:16).

CHRISTIANITY IS CONTEMPORANEOUS

Sören Kierkegaard (1813-1855) may not be the best model for an evangelical apologist, but he was correct in one aspect: Christ and the believer must be contemporaneous. But for Kierkegaard this seems to have been envisioned as a task for the believer himself, though in actuality it is simply to affirm that time and space do not confine the ascended Lord of heaven and earth. Neither do we agree with Kierkegaard when he seemingly disassociated the contemporaneous Christ from the Christ of history. The contemporaneous Christ is not a figment of the imagination but identical with the buried, resurrected, and ascended Lord. This means that Christians do not worship

12. Herman Dooyeweerd, *In the Twilight of Western Thought*, p. 191.

only a first-century figure, but that the God who walks and talks with me today is one in Being with the incarnate One of the first century. It means we have the same demanding and covenantal relationship as first-century Christians with Jesus of Nazareth since He "is the same yesterday and today and forever" (Heb. 13:8).

This must be true of the Christian apologist. He cannot merely point to such dynamic relationships with the living God in the Bible. This knowledge of God must be personal. Resurrection is more than a historical accuracy. As A. H. Ackley, the hymn writer, has put it in undeniable testimony, "You ask me how I know He lives? He lives within my heart." This one living "in" the apologist's heart is the objective postresurrection Jesus who promised His disciples He would be with them "always, to the very end of the age" (Matt. 28:20).

God *is* contemporaneous. His is the eternal now. To Moses, to Pharisees, to us; Father, Son, and Holy Spirit are the ever contemporaneous "I am."

5

GREAT APOLOGETIC PRECURSORS

The purpose of this chapter is to sketch in chronological order and in some detail the apologetic orientation and framework of five of the most influential Christian thinkers: Saint Augustine, Thomas Aquinas, John Calvin, Blaise Pascal, and Sören Kierkegaard. This will give a "big picture" of apologetic alternatives before we attempt to digest the more random data of the New Testament and the emphases of the church Fathers in chapters 6 and 7, respectively. These five men were all fervent Christian apologists, but in many ways they differed from each other. A Both/And apologetic is obviously not neutral and thus some polemics will doubtless show amidst what is meant to be primarily an expositional work. This chapter, like the rest of the book, will not deal with individual twentieth-century apologetic frameworks except in passing reference to the rationalistic and fideistic polarities of Calvinistically inclined apologists. This book is an obvious attempt at mediation between those polarities.[1]

1. Two evangelicals who have excellently analyzed the views of twentieth-century apologists are Norman Geisler, *Christian Apologetics*, and Gordon R. Lewis, *Testing Christianity's Truth Claims*.

Apologetic strategies are limited in number. As delineated in chapter 3, there are three primary means of acquiring knowledge in general and knowledge of God in particular: logic (reason), empiricism, and intuition. Philosophies of religion are based on variations of these means, as are apologetic strategies. The history of philosophy is for the most part a history of the differences that arise among the three primary methodologies: a priori deductive and a posteriori inductive methodologies in the West, and an experiential intuitiveness in the East that denies both Western methodologies.

Christian apologists usually follow one of these three paths, though in numerous ways that defy all attempts at precise classification. Inductive empiricism will be the basis for apologists oriented to natural theology who stress the classic theistic arguments. Evidentialists who stress historical evidences and fulfilled prophecies to the neglect or denigration of theistic arguments because of their disdain for philosophy are also rooted in inductive empiricism. This is particularly true in evangelical circles, though Norman Geisler is a notable exception. A priorists will include rationalistic defenders of Anselm's argument as well as those who may almost deny the role of logic in their revelational presuppositionalism. Lastly, some will reject both epistemological paths as totally inadequate for any knowledge of God that must be personal and subjective. Our five apologetic precursors, not just predecessors, can also be delineated as followers of one or the other of these paths (at least for the most part), but the real significance of these "giants" is how they have shaped and determined the three fundamental apologetic orientations: special revelation, natural theology, and personal experience.[2] We begin with Augustine.

AUGUSTINE

Augustine (354-430), a professor of rhetoric, was the son of a warmhearted Christian mother, Monica, and a good-humored but heathen father, Patricious. His late adolescence and early adulthood, as he confesses, were filled with debauchery and

2. This neglects the frequent evangelical Christian evidence approach that is not really philosophical apologetics, though it is usually an unsophisticated combination of all three orientations.

mischieviousness. By one mistress he had a son (*Confessions* 6.15). He did apparently make a genuine search for meaning in life. After rejecting skepticism, he turned first to the excessive dualism of Manicheanism and then to the absolute monism of Neo-Platonism. He testifies to the vanishing of spiritual doubt and the security of eternal life when he obeyed a voice that instructed him to "take up and read," upon which he turned to Romans 13:13-14, "not in orgies and drunkenness, not in sexual immorality and debauchery, not in dissension and jealousy. Rather, clothe yourselves with the Lord Jesus Christ, and do not think about how to gratify the desires of the sinful nature" (*Confessions* 8.12.29). He was ordained in 391 and served as Bishop of Hippo from 394 until his death.

He is probably Christianity's single most influential theologian, affecting all segments of the church if in different ways in Catholicism (ecclesiology) and Protestantism (soteriology). A wonderful facet of his life is the graphic display of God's marvelous grace in transporting him from the depths of immorality to the heights of theological insight and apologetic acumen. He set the Christian intellectual agenda for the next 800 years. As B. B. Warfield wrote: "He stood on the water-shed of two worlds. The old world was passing away; the new world was entering upon its heritage and it fell to him to mediate the transfer of the culture of the one to the other."[3]

Our treatment of Augustine must be limited to simply sketching his primary epistemological conclusions that bear on the knowledge of God and the presentation of Christian truth to the unbeliever. His great historical apology in the midst of Roman decay, *City of God*, is referred to only in light of our primary concerns. His insights into the problem of evil, predestination, language symbols, the Trinity, and so on, must be left to another.

Having once personally known the cul-de-sac of skepticism, Augustine anticipates Renè Descartes (1596-1650), the father of philosophical rationalism, when he writes:

> For if I am deceived, I am. For he who is not, cannot be deceived; and if I am deceived, by this same token I am. And since I am if I

3. Benjamin B. Warfield, *Calvin and Augustine*, p. 310.

am deceived, how am I deceived in believing that I am? for it is certain that I am if I am deceived. Since, therefore, I, the person deceived, should be, even if I were deceived, certainly I am not deceived in this knowledge that I am. And, consequently, neither am I deceived in knowing that I know. For, as I know that I am, so I know this also, that I know. (*City of God* 11.26)

Thus with one sweep Augustine rid himself of skepticism and assured himself of himself—the actual if not logical starting point. But where does one go from here? Though Augustine never denied the legitimacy of empirical knowledge, he was wary of the senses in light of an incipient Platonism he inherited through the thought of Plotinus (c. 205-270). He passed this Platonism on to the church, much to Christianity's chagrin and the resultant underestimating of the ontological significance of the created order. So, because sensible things are changeable, the eternal and necessary things are known by another and far superior "sense" independent of the five senses (*City of God* 11.27). These truths were not made but discovered. These truths, however, were not the ultimate ontological reality, but were dependent on the personal God of Christian revelation. The knowledge of God is the first truth.

Men are equipped by God, who made mankind in His image, to innately comprehend necessary truths such as mathematics or the law of noncontradiction (*Confessions* 13.22.32). Augustine thus stands in the a priori orientation. These principles of thought are not just conveniences constructed by man but are universal, for this is the way man was made by God. Logic, then, is not man-made but God-made. Logic, in one sense, is "God-thinking." Coherence becomes the *test for truth* in the Augustinian tradition. Man, by using his logic, which is identical with God's, can literally "think God's thoughts after him." The truth of these principles makes propositional revelation possible. But reason alone is not sufficient; revelation is indispensable. Augustine writes:

Seeing, then, that we were too weak by unaided reason to find out the truth, and for this cause needed the authority of the holy writings, I had now begun to believe that Thou wouldest by no means have given such excellency of authority to those Scriptures throughout all lands, had it not been Thy will thereby to be believed in, and thereby sought. (*Confessions* 6.5.8)

The universal validity of reason is admitted, but because of a strong doctrine of the Fall of man and the subsequent corruption of the will (see *Free Choice of the Will*), Augustine took an ambivalent position toward the theistic arguments. Nevertheless, because the principles of thought are identical between God and man, Augustine could look within and objectively find God there. Again in *Confessions* he writes:

For He did not create them, and then depart; but they are of Him, and in Him. Behold, there is He wherever truth is known. He is within the very heart, but yet hath the heart wandered from Him. Return to your heart, O ye transgressors, and cleave fast unto Him that made you. Stand with Him and you shall stand fast. Rest in Him, and you shall be at rest. (4.12.18)

The emphasis on the universality of logic, but the necessity of Scripture for proper understanding, is not as paradoxical as it may seem. Two basic Christian and Augustinian tenets resolve the tension: creation and Fall. God created the world *ex nihilo*, out of nothing. Therefore nothing can be understood apart from the meaning He gives to it. In *City of God* (10.2), Augustine has Plotinus agree with John 1:6-9 in his analogy that as the moon gets its light from the sun, so our rational soul has no superior nature other than God from which to be illumined. Therefore the necessity of revelation even before the Fall, let alone after it, when man and God became totally separate. In this circumstance, man will never use logic to understand the world theistically. Thus, though believers and unbelievers live in the same world and are each God's creation, they cannot and will not understand themselves or the world in identical fashion. Here is why all twentieth-century presuppositionalists hark back, at least to some degree, to Augustine. (They do this not solely for ontological and epistemological reasons, but for anthropological and soteriological reasons as well.)

Perhaps the most researched Augustinian topic, in Christian circles at least, is the relationship of faith and reason. Certainly this is at the center of apologetic concerns. Augustine's famous phrase *credo ut intelligam* (I believe in order that I may know), later developed by Anselm, united philosophy and theology as the former became the rational explanation of the content of faith. Because all men know intuitively there is a God (through God's image), Augustine believed it was very easy to prove God's existence, though he never did so in an absolutely formal manner. Because truth is superior to reason, and truth exists, then God exists since truth and God are one. Nevertheless, "no one can become fit for finding God unless he believes what he shall know afterward" (*On Free Choice of the Will* 2.2.19). Or more directly in *Sermon* 126:

> The mysteries and secrets of the kingdom of God first seek for believing man, that they make them understanding. For faith is understanding's step; and understanding, faith's attainment. This the prophet expressly says to all who prematurely and in undue order look for understanding and neglect faith. For he says, *Unless ye believe, ye shall not understand.*

This apparent priority of faith over reason has led many in the history of apologetics into a sort of Augustinian fideism. Faith, as a gift of God to His elect, is independent of any and all rational evidence. But Augustine did not mean that, though as Cornelius Van Til points out there is some tension between Augustine's tendencies to both rationalism and irrationalism.[4] Augustine simply realized, as previously noted, that all things have their meaning from God. Therefore, one must have faith in God and comprehend His Scriptures to truly know and understand. Nevertheless, evidence is abundant as to the reality of God to the unbeliever. Thus in one sense reason is prior to faith. On this Augustine writes:

> For no one believes anything unless he has before thought it worthy of belief ... it is yet necessary that everything which is believed should be believed *after* thought has preceded; although even belief itself is nothing else than to think with assent. For it is not everyone who thinks that believes, since many think in order that they may not believe; but everybody who believes, thinks—

4. Cornelius Van Til, *A Christian Theory of Knowledge*, pp. 119-35.

both thinks in believing and believes in thinking. (*On Predestination of the Saints* 5, italics added)

Elsewhere, Augustine notes:

Nevertheless unless they *understand* what I am saying *they cannot believe.* Hence what he says is in some part true, "I would understand in order that I may believe." And I, too, am right when I say, as does the prophet, "Nay, believe in order that thou mayest understand." We both speak the truth: We are in agreement. Therefore, understand in order to believe; believe in order to understand. Here is a brief statement of how we can accept both without controversy. Understand in order that you may believe my word; believe in order that you may understand the word of God. (*Sermon* 43, italics added)

Revelation is absolutely needed for the right knowledge of God and His world. Nevertheless, propositional revelation presumes its own rational intelligibility to fallen creatures made in God's image as He is the source of logic and its axioms. Therefore, it "is in some part true, 'I would understand in order that I may believe.' " But it is also true that one must "believe in order [to] understand." This would seem to mean that spiritual comprehension is based on rational comprehension, but is not identical with it, nor inherent to man in his fallen state. Such spiritual comprehension is the gift of God through the Holy Spirit's teaching of Scripture and regeneration (*Confessions* 12.10.10; 12.11.11). In other words, man could but would not accept the gospel in his sinful condition. This simply means that man is not so ruined by the Fall that he is less than man made in God's image and thus ontologically incapable of responding to God. Rather, it means that man is God's enemy (Rom. 5:10) and therefore "separated from the life of God because of the ignorance that is in them due to the hardening of their hearts" (Eph. 4:18) and thus will not positively respond to God's Word and will. The Fall totally destroyed man's ability to do good before God. Mankind is not simply a willful sinner because he sins, but he sins because he is willfully turned from God by actually "being in Adam sinning" (*City of God* 13.14). Faith is to think with assent. But assent is possible only by regeneration, even if all men can think. This gift of grace is not a substitute for man's voluntary action, but the condition upon which the will can begin to choose and do the good. With true freedom of action restored to it, the soul no longer wishes to resist its Creator.

Augustine thus anchors the being of man in the Being of God and the reason of man in the logic of God's mind. There have been some commentators who see some danger in Augustine's not properly differentiating man's essence from God's essence. In light of his emphasis on creation and the doctrine of the trinity, this does not really seem to be the case. He does assure actual communication between God and man, and as others have noted, Augustine was concerned with symbol and language long before the linguistic turn to philosophy in the twentieth century. His acceptance of both deductive reason and sense data presents a realistic view, if not totally balanced in light of the Platonic tendency to relegate sensation and the temporal world to second-class reality. His emphasis on sin and its debilitating effects on the intellect and the will is biblical. The stress on the intuitive knowledge of God in every man was based on the biblical doctrine of creation and general revelation, but was perhaps overdone; and if not, was still the initial impetus to the Christian mysticism of the Middle Ages at the expense of Augustine's emphasis on the Scriptures. A succinct summary of what we have called Augustine's epistemological conclusions is provided in his summary of Christian doctrine to his "beloved Laurentius":

> These are to be defended by reason, which must have its starting-point either in the bodily senses or in the intuitions of the mind. And what we have neither had experience of through our bodily senses, nor have been able to reach through the intellect, must undoubtedly be believed on the testimony of those witnesses by whom the Scriptures, justly called divine, were written; and who by divine assistance were enabled, either through bodily sense or intellectual perception, to see or to foresee the things in question. (*Enchiridion* 5)

Seven questions that are directly or indirectly dealt with in every apologetic framework were cited at the end of chapter 1. As mentioned there, at the conclusion of the discussion of each of the five apologists treated in this chapter an attempt will be made to answer these questions in a concise outline form. We thus present these questions and Augustine's answers:

1. What is the role of philosophy in Christian theology and apologetics?

   Because of Augustine's ontological and epistemological realism between God and man and his reliance on Platonic thought at many points, philosophy's questions are ultimately theology's problems also. The prime difference is probably methodological, as philosophy begins with man and his reason and finds at least inklings of God within man, and theology begins with God and His revelation and understands the relationship of God and creation. The radical doctrine of sin and its ravages short-circuits this mutuality for unregenerated man.

2. How are faith and reason related?

   For the believer these are mutually interdependent as faith is a response of the will based on creditable and noncontradictory evidence. For the unbeliever, since faith as trust is God's gift, these are functionally mutually exclusive.

3. Of what significance is the doctrine of sin for Christian apologetics?

   For Augustine it is very important as sin perverts the will and dulls the intellect. Therefore, divine illumination is really needed to properly understand everything as related to the Creator. This illumination is absolutely indispensable for revelation proper.

4. Do the theistic proofs have any worth for convincing the unbeliever?

   This is very difficult to assess as Augustine seems to accept them, even if never completely presented, due to his rationalistic tendencies. At the same time he limits their usefulness because of the effects of sin and man's inability to accept God in an unregenerate state. As usually interpreted in the history of philosophy and Christian apologetics, they are certainly not Augustine's first line of defense.

5. To what extent may a believer and unbeliever form a shared point of contact on common ground?

   Because both believer and unbeliever are God's creatures and live in God's universe they share the same real world and logical principles; however, since all facts are ultimately God-interpreted facts, only the believer illumined by special revelation truly "knows" the truth of God, himself, and nature. This perspective is adopted by all twentieth-century presuppositionalists and verbalized to mean that believer and unbeliever have a common ontological ground but no common epistemological ground.

6. Are historical Christian evidences important, or even possible, as evidence for the unbeliever?

   Miracles and fulfilled prophecies are the proofs and evidences that must appeal to the rational man prior to faith. There are reasons behind miracles even though we cannot comprehend them with our limitations.

7. What degree of certainty is there in the truthfulness of Christianity?

   The believer can have absolute certainty through the witness of the Holy Spirit by means of special revelation.

THOMAS AQUINAS

The youngest son of the Count of Aquino (near Naples) was educated at the university there as well as by the Benedictine Order. Whether fact or fancy, his father supposedly held Thomas in the family dungeon to keep him from entering the priesthood, as the Count wanted his son to practice law. Thomas finally joined the Dominican Order, committing himself to a teaching ministry, and entered the University of Paris. There he came under the tutelage of Albert the Great, who reintroduced Aristotle to the West after a thousand-year absence. He received his doctor of theology degree in 1256 from the University of Paris, after spending time also in Cologne with Albert for the purpose of setting up a Dominican House. He taught at Paris and Naples, and had a direct relation to the Papal Court during his career. He died in 1274, having been born in 1225.

Thomas Aquinas is the father of Roman Catholic theology and apologetics. *Thomism* was declared to be the official philosophy of the Catholic Church by Pope Leo XIII (1878-1903) in the encyclical *Aeterni Patris* (1879).[5] Thomism is encapsulated

---

5. Denise Meadows, *A Short History of the Catholic Church*, p. 107.

in two texts: the *Summa Theologiae*, completed by fellow theologians of the Dominican Order, and *Summa Contra Gentiles*.

Aquinas's new synthesis replaced Plato with Aristotle. The Aristotelian metaphysical structure of the chain of being, with two givens of matter and form (ideas), and the constructs of potentiality and actuality, was totally adopted and made the absolute framework of theology/philosophy, and thus subsequently determined Aquinas's apologetic method. Pure matter, which was completely formless and thus total potentiality, did not really exist for Aristotle. The same must be said for pure actuality, which was completely matterless. Complete actuality was also identified as the unmoved mover, the realization of all potentiality, and the theoretical, if not really existent, cause of both being and the chain of being. Only that included in the chain of being was really existent, being made up of both matter and form. This can be represented as follows:

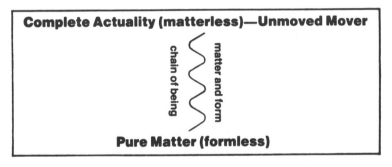

This structure was easily adapted to Christian theology. It definitely has merit. It makes the realm of nature *real* rather than merely the shadow of the *idea* (form) a la Plato. Reality is *here*, not *there*. But pure Aristotelianism also has dangers for Christian thought. Because "reality" is *here* and not *there*, Aristotle has been the fount of the naturalistic/empirical path of philosophy as Plato has been of the idealistic/rationalistic orientation. The loss of true transcendence is plainly evident if the unmoved mover does not really exist, regardless of Thomas's identification of such with the God of Christian theology. The Aristotelian perspective is as undermining of unnaturalistic reality, and therefore the biblical self-revealing personal God, as Plato's outlook is destructive of the reality of a true physical creation of the infinite-personal God. There is *no* biblical Both/ And in these two most important philosophers.

Obviously, the denial of God was absolutely anathema to Thomas Aquinas. Aquinas, as we shall see, used the chain of being to propose supposedly indubitable arguments for the reality of God. God will be the logically inferred necessity of the actuality of the chain of being. But if these arguments fail, after pinning the rational truth of the reality of God upon them, the viability of Christianity comes into question. That that did not happen until the eighteenth century does not provide much comfort. *It did happen* for countless individuals, leaving many with either no God and no salvation, or with a mystic and/or fideistic apologetic with no cognitive knowledge of God and no propositional revelation.

Aquinas's "indubitable" arguments were rooted in the *tabula rasa* (erased tablet) doctrine, later expounded by John Locke (1632-1704), the father of modern empiricism. Aquinas, following Aristotle, taught that man started out with a blank "tablet"—an unformed mind—and that all knowledge of the "forms" was derived from sensation, as they are inherently embedded in matter. The mind was active and passive. The passive intellect recorded the sensation as a precept of the mind. The active intellect abstracted the universal form (essence) from the sensation and thus knowledge was intellectual (mental) as well as sensate (physical) (*Summa Theologiae* 1.76-79, 84-86). There is no innate knowledge. All knowledge is inferential. The knowledge of God was not different. The philosopher, following inductive reasoning, could come to the absolute knowledge of the reality of God. Thus "arguing up" the chain of being brought us to the "form of forms," total immutable actuality with no potentiality to change: God (*Summa Theologiae* 1.88).

Aquinas rejected the ontological argument because it began with God's essence and argued to His existence. Thus he held philosophy to be prior to theology, as the former proves God's existence by reason prior to the latter elucidating God's essence by revelation. To "prove" God's existence, Thomas proposed five arguments that demanded the reality of God. These were all based on the Aristotelian model of reality that, viewed with Aquinas's Christian spectacles, demanded not only a source of motion but an efficient cause, a necessary being if there is a contingent chain of being, a gradual completion of the chain of being to include complete goodness and perfection, and the necessity of a governor or designer of the chain of being. The arguments, variously formulated, have been the essence of natural theology approaches to Christian apologetics. The cause and design arguments are by far the most important. We will examine only the former because its validity is prerequisite to the viability of the latter. In *Summa Theologiae* (1.2), Thomas Aquinas wrote:

> In the world of sensible things we find there is an order of efficient causes. There is no case (neither is it, indeed, possible) in which a thing is found to be the efficient cause of itself; for so it would be prior to itself, which is impossible. Now in efficient causes it is not possible to go on to infinity, because in all efficient causes following in order, the first is the cause of the intermediate cause, and the intermediate is the cause of the ultimate cause, whether the intermediate cause be several, or one only. Now to take away the cause is to take away the effect. Therefore, if there be no first cause among efficient causes, there will be no ultimate, nor any intermediate, cause. But if in efficient causes it is possible to go on to infinity, there will be no efficient cause, neither will there be an ultimate effect, nor any intermediate efficient causes, all of which is plainly false. Therefore it is necessary to admit a first efficient cause, to which everyone gives the name of God.

The argument is straightforward. Since there are obviously various effects, and nothing can be uncaused or the cause of itself, there must be a *final* cause or the continuum of cause and effect would "go on to infinity." The denial of the possibility of an unending sequence of causes and effects would seem to be an assumption "smuggled" into, and not logically demonstrated by, the argument. Paul Edwards, the editor of the *Encyclopedia of Philosophy*, contends that the argument fails "to distinguish between the two statements: (1) A [defined by Edwards as the first efficient cause] did not exist and (2) A is not uncaused."[6] To accept an infinite series of cause and effect

6. Paul Edwards, "The Cosmological Argument," in William L. Rowe and William J. Wainwright, eds., *Philosophy of Religion: Selected Writings*, p. 138.

is to assert that A is not uncaused, but not that A does not exist. Edwards succinctly writes: "The believer in the infinite series is not 'taking A away.' He is taking away the privileged status of A; he is taking away its 'first causiness.' He does not deny the *existence* of A or of any particular member of the series. He denies that A or anything else *is the first member of the series.*"[7]

The cosmological argument thus ultimately begs the question by concluding that God is the first efficient cause, but also an uncaused member, the existence of which was absolutely denied at the beginning of the argument. This is certainly a greater logical inconsistency than accepting an infinite series of causes! Infinite regress, however, is not really a sufficient explanation either. As Frederick Ferre writes,

> The fact remains that infinite regress is not so much an explanation as a rejection of the demand for an explanation. And as such it poses a moral threat to scientific as well as metaphysical investigation. Both metaphysics and science exist within, depend upon, man's questing, curious impulses; and appeal to infinite regress is, if successful, curiosity's assassin. The mind may be hypnotized into passivity by staring back, and back, and back . . . into the endless depths of time, but this is no way to obtain a sufficient explanation for any specific question.[8]

In summary, infinite regress is an unacceptable explanation, and the cosmological argument *does not prove* one efficient cause at the end of the causal series but merely assumes this is the case. Very similarly, this argument in the hands of a Christian theologian, including Thomas Aquinas, simply assumes that this supposed "First Cause" is the God and Father of our Lord Jesus Christ. Although the argument puts us on the horns of the dilemma that either there is a First Cause or the universe is a brute fact, it provides no rational reason demanded *by the argument* for why I must grab the First Cause horn other than prior theological assumption or "gut" feeling.

This "gut" feeling is important to the evangelical apologist. The intuitive attraction of the cosmological argument is the per-

---

7. Ibid.
8. Frederick Ferre, Editor's Introduction, *Natural Theology: Selections*, by William Paley, pp. XXIII-XXIV.

suasive and pervading reality of general revelation. General revelation, however, is an a priori fact concomitant with creation and not the derivative of an a posteriori argument from the fact of existence to the cause of such existence. Certainly the "phenomena disclose the noumena of God's transcendent perfection and specific activity." But "it is not a finite cause that the work of creation manifests but the eternal power and divinity of the Creator."[9] Thus cosmological argumentation in the context of general revelation is similar to historical evidential argumentation of the reality and truthfulness of God's redemptive activity based on special revelation. Both are probable, not logically necessary arguments, though the greater conclusiveness of historical evidence is a function of the necessity of special revelation as an indispensable supplement to general revelation.[10] A priori general revelation therefore *must never* be confused with a posteriori natural theology, even though the former implicitly predisposes us to think the latter has cognitive validity. There is a 180-degree difference in seeing nature as pointing to the reality of God on the basis of a doctrine of creation, and a logical argument that is created to prove God totally irrespective of a doctrine of creation.

What, then, are the primary apologetic assumptions and implications of Thomas's attempts to prove God rationally? The most apparent implication is the independence of reason and faith. Reason is neither inherently nor volitionally limited. The philosopher can come to the same conclusion by reason as the theologian does by revelation and faith. These paths are mutually exclusive. That is, if the reality of God is known through the philosophic-theistic arguments, God cannot be known by revelation. Or, in reverse, those who are incapable of following the logical demonstration of the arguments, or who have no time to do such if capable, can still individually know God by the response of faith to propositional revelation (*Summa Theologiae* 2.2.2). Some Christian truths are impossible to logically demonstrate and thus have to be accepted by faith by the philosopher, theologian, priest, and layman (*Summa Theologiae*

9. John Murray, *The Epistle to the Romans*, 1:40.
10. Helpful in this regard is the book by Bruce R. Reichenbach, *The Cosmological Argument: A Reassessment.*

2.2.36). These include historical truths such as the incarnation and resurrection of Christ and the doctrines of the Trinity, creation, and redemption (*Summa Theologiae* 2.2.8). The fact that creation is known by faith through special revelation *proves* that general revelation is not identical with natural theology. Natural theology based on the theistic arguments is developed independently of special revelation and the knowledge thereby of creation. General revelation, as noted earlier, is concomitant with creation and is apologetically unintelligible without the acceptance of such.

Believer and unbeliever thus can equally know the reality of God, if not all Christian truths. Reasoning is unspoiled in both. The Fall of man in disobedience to God is much less severe and radical here than in Augustine. The image of God in man is not effaced in the slightest, but rather man has lost his pristine relationship with God and the innate grace of original righteousness that made the relationship possible (*Summa Theologiae* 2.85). Thus only individual abilities or limitations of time put one on the path of faith to know the reality of God rather than having philosophical access to God by reason. Revelation is necessary for salvation but, unlike Augustine, not for the knowledge of God. Thomas's answers to our questions determinative of apologetic structure would be as follows:

1. What is the role of philosophy in Christian theology and apologetics?

   Philosophy is independent of and thus considerably more than the handmaiden of theology. Its function is to demonstrate rationally the *praeambula fidei*, that is, presuppositions of revelation and theology, and thus prepare the mind of man to receive Christian revelation by faith. Philosophy proves God's existence prior to theology discussing God's essence. Nevertheless, philosophy can and does logically elucidate the Christian revelation as well as defend its truths.

2. How are reason and faith related?

   Faith and reason are mutually exclusive. For the most part, reason is the means of knowing the mundane things and faith the means of knowing the things of special revelation. It might also be said that reason is superior to faith in the clarity and exactness of knowledge, but that faith is preferred by means of the character of the knowledge it knows.

3. Of what significance is the doctrine of sin for Christian apologetics?

   Sin did not leave man rationally or volitionally incompetent as only original righteousness was lost in the Fall. Thus a true philosophy can be constructed, theistic proofs are valid, and a system of ethics is possible based on natural law.

4. Do the theistic proofs have any worth for convincing the unbeliever?

   Theistic proofs are seemingly more than inductively probable, they are rationally demonstrable. They are the first line of argument to use with the unbeliever.

5. To what extent may a believer and unbeliever form a shared point of contact on common ground?

   There is most definitely an epistemological common ground between believers and unbelievers as the methodology of natural theology must assume. This epistemological common ground is possible because all men have the possibilities and usage of reason untainted by the Fall.

6. Are historical Christian evidences important, or even possible, as evidence for the unbeliever?

   Special revelation is indispensable for Christianity if not for theism. Proof of special revelation is the traditional evidences of God's supernatural work as seen in fulfilled prophecy, miracles, and so on.

7. What degree of certainty is there in the truthfulness of Christianity?

   At the point of evidence, reason by means of demonstration is more certain than faith; however, as stated in question (2), faith is superior to reason because it puts man in contact with the supernatural realm as expressed in special revelation, especially the incarnation and the resurrection—the heart and soul of the Christian religion. In regard to the theistic arguments alone, Thomas believed that there certainty was a logical necessity and not simply an inductive probability.

JOHN CALVIN

John Calvin (1509-1564), one of the two greatest leaders of the Protestant Reformation, was the son of a man who was the secretary to the bishop of Nayon, France. His mother died when Calvin was still a child. When John was twelve, his father obtained a benefice providing a study endowment for him. Two years later he entered the University of Paris for Latin studies where he received, like Luther at Erfurt, instruction in philosophical nominalism as well. In 1528, he studied law at Orleans on his father's wishes, but returned to Paris and more humanist studies after his father's death in 1531. In 1532 he published his first work on Seneca's *De Clementia*. This was the same year he experienced his "sudden conversion," of which little is known.

By 1535 his Protestant leanings found him in Basel, and by the spring of 1536 the first small edition of the *Christianae Religionis Institutio* was published. Beckoned by Guillaume Farel (1489-1565) to aid in the organization of the Reformation in Geneva, Calvin gave up the quiet life of the scholar for the tumultuous life of the Reformer. He was exiled from Geneva to Strasbourg during 1538-1541, where he labored with Martin Bucer (1491-1551), another Protestant reformer, published a much enlarged second edition of the *Institutes* and his first biblical commentary on the epistle to the Romans, and married the widow of an Anabaptist, Idelette de Bure. He returned to Geneva on September 13, 1541, where he continued the work of reformation, publishing the last edition of the *Institutes* in 1559. He died on May 27, 1564.

Of the five apologetic systems discussed in this chapter, none has directly influenced American evangelicals as greatly as Calvin's. For this reason, this section will be slightly longer than either the preceding or following ones. Brief attention will be focused on the debate within Calvinistic apologetics as to the relationship of the Holy Spirit to Christian evidences as well as to the question of the analogic nature of the language of Scripture. We turn now to the opening paragraph of the *Institutes:*

> Our wisdom . . . consists almost entirely of two parts: the knowledge of God and of ourselves. But as these are connected together by many ties, it is not easy to determine which of the two precedes, and gives birth to the other. For, in the first place, no man can· survey himself without forthwith turning his thoughts towards the God in whom he lives and moves; because it is per-

> fectly obvious, that the endowment which we possess cannot pos-
> sibly be from ourselves; nay, that our very being is nothing else
> than subsistence in God alone. . . .[In light of the Fall] every man,
> being stung by the consciousness of his own unhappiness, in this
> way necessarily obtains at least some knowledge of God . . . every
> person, therefore, on coming to the knowledge of himself, is not
> only urged to seek God, but is also led as by the hand to find him.
> (*Institutes* 1.1.1)

Calvin was very sensitive to the problem of starting point. Nearly all apologetic disputes can be traced to this issue—do we start inductively from man and argue to God, or do we argue deductively from the reality of God to ourselves and everything else? Calvin was cognizant that it is not as clear or simple as many apologists of either color have made it to appear: "It is not easy to determine which of the two precedes, and gives birth to the other." How can man *actually* begin with God? He is man and not God. And still, if we begin with man, there is an impelling ascension to God "because it is perfectly obvious, that the endowments which we possess cannot possibly be from ourselves." These two must be held together! Though it is obvious that man cannot properly know himself without knowing God, the reverse is also true, for Calvin writes that "we cannot clearly and properly know God unless the knowledge of ourselves be added" (*Institutes* 1.15.1).

That is the foundational assumption of the Both/And approach. Apologetics cannot be solely presuppositional by beginning with God to the practical exclusion of man, nor is it able to begin with supposedly agnostic man as if independent of God and find God by either the inductive proofs or the historical evidence of special revelation. God cannot be known apart from the recognition of His creation, for it is we, the creatures, who are knowing. Likewise, nature cannot be used in an agnostic manner when nature is only possible, and rightly and ultimately understood, as created. In historical actuality, then, we must start with ourselves, though logically God is the primary reference point. Van Til states this well, though we may apply it differently, when he writes that if "the human consciousness must, in the nature of the case, always be the proximate starting point, it remains true that God is always the most basic and therefore the ultimate or final reference point in human interpretation."[11]

For Calvin, God is really not known where there is no worship or personal piety. To know God is not to know Him as the conclusion of an argument that seemingly demonstrates the priority of human reason, but rather to be touched by our own insignificance in contrast to the majesty of God (*Institutes* 1.1.3). God is known first as Creator in Scripture as well as in nature. The effect of so knowing God as Creator should be "to teach reverence and fear" and to encourage in reverence "to ask every good thing from him, and when it is received, ascribe it to him" (*Institutes* 1.2.2). The knowledge of God as Creator incipiently and necessarily implies His absolute authority as His will ought to be, and was originally meant to be, "the law of our lives" (*Institutes* 1.2.2). We keep from disobedience and sin, therefore, not out of fear of judgment, but because of the dread of offending the Creator. Genuine religion is both confidence in, and fear of, God.

All men have a natural knowledge of God because it is the stamp of their creation status. Calvin writes:

> That there exists in the human mind, and indeed by natural instinct some sense of Deity, we hold to be beyond dispute, since God himself, to prevent any man from pretending ignorance, has endued all men with some idea of his Godhead, the memory of which he constantly renews and occasionally enlarges, that all to a man, being aware that there is a God, and that He is their Maker, may be condemned by their own conscience when they neither worship him nor consecrate their lives to his service. (*Institutes* 1.3.1)

There are thus no true atheists for Calvin. All men have a sense of deity no matter how maliciously they attempt to stifle it or how extensively it may be corrupted in ignorance. For though there may be many who deny the being of God, "yet whether they will or not, they occasionally feel the truth which they are desirous not to know" (*Institutes* 1.3.2) for the "sense of Deity is indelibly engraven on the human heart" (*Institutes* 1.3.3).

Men, therefore, have an innate orientation toward God

11. Cornelius Van Til, "Apologetics," p. 45.

through creation, but because of the Fall they replace the holy God with an idol of their own imagination. Rather than worshiping the true God who demands their entire person and absolute obedience, they superstitiously worship a god of their own creation. Man believes erroneously that it is enough to have zeal for some religion, rather than accepting conformity to the will of the Creator/Redeemer. But however much he may try to deny it, the natural revelation of God, "indelibly engraven on the human heart," must be acknowledged by even the reprobate (*Institutes* 1.4.4). As Calvin states it, "We see many, after they have become hardened in a daring course of sin, madly banishing all remembrance of God, though spontaneously suggested to them from within, by natural sense" (*Institutes 1.4.2*).

Regardless of the pervasiveness of the knowledge of God through natural revelation by creation, Calvin saw little significance for the theistic proofs of natural theology. Even if the arguments were valid, on which question Calvin said little, that would be inconsequential as the essential issue is not that we know God exists (in fact in our more sober moments we innately "know" that He does), but that we love, obey, serve, and worship Him. In fact, not only is natural theology rejected, but natural revelation is inadequate because of the sinful suppression of such by fallen man. Calvin appealed to Hebrews 11:3 to document that faith and internal revelation are necessary for us to perceive God in the visible displays of created nature (*Institutes* 1.5.14). Calvin understood natural revelation to condemn man because the incorrect interpretation of the glory of God's creation is not caused by the revelation itself, but by man's willful suppression of that revelation and the dullness of man's natural powers. He writes:

> Therefore, though the effulgence which is presented to every eye, both in the heavens and on the earth, leaves the ingratitude of man without excuse, since God, in order to bring the whole human race under the same condemnation, holds forth to all, without exception, a mirror of his Deity in his works, another and better help must be given to guide us properly to God as a Creator. Not in vain, therefore, has he added the light of his Word in order that he might make himself known unto salvation, and bestowed the privilege on those whom he was pleased to bring into nearer

> and more familiar relation to himself. . . . So Scripture, gathering
> together the impressions of Deity, which, till then, lay confused in
> their minds, dissipates the darkness, and shows us the true God
> clearly. (*Institutes* 1.6.1)

Scripture is the heart of the apologetic of Calvin. Without
Scripture, though man is made in God's image and lives in
God's universe, man cannot know God rightly. Scripture alone
distinguishes "God, as the Creator of the world, from the whole
herd of fictitious gods" (*Institutes* 1.6.1). Man will not even
interpret his innate knowledge of God rightly without Scripture. Not even the smallest particle of true divine knowledge
can be obtained without Scripture. "Since the human mind,
through its weakness, was altogether unable to come to God if
not aided and upheld by his sacred word, it necessarily followed that all mankind, the Jews excepted, inasmuch as they
sought God without the Word, were labouring under vanity and
error" (*Institutes* 1.6.4).

This brings us to the point where the Reformed apologists
cannot agree—the relationship of faith and reason, or put within the context of the *Institutes*, the relationship between chapters 7 and 8 of Book 1, that is, the Holy Spirit and Christian
evidences. Succinctly stated, does the Holy Spirit work through
the evidences on the mind of the unbeliever as Princeton
Calvinsim taught throughout the nineteenth century and as is
exemplified by Benjamin B. Warfield? Or, are Christian evidences confirmatory to the believer only after he has been giv-
en faith by the Holy Spirit?—a perspective more conducive to
Dutch Calvinism best expressed by Abraham Kuyper.[12] In actuality, it is the a priori/a posteriori controversy raising its head
within the bastion of Calvinism.

It seems impossible to solve that ongoing division within Calvinistic apologetics by referring to the master. John Calvin is
interpreted favorably by both sides. It seems that Calvin does
give hints going in both directions. Perhaps he realized the a
priori/a posteriori dilemma was inextricably intertwined in
regard to Scripture and evidence as he did in the question of

---

12. For a detailed analysis of this debate see Stephen Spencer, "A Comparison
and Evaluation of the Old Princeton and Amsterdam Apologetic."

beginning with ourselves or with God in the first paragraph of the *Institutes*. In chapter 7 we find some statements seemingly supporting the priority of evidence and others that support the priority of the Holy Spirit (all italics added):

Evidence

... compelled to confess that the *Scripture exhibits clear evidence* of its being spoken by God ....(1.7.4)

Still, however, it is preposterous to attempt, by discussion, to *rear up a full evidence* in Scripture. (1.7.4)

But although we may *maintain* the sacred Word of God *against* gainsayers, it does not follow that we shall forthwith implant the certainty which faith requires in their hearts. (1.7.4)

Spirit

But I answer, that the testimony of the spirit is superior to reason. For as God alone can properly bear witness to his own words, so these words will not obtain full credit in the hearts of men, *until they are sealed by the inward testimony of the Spirit*. The same Spirit, therefore, who spoke by the mouth of the prophets, must penetrate our hearts, in order to convince us that they faithfully delivered the message with which they were divinely intrusted. (1.7.4)

Let it therefore be held as fixed, that those who are inwardly taught by the Holy Spirit acquiesce implicitly in Scripture; that Scripture, *carrying its own evidence along with it, deigns not to submit to proofs and arguments; but owes the full conviction with which we ought to receive it to the testimony of the Spirit*. Enlightened by him, we no longer believe, either on our own judgment or that of others, that the Scriptures are from God; but, in a way superior to human judgment, feel perfectly assured—as much so as if we beheld the divine image visibly impressed on it—that it came to us by the instrumentality of men, from the very mouth of God. *We ask not for proofs or probabilities* on which to rest our judgment, but we subject our intellect and judgment to it as too transcendent for us to estimate. (1.7.5)

Such, then, is a conviction which asks not for reasons; such a knowledge which accords with the highest reason, namely, knowl-

> edge in which the mind rests more firmly and securely than in any
> reasons; such, in fine, the conviction which revelation from heav-
> en alone can produce. (1.7.5)

It appears that these statements are supportive of neither an exclusively a priori fideism nor an a posteriori evidentialism. Faith and evidence are not mutually exclusive. The evidence for Scripture is obviously the revelatory historical events it records and interprets. Thus, "Scripture exhibits clear evidence of its being spoken by God. . . .carrying its own evidence along with it." But such evidence is not "full evidence." Historical probabilities and rationalistic proofs cannot replace or dispense with the necessary testimony of the ultimate author of Scripture, God the Holy Spirit. Therefore, though one can certainly argue and rationally maintain the uniqueness of the Bible against its detractors, they will never be absolutely convinced until such evidence is *used by the Holy Spirit* in conviction and subsequent regeneration. This conviction by the Holy Spirit is different in kind from all human reasons for believing Scrip-ture, since it "accords with the highest reason" — the Being and authority of God. Just as no one can bear witness to the words on this page other than myself, so no human reasoning can bear totally adequate testimony to the Scriptures since "God alone can properly bear witness to his own words." The Scrip-tures are ultimately self-authenticating. The Author of Scrip-ture must uniquely testify to the divine authorship through the instrumentality of men "to convince us that they faithfully delivered the [divine] message." Therefore, since the Bible looks like any other book as far as physical paper and ink, human presumption can only be overridden by such supernat-ural testimony. Without it, the Bible remains letter only and not Spirit also!

Apologetics is not useless, as some Calvinists have con-tended in the past. Calvin was not a fideist, or the long list of evidences for Scripture in chapter 8 of *The Institutes* (even if taken as primarily for confirmation of the believer), his many debates with agnostics, and the exegetical evidence produced for preaching and commentary would all border on insignificance and perhaps meaninglessness. Cornelius Van Til, no evidentialist or rationalist himself, declares that

Warfield was correct as to the objective rationality and defensibility of Christianity. He writes:

> Warfield stresses the objective rationality of the Christian religion. This is not to suggest that Kuyper does not also believe in such an objective rationality. But by pointing out again and again that the Christian faith is belief on evidence not blind belief, Warfield makes plain that Christianity is "rationally defensible." This has direct significance for apologetics. Kuyper seems sometimes to argue from the fact that the natural man is blind to the truth, to the uselessness of apologetics. But Warfield points out that this does not follow. On this point he closely follows Calvin.[13]

Thus the Reformed apologist need not give up his calling. Though man is dead in sin, this deadness is an ethical not an ontological deadness; it is not a metaphysical escape from the reality of God. Because man is made in God's image, and "therefore endowed with the sense of deity, man can very well understand intellectually what is meant when the preacher tells him that he is a sinner and that he ought to repent."[14] These intellectual and ethical dimensions must not be forgotten or overlooked. Man is separated and alienated from God and holds himself as the proximate *and* final reference point for understanding reality. Regardless of his practice, man is no more independent of God (the one final reference point) for even his personal reality than a "terrible two" is independent of his mother, or a budding adolescent is of his father. There are those who interpret "you were dead in your transgressions and sins" (Eph. 2:1) by the analogy *What did you ever see a physically dead man do or understand?* To them this eliminates the need for presentation of evidence to unbelievers, whether by apologetics, evangelistic preaching, or even missions. However, to follow this course of action is to miss the Scylla of rationalism only to flounder in the fideistic whirlpool of Charybdis because of a perverted Calvinism based on erroneous exegesis and a false biblicism. Van Til correctly warns of either danger as they may be occasionally expressed in the ongoing Warfield/Kuyper debate by new disciples:

13. Van Til, *Theory of Knowledge*, p. 243.
14. Ibid., p. 245.

> Warfield has greatly stressed the point that God's revelation is present to every man and sometimes draws from it the illegitimate conclusion that therefore the natural man, disregarding his ethical alienation from God, can give an essentially correct interpretation at least of natural revelation. Kuyper has stressed the natural man's ethical alienation from God and sometimes draws from it the illegitimate conclusion that the natural man is unable to understand the intellectual argument for Christianity in any sense.[15]

The goal of the Both/And apologetic, difficult as it may be, is to stress the need of an evidential/rational presentation of the gospel to unbelievers, while never forgetting their ethical egocentric predicament in their depravity, not innocence; in their bondage, not freedom; in their lawlessness, not obedience.

This tendency of Reformed apology and theology to polarize at either rationalistic or fideistic extremes is not due only to the question of the interrelationships of the Holy Spirit, rational evidence, and faith. Calvin himself penned a few succinct sentences that in isolation from each other tend to incline to one pole or the other. He wrote both, however, and thus Calvin himself seems to hold faith and reason in a dialectical and uncomfortable tension. For instance, in 1.5.8 of the *Institutes*, Calvin wrote that the excellency of the divine wisdom was seen in God "conducting all things in perfect accordance with reason." This phrase is innocent enough, but it has caused some philosophers and theologians to suppose that if God does *all things according to reason*, and *I am made and now restored in God's image with the gift of reason*, then *I can perfectly work out the mysteries of the divine-human relationship* through the exact ordering of the divine decrees in a manner that is as rationalistic in identifying logic and being as Parmenides or Hegel. Calvin warned of this danger of Christian or theistic rationalism in the very next paragraph when he wrote that "in seeking God, the most direct path and the fittest method is, not to attempt with presumptuous curiosity to pry into his essence, which is rather to be adored than minutely discussed, but to contemplate him in his works, by which he draws near, becomes famil-

15. Ibid., pp. 245-46.

iar, and in a manner communicates himself to us" (*Institutes* 1.5.9). Calvin, for the most part, followed his own instruction. Numbers of his disciples, beginning with his successor at Geneva, Theodore Beza, have not.

The idea that God does all things according to reason is directly responsible for the fine tradition of scholarship in Calvinistic circles in disciplines other than theology and biblical studies. All legitimate academic disciplines—such as astronomy, chemistry, or geology in the sphere of nature; or anatomy, history, and psychology in the realm of man—are also direct contemplations of God in His works. This is God's universe and in gaining knowledge man must think God's thoughts after Him. Christianity is not only a vertical relationship. Knowing the true God truly and personally in Christ means we can also know horizontally differently than we could prior to salvation because we now accept that "by him all things were created" and "in him all things hold together" (Col. 1:16-17).

The warning to refrain from prying into the divine essence presumptuously may also be understood fideistically, though this would be to misunderstand Calvin. Since God is infinite and we are finite, it is reasoned that "God's ways are not our ways" (a misapplication of Isa. 55:8, see pp. 36-38), and therefore we cannot comprehend God even in His works. Man must simply believe. God is inherently unintelligible in Himself as well as in His works. Any questions by an individual of a scriptural passage or a traditional doctrine are immediately taken as a sign of unbelief and, therefore, sin. (As we shall see, evangelicals frequently practice what they attack in Kierkegaard.) Even Scripture, which is to reveal and uncover God, is functionally set aside because Calvin also said we must "subject our intellect and judgment to it as too transcendent for us to estimate" (*Institutes* 1.7.5). The many volumes of his commentaries put a lie to a fideistic understanding of this statement. In context, Calvin is not telling us that God's revelation in the Bible is "beyond" us and therefore is not really revelation and is not a gracious and loving gift of our heavenly Father. Rather, Calvin is simply asserting that the fact that the Bible is a book like other books, and that at the same time it is not like other books in that it is the Word of God through "the instrumentality of men, from the very mouth of God" and is "too transcendent for us to estimate" (*Institutes* 1.7.5). That is a reference to biblical inspiration, not a self-defeating principle for hermeneutics.

There is one last facet to note in regard to Calvin before we attempt to answer our seven questions. The previous quotation, referring to the "very mouth of God," raises the question of anthropomorphisms and the univocal truthfulness of the revelation of God in Scripture. Though we do not "pry" into the divine essence, mind, and will, do we truly, if not exhaustively, know God Himself in His verbal revelation? Some, both nonevangelicals and the staunchest of evangelicals, have appealed to the following two *Institute* quotations to deny any knowledge of God as He really is:

> For who is devoid of intellect as not to understand that God, in so speaking, lisps with us as nurses are wont to do with little children? Such modes of expression, therefore do not so much express what kind of a being God is, as accommodate the knowledge of him to our feebleness. In doing so, he must of course stoop far below his proper height. (1.13.1)

> Because our weakness cannot reach his height, any description which we receive of him must be lowered to our capacity in order to be intelligible. And the mode of lowering is to represent him not as he really is, but as we conceive him. (1.17.13)

Probably no two references in Calvin have had more attention in the past few years. In the former reference, Calvin is attempting to deter excessive speculation concerning how much of God's image is revealed in man, because the doctrines of God's spirituality and immensity (freedom from space limitations) were being downplayed. The latter reference is a preface to understanding the biblical statements of God's repenting. Taken in this light, the anthropomorphisms of Scripture are accommodating God to our feebleness by depicting God in physical terms through analogy based on His image in man. Because man speaks, creates, and wills, man intuitively knows the truth of these analogies when they are referred to God. The God-given image fulfills the prerequisite of there being an ontological foundation for the possibility and need of God's revealing Himself. But remembering that God is spirit (John 4:24) and not body, and that therefore He transcends space, we are not to take these physical analogies literally. Nevertheless, they *do communicate true knowledge* of the infinite-personal God to us. We understand the Being of God by analogies of proportionality, previously discussed in chapter 3.

The second quotation does present an additional difficulty. Clearly the phrase "any description which we receive of him must be lowered to our capacity in order to be intelligible" can be understood as God's accommodation to us on a finite level of His infinite Being. This is similar to Calvin's comment on 1 Peter 1:21 that without Christ, God is a vast abyss and thus "God in a manner makes Himself little, in order to accommodate Himself to our comprehension."[16] This accommodation of Himself in Scripture, or incarnation, in no way need imply biblical errancy, as some contend.[17] However, the second sentence in the above quote may eliminate any need to contend over inerrancy because "the mode of lowering is to represent him not as he really is, but as we conceive of him." Is there, then, no actual, essential, and true knowledge of God in the Bible? If the Bible does not truly convey the nature of God in analogies, metaphors, parables, anthropomorphisms, and so on, in a univocal and true manner (recognizing the inherent limitations epistemologically because of the absolute and intrinsic ontological differences between the infinite and finite), then we need not worry about questions of inerrancy for we really *do not have a revelation of God.* If God is simply as man conceives Him to be in the Bible, and not in any sense the way He Himself is, *we have nothing* more after Moses, Isaiah, Matthew, John, and Paul, than we had before. No need to worry about inspiration or illumination for we have no normative revelation to start with. To say that God loves, speaks, or forgives us, or to say that He is holy, righteous, and personal, gives no knowledge of *He Who Is* or of *Who He is.*

Calvin has outdone himself here, as have those evangelicals who follow him. He preserves God's uniqueness and sovereignty at the expense of His knowability. Cornelius Van Til is the most notable theologian to deny man *any* univocal knowledge

16. John Calvin, *Hebrews and the First and Second Epistle of St. Peter*, p. 250.
17. Jack Rogers, "The Church Doctrine of Biblical Authority," in *Biblical Authority*, pp. 27-28.

of God.[18] But we cannot compromise the knowability of God, and the involvement of God with us in the process of knowing, or we are left with the same skepticism of ultimate reality as those who consciously reject Scripture for nihilism and meaninglessness, except now there is no revelation and/or Scripture to reject. Charles Hodge, a Calvinist who apparently forsook his mentor for the sake of rescuing both Scripture and man through a real knowledge of the infinite sovereign God, must be followed here rather than Calvin himself. Hodge wrote:

> God really is what we believe Him to be, so far as our idea of Him is determined by the revelation which He has made of Himself in His works, in the constitution of our nature, in His word, and in the person of His Son. To know is simply to have such apprehensions of an object as conform to what that object really is. . . . In this sense God is an object of knowledge. *He is not the unknown God, because He is infinite.* Knowledge in Him does not cease to be knowledge because it is omniscience; power does not cease to be power because it is omnipotence.[19] (italics added)

1. What is the role of philosophy in Christian theology and apologetics?

   There is no explicit answer to this question in the *Institutes*. It would appear that because of the innate knowledge of God in all men, and because of the universal Fall of man, the philosophical proofs of God's existence are not only not needed but also unachievable. Though there is thus no philosophical contribution to the knowledge of God, Calvin was well acquainted with the philosophers through his early humanistic studies, being especially fond of Plato, and was cognizant of the fact that the theologian would use philosophical concepts and language in explicating the doctrines of Scripture.

2. How are reason and faith related?

   In light of the long-standing debate on this issue by con-

---

18. The purpose of this book is not to refute contemporary apologists. Robert L. Reymond, a confirmed Calvinist like Van Til, takes Van Til to task for his position on univocal knowledge in *The Justification of Knowledge*, pp. 98-105. Gordon Lewis also deals with this, if less extensively (pp. 133-35).
19. Charles Hodge, *Systematic Theology*, 1:338.

vinced Calvinists, a dogmatic answer is not possible. The interpretation offered above has been to emphasize Calvin's balance of reasonable evidence and Spirit-given faith. Saving faith is certainly not the product of reason and evidence but the gift of the Holy Spirit, even if He uses rational evidence in the process of conviction and calling. In 3.2.34 of the *Institutes*, Calvin wrote that "indeed, it is only when the human intellect is irradiated by the light of the Holy Spirit that it begins to have a taste of those things which pertain to the kingdom of God; previously it was too stupid and senseless to have any relish for them."

3. Of what significance is the doctrine of sin for Christian apologetics?

It is all-important! Valid general revelation is unreadable because of man's willful depravity and effacement of God's image and thus produces neither a true knowledge of God nor the rightful worship due Him. The answer to question two above demonstrates that special revelation is spiritually uninterpretable because of sin apart from illumination by the Holy Spirit.

4. Do the theistic proofs have any worth for convincing the unbeliever?

No, it is not knowledge of the bare existence of God that man desperately needs, but personal knowledge of God that culminates in true worship, piety, obedience, and changed attitudes and ambitions.

5. To what extent may a believer and unbeliever form a shared point of contact on common ground?

Because of the witness of the Spirit there is not a common ground of knowledge of God, but because we all live in God's universe and are God's creatures there is a "kind" of common ground because no man can really know himself without first knowing God.

6. Are historical Christian evidences important, or even possible, as evidence for the unbeliever?

The answer to this is a correlative to the answer to question two, which is a far from unanimous answer among the very best of Calvinist theologians and apologists. It seems to me that Calvin was saying that although there are distinctive evidences that manifest the divine origin of the Scriptures

and the truth of Jesus Christ (*Institutes* 1.8), these are not in
their own right, apart from the work of the Holy Spirit, sufficient to break through the shell of depravity and willful sinfulness. Evidences are particularly useful and intellectually
confirmatory to the believer.
7. What degree of certainty is there in the truthfulness of
Christianity?

Absolute certainty is available by means of the witness of
the Holy Spirit, who enables us to see scriptural revelation as
special revelation. There is no apparent differentiation, common today, between objective certainty and subjective
certitude.

BLAISE PASCAL

Blaise Pascal was a precocious child, though the story that he
independently discovered the principles of geometry while
reading Greek and Latin texts under the instruction of his
father is probably apocryphal. Nevertheless, he did write an
article on conic sections at sixteen and later invented an adding
machine to aid his father in tax assessments. He also conducted
experiments to prove the theory of the vacuum. In 1654 Pascal
had a radical conversion experience at the age of thirty-one,
only eight years before his death in 1662. This happened
through the Cistercian convent at Port Royal outside Paris,
which had come under the Augustinian influence of Cornelius
Jansen (1585-1638). *Jansenism* emphasized conversion and the
irresistibility of grace along Augustinian lines, though Jansen
maintained that the extension of the incarnation through which
alone salvation was dispersed was the Roman Catholic church.
Pascal had been attracted to the community, though he never
officially joined the Jansenists, by the conversion of his sister
Jacqueline two years prior to his own. Upon conversion, Pascal
did not give up his scientific and mathematical pursuits as
worldly, but he did understand them in a new light as interpreting God's world and bringing glory to the Creator.

Pascal was not a theologian or trained biblical scholar, but he
was deeply devoted and a very perceptive and talented writer.
His apologetic "notes" known as the *Pensees* (*Thoughts*), are a
French classic. They were collected from various scraps of

paper and brief discourses Pascal had written in anticipation of writing an apologetic text, but which his premature death at thirty-nine prevented. Though we could wish for a more orderly and systematic presentation, few works have had more influence in the history of Christian thought. By the very nature of the case, more direct quotation from the *Pensees* is needed to "feel" the pulse of Pascal's apologetic thoughts than was needed with our three previous apologists.

In No. 60,[20] Pascal outlines his projected book as first the "misery of man without God" or "that nature is corrupt, proved by nature itself," and second, "happiness of man with God" or "that there is a Redeemer, proved by Scripture." These are Pascal's basic motifs—the depravity of man and the grace of God in providing Jesus Christ as man's Redeemer, two very Augustinian emphases. These Augustinian themes, acquired through the Jansenist influence, can be clearly seen in No. 556:

> The Christian religion, then, teaches men these two truths; that there is a God whom men can know, and that there is a corruption in their nature which renders them unworthy of Him. It is equally important to men to know both these points; and is equally dangerous for man to know God without knowing his own wretchedness, and to know his own wretchedness without knowing the Redeemer who can free him from it. The knowledge of only one of these points gives rise either to the pride of philosophers, who have God, and not their own wretchedness, or to the despair of atheists, who know their own wretchedness, but not the Redeemer.

These two points are the essence of the Christian religion as far as Pascal is concerned. Religious error can only be one of these two extremes. Christians can be guilty of neither since "we cannot know Jesus Christ without knowing at the same time both God and our own wretchedness" (No. 556). Religions that attempt to find God in nature either gain no knowledge of God or think they have a means of knowing God without a

---

20. Pascal's *Pensees* are always noted by number. Unfortunately, not all the editions have the same numbering. The material quoted here is from the Brunschvicg edition.

mediator; the former is atheism, the latter deism. Christianity abhors both almost equally.

The tendency toward what we are calling the Both/And approach is clearly seen in Pascal's Augustinian-influenced anthropology. He writes:

> The greatness of man is so evident, that it is even proved by his wretchedness. For what in animals is nature we call in man wretchedness; by which we recognise that, his nature being now like that of animals, he has fallen from a better nature which once was his. (No. 409)

> Wretchedness being deduced from greatness, and greatness from wretchedness, some have inferred man's wretchedness all the more because they have taken his greatness as a proof of it, and others have inferred his greatness with all the more force, because they have inferred it from his very wretchedness. . . . The one party is brought back to the other in an endless circle, it being certain that in proportion as men possess light they discover both the greatness and the wretchedness of man. In a word man knows that he is wretched. He is therefore wretched, because he is so; but he is really great because he knows it. (No. 416)

> It is dangerous to make man see too clearly his equality with the brutes without showing him his greatness. It is also dangerous to make him see his greatness too clearly, apart from his vileness. It is still more dangerous to leave him in ignorance of both. But it is very advantageous to show him both. Man must not think that he is on a level either with the brutes or with the angels, nor must he be ignorant of both sides of his nature; but he must know both. (No. 418)

Man, the "thinking reed" (No. 347), is thus one reality with two dimensions that are neither totally animalistic nor quite angelic. He reflects both, but is more than the former and less than the latter. Philosophies tend to make him one or the other and thus make him less than a "real man" (No. 525). The tension of being so great and yet so potentially vicious, and more frequently and usually so vile and yet so inherently great, is the paradoxical essence of man. Christianity alone both explains and fulfills this dual nature in man as it "bids man recognise that he is vile, even abominable, and bids him desire to be like

God. Without such a counterpoise, this dignity would make him horribly vain, or this humiliation would make him terribly abject" (No. 537). True humility comes not from man's nature, however, but from penitence that will lead to greatness; likewise, feelings of greatness are not from merit as the philosophers taught, but from grace that will pass on to humiliation (No. 525). Man thus knows both his misery and majesty through the incarnation, which "shows man the greatness of his misery by the greatness of the remedy which he required" (No. 526). Man cannot solve this desire for happiness and greatness himself. His very inability shows us that "there was once in man a true happiness of which there now remains to him only the mark and empty trace, which he in vain tries to fill from all his surroundings..." (No. 425). It can, however, be done! An "infinite abyss can only be filled by an infinite and immutable object, that is to say, only by God Himself" (No. 425). In Jesus Christ, and Jesus Christ alone, man finds both himself and God. Pascal writes in No. 527:

> The knowledge of God without that of man's misery causes pride. The knowledge of man's misery without that of God causes despair. The knowledge of Jesus Christ constitutes the middle course, because in Him we find both God and our misery.

What are the epistemological means of so knowing God in the person of Jesus Christ? Pascal, as is well-known, spoke of the heart having "its reasons, which reason does not know" (No. 277). Does this make him an irrationalist? Certainly it is true that, though he was a contemporary of René Descartes for twenty-seven years, he was never caught up in the French enthusiasm for Cartesian rationalism. He put little stock in the theistic proofs because they were too complicated, and because their demonstrative service had benefits limited to the time of such demonstration, and subsequently the unbeliever could again be overtaken with the fear of having been mistaken (No. 543). Blaise Pascal, however, was no fideist or even a forerunner of twentieth-century existentialists, as he has been frequently portrayed in either the history of philosophy or Christian apologetics. He succinctly says there are "two extremes: to exclude reason, to admit reason only" (No. 253). Christianity is thus more than the practice of rationalism, but that does not reduce it to irrationalism. It is both capable of proof and beyond proof. He wrote: "If we submit everything to reason, our religion will have no mysterious and supernatural element. If we offend the principles of reason, our religion will be absurd and ridiculous" (No. 273).

Pascal thus identifies "three sources of belief: reason, custom, inspiration." Though the Christian religion "alone has reason," it does not accept as her true children "those who believe without inspiration" (No. 245). True faith is thus reasonable and "opened to proofs," but it is also more than reason as inspiration (the work of the Holy Spirit) "alone can produce a true and saving effect" (No. 245). Similarly, faith is not contrary to the senses but beyond them, for he writes that "faith indeed tells what the senses do not tell, but not the contrary of what they see. It is above them and not contrary to them" (No. 265). Empirical proofs are important but by their very nature are not absolute. But nothing is ever proven absolutely, nor are first principles capable of rational proof, e.g., space, motion, time, and number, though they are assumed in all reasonable endeavors (No. 282). Thus knowledge of the reality of Christianity is identical with knowledge of other historical realities. Christianity is never accepted or rejected on reason alone, however, since the truth of Christianity points beyond the historical and empirical. Thus Pascal writes perceptively of Christian evidences:

> The prophecies, the very miracles and proofs of our religion, are not of such a nature that they can be said to be absolutely convincing. But they are also of such a kind that it cannot be said that it is unreasonable to believe them. Thus there is both evidence and obscurity to enlighten some and confuse others. But the evidence is such that it surpasses, or at least equals, the evidence to the contrary; so that it is not reason which can determine men not to follow it, and thus it can only be lust or malice of heart. And by this means there is sufficient evidence to condemn, and insufficient to convince; so that it appears in those who follow it, that it is grace, and not reason which makes them follow it; and in those who shun it, that it is lust, not reason, which makes them shun it. (No. 564)

Pascal was hardly an irrationalist in light of this and the

above references. How then do some take him to be such? There is only one reason, the misunderstanding of the intent of *Pascal's wager*—"if you gain, you gain all; if you lose, you lose nothing. Wager, then, without hesitation that He is" (No. 233). But remember that Pascal's wager, or No. 233, was simply a note, as are all the other remnants of the *Pensees*. How would he have used it? Where would he have placed it? All answers are, of course, speculative. In light of the preceding analysis, I believe that the "wager" would have been placed at the end of his projected work. Gamblers wager on the basis of the odds. Pascal was an early investigator of probability theory. Gamblers might not ever bet on *sure* things, but they do determine their odds on the basis of probability. Few wager on 200-1 odds in a horse race, but 3-2 odds, though paying less, are much more likely to pay. So the evidence for Christianity, although not a "sure thing," and thus open to probability (No. 564), has a "very likely" probability and is a reasonable "bet." We neglect His probability signs at our own peril. "Seek them, therefore; it is well worth it" (No. 236). Thus smart gamblers would "bet" on God and the truth of His revelation in Christianity.

Does this mean that the Christian believer only has probability of the truthfulness of his faith? Never! Recall No. 245, where Pascal noted that the "the mind must be opened to proofs," but that inspiration "alone can produce a true and saving effect." Thus the Christian religion "does not acknowledge as her true children those who believe without inspiration" (No. 245). There is therefore an enablement and a certitude beyond reason. Christianity is neither only rational nor beyond reason, it is *Both/And*.

1. What is the role of philosophy in Christian theology and apologetics?

Since philosophy basically means Cartesianism and the use of theistic arguments, there is no absolute relationship between philosophy and Christian apologetics. As a man who used reason and realized the intuitive nature of first principles, Pascal was not ignorant of the philosophical implications of Christianity. In one sense, we might say that philosophy makes room for faith.

2. How are reason and faith related?

There is very little relationship between faith and reason if

the latter is understood as midseventeenth-century deductive rationalism as noted in question one. Reason, understood as the comprehension of evidence, is necessary for a
reasonable faith, but faith is more than rational assent and is
not simply the product of rational inference but divine grace.
3. Of what significance is the doctrine of sin for Christian
apologetics?

In light of man's wretchedness, which is his acquired—not
original—state, sin is very important in Pascal's apologetic.
Though it does not make miracles and proofs completely
unintelligible to fallen man, man does reject such because of
his sinful inclinations and inherent self-centeredness.
4. Do the theistic proofs have any worth for convincing the
unbeliever?

Pascal recognized their worth as an initial thought provok-
er, but believed the evidence was ambivalent. In No. 229,
speaking of seeing God in nature, he wrote that "seeing too
much to deny and too little to be sure, I am in a state to be
pitied; wherefore I have a hundred times wished that if a
God maintains nature, she should testify to Him unequivo-
cally, and that if the signs she gives are deceptive, she should
suppress them altogether; that she should say everything or
nothing, that I might see which cause I ought to follow."
Thus Pascal essentially rejected them as totally insufficient
for religious purposes. To rightly know God, given man's
two-sided dimension of greatness/wretchedness, man can
and must know God only through a mediator.
5. To what extent may a believer and unbeliever form a shared
point of contact on common ground?

Pascal would appear to give a Both/And answer to this
question; from an ontological dimension he would seem to
answer that both believer and unbeliever share in the realities of God's image (greatness) and man's Fall (wretchedness), and second, that the objective historical evidence of
the miracles and fulfilled prophecies are there for everyone
to see. From an epistemological perspective Pascal would
answer that the unbeliever does not share the "reasons of
the heart" with the believer.
6. Are historical Christian evidences important, or even possible, as evidence for the unbeliever?

Obviously, in light of question five, Christian evidences are important to objectively differentiate Christianity from all the false religions, providing cognitive reasonableness of the truth of Christianity for the unbeliever. Such cognitive reasonableness is not identical with, nor mutually exclusive of, saving faith.

7. What degree of certainty is there in the truthfulness of Christianity?

There can only be a degree of probability about the historical evidences of Christianity. Although Pascal rejected the absolute deductive certainty of Cartesian rationalism derived from the theistic proofs, the believer has absolute personal certitude as the "heart has its reasons, which reason does not know" (No. 277).

SÖREN KIERKEGAARD

Sören Kierkegaard was born to older (his father was fifty-six, his mother forty-four) but well-to-do parents in Copenhagen, Denmark in 1813. A tender-spirited and physically weak child, he was also overprotected by his parents and much too close to a father given over to morbid remorse and self-criticism due to believing he had committed the unpardonable sin as a young man. Kierkegaard seemingly inherited this melancholy spirit, sensitive disposition, and hesitancy of self-acceptance. In 1847 he described himself: "From my early childhood the arrow of suffering has been planted in my heart. So long as it is there I am ironical—pull it out and I will die."[21] His university career was stormy, though he fell in love with Socrates and philosophy. His other love, Regina, a woman some ten years his younger, was induced to reject him after ill treatment by Kierkegaard. This rejection was subsequently interpreted by Kierkegaard as his self-sacrifice as a "knight-of-faith," a la Abraham, and with pen in hand he began a passionate crusade against the unbelief and dead orthodoxy of his time. His one duty, in his human solitude, was to "take up his cross daily" and be totally obedient to God in Christ. Convinced that his love for a woman would have destroyed the absoluteness of his love for God, he

---

21. Quoted in Robert Heiss, *Hegel, Kierkegaard, Marx*, p. 211.

fought a strenuous battle for Christianity against the rationalistic spirit of the age, and died a physically, if not spiritually, broken man in 1855.

Kierkegaard's two enemies, as is well-known, were the all-encompassing Hegelianism of the intellectual world, including theology and Christian preaching, and the easy equation of Danish-Lutheran citizenship with being a Christian. Kierkegaard rightly understood the New Testament to speak of Christianity as a separation from the world, a costly obedience, not something as universal as national citizenship. The kingdom of God and the kingdom of Denmark were not identical. If they were, there was no decision for Christ that was even possible. Faith was not necessary. There was no narrow way. Everyone was a Christian!

This identification of national citizenship with Christianity was neither dependent upon, nor originally caused by, the pervasive Hegelian outlook, but it certainly was abetted by it. Many of the most influencial clergy interpreted Christianity through the matrix of Hegel's system in a manner reminiscent of Aquinas's use of Aristotle. It was against these right-wing Hegelians, who made Hegel and Christianity amenable, that Kierkegaard so rightly, if excessively, reacted. He so rejected the rationalism of Hegel that he consciously adopted an irrational apologetic of extreme fideism. There is a growing tendency among Kierkegaardian interpreters to believe that he consciously and purposely overstated his case as an ironic *tour de force* to make his point that faith is essential to Christianity as a way of life and is neither merely commitment based on objective evidence nor commitment totally devoid of such. Though there may be *some* truth to this, I cannot accept it in light of Kierkegaard's perception of traditional apologetics as destroying Christianity: "If one were to describe the whole orthodox apologetic effort in a single sentence, but also with categorical precision, one might say that it has the intent to make Christianity *plausible*. To this, one might add that, if this were to succeed, then this effort would have the ironical fate that precisely on the day of its triumph it would have lost everything and entirely quashed Christianity."[22]

22. Kierkegaard, *On Authority and Revelation*, p. 59.

Our purpose here is the same as with the previous four apologists, though it may be more difficult to avoid exaggerating Kierkegaard due to limiting ourselves to apologetics. For example, Kierkegaard's *Stages on Life's Way* portrays man as an aesthetic, moral, and religious being, and is central to his anthropology. However, we will focus exclusively on the epistemological issues of man as a religious being—specifically in relation to Christianity. Important ethical issues such as the teleological suspension of the ethical advocated in *Fear and Trembling*, as well as questions revolving around Kierkegaard's tactic of "indirect communication," will hardly be touched.

Kierkegaard emphasized the transcendence of God, perhaps excessively, to confute the total immanence of God in the theological expositions of Hegelian idealism. Therefore the possibility of natural theology is absolutely rejected. God is not known at the end of an inferential series of rational statements. God is not an object we manipulate by our reason, nor is He to be identified as "reason personified" and thus synonymous with logic, per Hegel. Reality is more than an impersonal expression of Anselm's ontological argument.

Rather, God is Subject. In His transcendence God is *Deus absconditus* (the hidden God) and thus can be known in no other way than the way a person can be known, that is by personal meeting or encounter. Since God is Other than us, He cannot be known by either Socratic recollection or Hegelian dialectic as if man possessed the truth within himself. Since God is outside of us, transcendent, He can only be known in the moment of meeting when man "becomes another man." He becomes "a man of a different quality." This is conversion, repentance, new birth. In *Philosophical Fragments*, his most important book for our purposes, Kierkegaard wrote that "such a moment has a peculiar character. It is brief and temporal indeed, like every moment; it is transient as all moments are; it is past, like every moment in the next moment. And yet it is decisive, and filled with the Eternal."[23]

It is this "moment," or history, that gives Kierkegaard his

---

23. Kierkegaard [Johannes Climacus], *Philosophical Fragments*, p. 22. Johannes Climacus is one of Kierkegaard's frequently used pseudonyms.

problems. Gotthold Lessing (1729-1781), a unique theological critic and dramatist, had stated that "the accidental truths of history can never become proofs of necessary truths of reason."[24] This is an obvious truism. The early nineteenth-century quest for the historical Jesus had demonstrated it. But living in such a rationalistic era, Kierkegaard thought that the unconditioned, eternal God, the logically necessary Being, must rationally be precluded from involvement with the conditioned contingencies of temporal history. Nevertheless, such involvement had occurred. God had appeared as the servant.[25] Therefore Jesus Christ, as the God/Man, was the "Absolute Paradox." He could not be understood, only believed.

Neither Kant nor Hegel had seen the uniqueness of Jesus as the One and Only God incarnate. For Kant, the historical revelation in Jesus was simply the historical particularized communication of moral truths that were also universally accessible, at least in principle, by reason. Jesus Christ was thus understood by Kant as the finest ethical teacher, not the acme of God's personal revelation, in *Religion Within the Limits of Reason Alone*. For Hegel, there could be no conflict of logical necessity and contingent historical facts as all history was the necessary dialectical unfolding or actualization of the Absolute. Idealism and Christianity are the same, the former the literal expression of ultimate reality, the latter the religious or symbolic understanding of what is. Christianity, for Hegel, is only the religious expression of the Absolute. Historical existence was simply the necessary expression of Being, or theologically expressed, God. All was immanence. God was not different from, or other than, everything else.

Kierkegaard rightly rejected both Kantian and Hegelian versions of Christianity. Biblical Christianity was neither reducible to good, even objective, ethics, nor were God and man ultimately one with man simply needing to look within himself to find God. These are the two strains of Christian liberalism — whether interpreted as ethics a la Albrecht Ritschl (1822-1889)

---

24. The original quotation is found in G. E. Lessing, *Über den Beweis des Geistes und der Kraft*. It is taken from Martin Kähler, *The So-Called Historical Jesus and the Historic Biblical Christ*, p. 138n.
25. Kierkegaard, *Philosophical Fragments*, pp. 39-43.

or as Friedrich Schliermacher's (1768-1834) "feeling of dependence." His rejection of these alternatives is why Kierkegaard was so warmly grasped in the beginnings of a new orthodoxy in the first decades of the twentieth century. Kierkegaard seemingly endorsed the orthodox doctrines, but not in the usual manner of historic Christian apologetics. Jesus was the Christ. But Jesus, the Christ, was also unintelligible, or at least unknowable. Kierkegaard answered his own question as to whether Christ could be known through history:

> No. And why not? Because one cannot "know" anything at all about "Christ"; for he is the paradox, the object of faith, and exists only for faith. But all historic information is communication of "knowledge." Therefore one cannot learn anything about Christ from history. For whether now one learn little or much about him, it will not represent what he was in reality.... History makes Christ look different from what he looked in truth, and thus one learns much from history about—Christ? No, not about Christ, because about him nothing can be "known," he can only be believed.[26]

He continues:

> "History," says faith, "has nothing to do with Christ." With regard to him we have only Sacred History (which is different in kind from general history), Sacred History which tells of his life and career when in debasement and tells also that he affirmed himself to be God. He is the paradox which history never will be able to digest or convert into a general syllogism.[27]

And last, but very similar:

> Ah, wicked thoughtlessness which thus interprets Sacred History like profane history, which makes Christ a man! But can one, then, learn anything from history about Jesus? No, nothing. Jesus Christ is the object of faith—one either believes in him or is offended by him, for "to know" means precisely that such knowledge does not pertain to him. History can, therefore, to be sure,

---

26. Sören Kierkegaard, *Preparation for a Christian Life*, as found in *Selections from the Writings of Kierkegaard*, trans. Lee M. Hollander, p. 169.
27. Ibid., p. 174.

give one knowledge in abundance; but "knowledge" annihilates Jesus Christ.[28]

Obviously, Kierkegaard's problem of historical knowledge of Christ was not due to a skepticism of history, which can give "one knowledge in abundance," but because of the separation of Christ's history from all other history, a tenet we previously denied (p. 69). With the radical separation of Christ from history, Kierkegaard runs the danger of making Christ a figment of the imagination—an "object of faith" exclusively. *Knowing* and *believing* are always mutually exclusive for Kierkegaard, since knowing is to accept something on an objective and rational basis, but believing is to risk all on an objective uncertainty. Knowing leaves the person as he was, believing changes him. Christ, then, must be believed, not known. Faith cannot be knowledge, since knowledge has to do with either "the Eternal, excluding the temporal and historical as indifferent, or it is pure historical knowledge. No knowledge can have for its object the absurdity that the Eternal is the historical."[29] Christ, however, is this Absolute Paradox, the Absurd, and the sole object of faith because He "unites the contradictories and is the historical made eternal, and the Eternal made historical."[30]

No "Absolute Paradox" would have existed if Kierkegaard had not unconsciously adopted two unbiblical assumptions. First, he identified God's existence with His essence; in a Hegelian climate, this implied God's *logical* necessity rather than factual necessity and thus the contradictoriness of attempting to prove the logical "necessary truths of reason" by the historical, existential (accidental) truths concerning the person of Jesus Christ.[31] Second, Kierkegaard adopted a Socratic qualitative differentiation between time and eternity rather than the biblical conception of "ages of ages," where history is one segment

28. Ibid., p. 177.
29. Kierkegaard [Climacus], *Philosophical Fragments*, p. 76.
30. Ibid.
31. Very helpful in distinguishing logical from factual necessity in regard to the being of God is John Hick's article "Necessary Being," in William L. Rowe and William J. Wainwright, eds., *Philosophy of Religion: Selected Readings*, pp. 14-27. See also above, p. 20.

of an unlimited (eternal) linear timeline.[32] History and eternity
are not mutually exclusive in the Bible. Kierkegaard, however,
refused to take the paradox away. For him paradox was indispensable, not simply as apparent contradiction, but as absolute
contradiction because "the absurd is the Object of faith, and
the only object that can be believed."[33] Jesus the Christ was not
simply objectively uncertain as a fact of history, but absurd and
thus to be received as the truth only by "an appropriation process of the most passionate inwardness."[34] This "passionate
inwardness" was both the reception of faith and Kierkegaard's
criterion of truth. Malcolm Diamond notes that Kierkegaard's
fate was sealed by his intense desire to make his fellow Danes
take Christianity seriously on the personal, subjective (not subjectivistic) level. He was so concerned, Diamond relates, with
the *how* of faith that he lost the distinctive Christian *what* of
faith. The analysis of truth as subjectivity implied "that when
dealing with an existential decision which cannot be handled
objectively, any *what* will do, as long as you have an authentic
how."[35] The Absolute Paradox must be a contradiction or it
becomes objectively definable *after* the "leap of faith" in "passionate inwardness," and thus truth could no longer be defined
as subjectivity. Diamond concludes:

> Ironically that makes his formulation of Christian truth impossible
> for us. No amount of passionately subjective appropriation can
> make sense of a "paradox" that is really a contradiction. Kierke-
> gaard might as well urge us to attain authentic individuality by
> passionately appropriating the "paradox" of the three sided
> square.[36]

This does not mean Kierkegaard is of no assistance whatever
in the construction of an evangelical apologetic. Though history
cannot be rejected so glibly or we reject Luke and John, it is at
the same time a healthy reminder that all the objective evidence possibly conceivable is not capable of regenerating a per-

32. See Oscar Cullmann, *Christ and Time.*
33. Sören Kierkegaard, *Concluding Unscientific Postscript*, p. 189.
34. Ibid., p. 182.
35. Malcolm Diamond, *Contemporary Philosophy and Religious Thought*, p. 155.
36. Ibid., p. 169.

son and turning him from sin, Satan, and self to the Creator, Savior, and Lord. There is still the radical problem of sin and alienation from God. Kierkegaard knew that well and, perhaps better than anyone since Augustine, made us face ourselves in *The Concept of Dread* and *The Sickness unto Death*.

There is, then, a very personal, subjective, element to salvation. As noted earlier (p. 76), there is a sense in which revelation is recognized for what it is and it "becomes" a normative practicing absolute as God's Word "for me." There is also indisputable personal testimony, even if it is not sufficient unto itself. As put by A. H. Ackley, "You ask me how I know He lives? He lives within my heart." That is an answer very similar in structure to Jesus' answer concerning the dead: the Lord is " 'the God of Abraham, and the God of Isaac, and the God of Jacob.' He is not the God of the dead, but of the living, for to him all are alive" (Luke 20:37-38). Kierkegaard's motives and intentions were thus absolutely pure in both the refutation of an impersonal metaphysic and the prayed-for revival of Danish Christianity. His method, however, was overstated at best, totally misconceived at worst. We must learn, however, from his sincere passion for and keen insight into the reality of unsaved man. We must construct a more *balanced* apologetic that neither costs us the objective Christ for a subjective experience, nor forgets that a confrontation with the resurrected Lord of glory is inherently personal and transforming. For, like the disciples on the road to Emmaus, our hearts (i.e., our total beings) must "burn within us" as we meet Him personally in the midst of our lives as the living, ascended Christ—through the pages of holy Scripture.

1. What is the role of philosophy in Christian theology and apologetics?

    It has no role, since philosophy takes the path of reason to knowledge and theology follows faith to the Absolute Paradox.

2. How are reason and faith related?

    Reason and faith are not only *not* related, they are mutually exclusive. Faith is the passionate subjective acceptance of the absurd; reason is the objective calculation of the uncertain for the purpose of obtaining knowledge. Knowledge, however, destroys the subject of faith, Jesus Christ.

3. Of what significance is the doctrine of sin for Christian apologetics?

Sin is the source of man's separation from God and other men, resulting in solitude and despair. Only the "leap of faith" to God through the Paradox of Jesus Christ can cure man of his inherent sickness.

4. Do the theistic proofs have any worth for convincing the unbeliever?

Though Kierkegaard affirms creation, the "hidden" God is not seen when nature or man is observed. The proofs make God an object at the end of the reasoning process and thus are of no value in knowing the transcendent, personal God.

5. To what extent may a believer and unbeliever form a shared point of contact on common ground?

Since only the believer has taken the leap of faith, and one cannot take the leap and remain an unbeliever, there is absolutely no shared point of contact. Faith is incommunicable, and therefore no argument is possible. In terms of one of the titles of Kierkegaard's primary books, it is *Either/Or*.

6. Are historical Christian evidences important, or even possible, for the unbeliever?

They are worthless, but for a different reason than the problem of the unbelieving subject's being unable to believe and accept the evidence in an unregenerate state. Rather, they are ambiguous because of the subject to which they point, Jesus Christ, the contradiction of Eternity in time, the Absurd, for which there is no evidence or knowledge possible.

7. What degree of certainty is there in the truthfulness of Christianity?

In light of the above questions, it is clear that for Kierkegaard there was absolute ambiguity objectively and absolute certitude subjectively through the passionate inwardness of faith.

6

NEW TESTAMENT PRACTICES

We must now retrace our steps from the examples of the great theologian-apologists to the absolute norm for apologetic methodology—the New Testament. The five examples from church history each approached the apologetic enterprise differently, though there is an obvious affinity in the emphases of Augustine, Calvin, and Pascal. In examining the New Testament—particularly the apostolic practices and sermons recorded in the book of Acts—and the second century Fathers of the church (see chapter 7), there is no attempt to present Paul and Peter, or Justin Martyr and Irenaeus, as systematically and concisely as the men of chapter 5. Rather, the approaches to different audiences will be looked at for definitive instruction and generalization to our own day. An attempt will be made to determine if these men can be labeled as evidentialists, presuppositionalists, natural theologians, or fideists.

The role of written Old Testament revelation in the first century events in Palestine will be of prime importance as we examine the early preaching of Peter and John in chapters 2-5 of Acts. Our style will be purposely freer than it was with the apologists, so that the reader can come to some of his own conclusions about the apostolic and early church practices in regard to (1) a priori or a posteriori methodology, (2) the questions of the relationship of faith and reason, and (3) the extent to which God's image in man was damaged by the Fall. Doubtless the presentation will be colored by conclusions the author believes to be biblical. Chapter 4 has already delineated "Biblical Theological Necessities," and thus these emphases are believed to be true of apostolic practice as recorded in Acts, even if there was a conscious effort previously to draw on the other portions of the New Testament. But biblical apostolic practices are normative and must be the measure of any apologetic framework. Therefore, one must go back to the primary evangelistic and preaching passages of Acts to fit theological understanding with biblically sustained practices.

Some may question a perceived imbalance with greater emphasis on the New Testament to the apparent neglect of the Old Testament. This is frequently the cardinal sin of evangelical theology and apologetics. We plead innocent. Though there is not a separate chapter and thus totally equal treatment of the Old Testament, there has been ample reference to the Old Testament in chapters 2 and 3 in the discussions of ontology and epistemology as well as additional reference in chapter 4 in the discussion of the historical and supernatural dimensions of biblical religion. Also, by the very nature of the Christian gospel, Christian apologetics and evangelism must put primary emphasis upon New Testament doctrines and practices because of the finality of the Christ-event (Heb. 1:1-2).

A brief synopsis of the apologetic nature of various New Testament books before examining the apologetic models and techniques in detail should prove helpful. The gospels, regardless of the exact date of writing, were among the earliest apologetic literature. Though Mark's gospel contains little that is purely apologetic, Matthew and Luke, like the two primary missionary thrusts in Acts, were addressed to Jews and Gentiles, respectively. Matthew certainly portrays Jesus as the Messiah, the long-awaited King, in the detailed genealogy from Abraham through David and Solomon. He also precedes an explicit reference to Isaiah 7:14 with an "editorial comment" that "all this took place to fulfill what the Lord had said through the prophet" (Matt. 1:22). Matthew's apologetic, which makes repeated use of fulfilled prophecy as a primary means of illustrating and defending the truth, was deemed successful by the early church. It was given the first position among the gospels and was frequently referred to as "the gospel" at the turn of the first century.

Luke, on the other hand, addresses himself to Gentiles. There is great emphasis on distinctly dating the time of Christ's appearance by reference to Roman rulers and events, illustrated easily in the gospel by the census record in Luke 2:1-3 and the listing of Gentile authorities in Luke 3:1-2. That procedure is also prevalent in the history of the apostles (Acts). Luke also typically expands the coverage of Gentile blessings. Examples of that include Luke's reference to the ministries of Elijah and Elisha (Luke 4:26-27), the more extended treatment given the healing of the centurion's son (Luke 7:1-10), perhaps the exorcism of the demon-possessed man among the Gerasenes (Luke 8:26-39), and the parable of the Good Samaritan (Luke 10:25-37). There may even be an anti-Jewish polemic present, since the Jews are made to bear the responsibility for Christ's death a bit more actively, and Pilate, as the Gentile representative, appears a bit more passive.

There are apologetic overtones in other New Testament books as well. Apologetic notes are certainly sounded in 1 Corinthians and Colossians (see pp. 10-12). Romans presents an apology for the place of the Jewish people (this will be dealt with later in this chapter). The gospel of John and Hebrews require a little more treatment. The gospel of John has two distinctively apologetic passages: 1:1-14 and 20:31. The prologue of John attempts to straddle the two halves of the ancient world by the term *logos*, or "word." The term was current in the philosophical literature from Heraclitus down through the Stoics to Philo, a Jewish philosopher during the first half of the first century. *logos* always meant, though understood differently by the respective philosophers, the meaning, purpose, and plan of the universe. It thus was a very useful term with definite apologetic significance and value for commending the gospel to the Gentile world. It was also of value for an entrance into the Jewish community where the concept of the "Word of the Lord" gave the term immediate meaning. It was doubtless the Old Testament context that was the background for John's use of the term. Nevertheless, it gives ample apostolic sanction to the dangerous but necessary endeavor of communicating the gospel in current intellectual concepts and terminology while maintaining resolute fidelity to the truth.

John's use of *logos* as "the Word became flesh" (1:14) unquestionably differentiated the Christian understanding of the concept from the philosophical. John also spelled out the purpose for his gospel in apologetic terms in regard to Jesus' miracles: "But these are written that you may believe that Jesus is the Christ, the Son of God, and that by believing you may have life in his name" (20:31). There is some textual disagreement as to whether John is saying that he writes so they "may continue to believe" or they "may [be able to] believe" as in the NIV and the NASB. In either case John's gospel is apologetic, if not evangelistic according to the former translation. Textual criticism would appear to prefer the latter translation. Thus John's purpose in writing is to defend the gospel and enable individuals to believe that Jesus is the Christ, the Messiah, who fulfills Old Testament prophecies and who is substantiated by God-wrought miracles (see John 11:45 for instance). For John *both* factual evidence *and* scriptural Word are equally indispensable.

Even if John's gospel had the purpose of Jewish evangelism by the *logos* motif and the interpretation of Jesus' miracles, Hebrews is still the preeminent apology to the Jews. J. K. S. Reid states in his history of apologetics that "of all the documents later recognized as canonically belonging to a New Testament and so set alongside the Hebrew Scriptures, the Epistle to the Hebrews is the clearest example of sustained apology for the Christian faith."[1] Though addressed to a predominantly Jewish community, an apologetic based on the typology and fulfillment of the Old Testament had an immediate and a continued appeal. The Old Testament was a necessary but preliminary step to the completion of salvation. The priestly practices were merely the shadow of the atonement reality in Jesus Christ (Heb. 10:1). The promises to the Hebrew patriarchs were completed in the person of the Messiah, the final High Priest (4:14-16; 7:11 — 8:6). Jesus Christ, in fact, is both high priest and sacrifice, introducing the new covenant (Jer. 31:31-34) and thus

1. J. K. S. Reid, *Chrisitan Apologetics*, p. 28.

setting in motion God's final promises to Israel (Heb. 8:6-13; 9:11-15). Jesus fully covers sin and thereby completely cleanses of it by giving His life, the literal shedding of blood (10:19-22). We now "have been made holy through the sacrifice of the body of Jesus Christ *once for all* . . . because by one sacrifice he has made perfect forever those who are being made holy" (Heb. 10:10, 14, italics added). Jews need not give up their Old Testament faith when accepting Christianity. They need only realize that anticipation has become actualization, that shadow has been replaced by reality. Christianity does not replace or obliterate Judaism but completes it. Christianity is Judaism fulfilled.

THE APOLOGETICS OF JESUS

There are no signs of a self-conscious apologetic in the thoughts and actions of Jesus as recorded in the gospels, yet on numerous occasions Jesus is recorded either as defending Himself and/or His disciples, or as giving an explicit reason for what He says or does. He answered John's disciples on two occasions: once to defend the non-fasting practices of His disciples contrary to the practices of John's disciples or the Pharisees (Matt. 9:14-17), and a second time to point out the empirical evidences of His messianic fulfillment that they themselves could hear and see—the lame walking, the blind seeing, the deaf hearing, the leper cleansed, and the dead raised to life again (Matt. 11:2-6; see Isa. 29:18; 35:5-6). He also defends His and the disciples' Sabbath practices such as plucking corn or healing (Mark 2:23—3:6).

In John 5:17-47 Jesus very cogently argued His equality with God. He began His twofold defense of word and deed by claiming that the "very work that the Father has given me to finish, and which I am doing, testifies that the Father has sent me" (v. 36), but "since you do not believe what [Moses] wrote, how are you going to believe what I say?" (v. 47). That tactic, if we may call it such, began very early in Jesus' ministry. One of the clearest manifestations of it is recorded in Mark 2:1-12, which is the familiar story of the paralyzed man lowered to Jesus through a hole in the roof, to whom Jesus said in response to his and his friends' faith, "Son, your sins are forgiven" (v. 5).

Jewish teachers immediately labeled this as blasphemy, as they said to themselves, "Who can forgive sins but God alone?" (v. 7). Jesus, knowing what they were thinking, questioned them as to which was easier, to forgive sins or heal the body. As if to illustrate that His word was God-sustained, He performed a God-ordained work so that people might *know* the reality of His person. The text reads most definitively: " 'But that you may know that the Son of Man has authority on earth to forgive sins. . . .' " He said to the paralytic, 'I tell you, get up, take your mat and go home' " (vv. 10-11). It is no wonder that those in attendance rightly concluded, "We have never seen anything like this!" (v. 12).

We need to look more closely at this relationship of Jesus' deeds and words. Doubtless Jesus did not do miracles to induce conviction or overcome doubt in an apologetic manner, though this was frequently the effect of His miracles. Nevertheless, when asked for a miracle as a sign simply for the sake of a sign, He refused on the grounds that only a "wicked and adulterous generation asks for a miraculous sign" (Matt. 12:39). This is characteristic throughout His ministry, perhaps because of the temptation experience, which consisted of Satan's asking for at least one sensational miracle simply for its own sake with no inherent redeeming value (Matt. 4:1-11). Jesus seemingly did miracles only where great need or great faith (or both) were present—not to create faith. However, John in particular links the miracles in a causative way with belief. Relating miracle and belief at the very beginning of Jesus' ministry, John wrote:

> This, the first of his miraculous signs, Jesus performed in Cana of Galilee. He thus revealed his glory, and his disciples put their faith in him. . . . Now while he was in Jerusalem at the Passover Feast, many people saw the miraculous signs he was doing and believed in his name. (John 2:11, 23)

If Hebrews is influential in the role fulfilled prophecy played in the apologies of the second century, then the gospel accounts that depict the result, if not the original intention, of any particular miracle are responsible for the role Christ's miracles have had in Christian apologetics. Miracle is closely related to belief by Jesus Himself in John 4:48. John shows the Jewish populace expecting miracles so that they might believe (John 6:30) and realizing that, since the Christ would do marvelous signs when He came, and such signs were among them through the man Jesus, Jesus must be the Christ (John 7:31). This effect of miracles was accepted by Jesus. His miraculous deeds are to be understood as supportive and absolutely indicative of the truth of His word concerning His identity. Jesus clearly implied that the death of Lazarus occurred so the disciples "may believe" (John 11:15); He was even more explicit when, in His prayer before Lazarus's tomb, He stated, "I said this for the benefit of the people standing here, that they may believe that you sent me" (John 11:42). Finally, in a very declarative manner, John records Jesus as saying on two different occasions:

> Why then do you accuse me of blasphemy because I said, "I am God's Son?" Do not believe me unless I do what my Father does. But if I do it, even though you do not believe me, believe the miracles, that you may learn and understand that the Father is in me, and I in the Father. (John 10:36-38)

> Believe me when I say that I am in the Father and the Father is in me; or at least believe on the evidence of the miracles themselves. (John 14:11)

There can be no escaping the supportive, and even causative, role of miracle to belief here. Word and deed *cannot* be separated. Jesus' deeds supported His word. One cannot disbelieve His claims if His works are the works of God. Such works are distinctive pointers to the true identity of His person. He cannot falsely claim to be God's Son and then do such miracles, for God would not permit it. The very doing of the miracles demonstrates the truth of His claims and word. Therefore Jesus demanded that they believe Him by the very "evidence of the miracles themselves." Notice that the apostle John believed by the empirical remains left after the resurrection (John 20:8).

It is no wonder that Jesus' miracles play such a large role in both the apostolic and patristic apologetic. (We will see this shortly in our treatment of Acts 2.) But, and this is very important, miraculous signs are not enough. "Even after Jesus had done all these miraculous signs in their presence, they still would not believe in him" (John 12:37). The following verses go on to quote Isaiah 53:1 and 6:10, which picture the hardening of the hearts of first-century Jews as being similar to God's dealings with Pharaoh in Egypt. It demonstrates, however, that as important as empirical evidence is, it is never entirely sufficient in its own right. Jesus' miracles moved many to intellectual belief as did the plagues in ancient Egypt, but it is not a logical necessity to believe even in the face of such overwhelming evidence. The episode ascribing Jesus' exorcism of demons to Beelzebub, the prince of demons, shows how blind to the evidence and illogical the unbelieving heart can be (Matt. 12:22-28). The use of such revelatory evidence may very likely have the same result today. But that cannot be an excuse to avoid providing empirical and historical evidence of the absolute uniqueness of Jesus Christ, the Son of God. As Jesus said, there is *only one proper interpretation* of the fact that demons are cast out "by the Spirit of God ... the kingdom of God has come upon you" (Matt. 12:28).

Thus the New Testament provides miracles as evidence for Jesus' being the incarnate Son of God, the anticipated Messiah. We must never turn this into a fideistic or neo-orthodox perspective that we believe in miracles because we believe in Christ. Neither Christ, nor the gospel writers, present the effect of the miracles in this epistemological order. As Jesus said, we believe He is the Christ because of "the evidence of the miracles themselves" (John 14:11).

There is another direct factor in our Lord's message that has apologetic significance. Jesus repeatedly connected His ministry and mission with the Old Testament. That this is a central fact of His preaching is evidenced by its blatant appearance in the Gentile-directed gospel of Luke as well as the more direct apologetic attempts toward Judaism in Matthew and John. In Luke 4:17-21 Jesus explicitly ascribes the fulfillment of Isaiah 61:1-2 to Himself. Throughout each of the gospel accounts, though perhaps to a lesser degree in Mark, Jesus is seen as living under a divine compulsion and necessity. Luke alone has the Emmaus Road experience where the risen Savior explained to His disciples that the entire Old Testament, from Moses through the prophets, bore witness to Him (Luke 24:25-27), helping us to better comprehend through the blessing of hindsight the aforementioned necessity that drove Jesus to "be about my Father's business" (Luke 2:49, KJV). John also pinpoints the early acceptance of Jesus of Nazareth as the One of whom Moses wrote (John 1:45). The appeal to Scripture, like miracles, does not necessitate belief. Many pious Jews did not see or understand Jesus as the Messiah, the long-awaited of Israel. The resurrection proved them wrong (Rom. 1:4). But it also showed that men, alienated from God, can always disbelieve if that is their wish—miracle or fulfilled prophecy notwithstanding. Peter's affirmation that Jesus is "the Christ, the Son of the living God" (Matt. 16:16) was not done solely by means of his own intellectual discernment and interpretation of fact, for such understanding "was not revealed to you by man, but by my Father in heaven" (16:17). There were only two alternatives: either Jesus was who He claimed to be and thus had to be accepted unconditionally; or the first-century autonomous Jews could reject Him as a blasphemer (Matt. 26:65; John 19:7). Pascal is doubtless correct that

> there is both evidence and obscurity to enlighten some and confuse others . . . . And by this means there is sufficient evidence to condemn, and insufficient to convince; so that it appears to those who follow it, that it is grace, and not reason, which makes them follow it; and in those who shun it, that it is lust, not reason, which makes them shun it. (*Pensees* No. 564)

THE APOLOGY TO ISRAEL

Before turning to the examples of apostolic preaching to Jewish audiences recorded in Acts 2-5, we must turn our attention to two central problems of first-century Jewish evangelism that had to be answered apologetically: How could the Messiah die on a Roman cross, and were the ancient promises revoked since the majority of Israelites rejected Jesus as their Messiah? We turn first to the stumbling block issue of a crucified Messiah.

In 1 Corinthians 1:23 Paul calls Christ's crucifixion "a stumbling block to Jews." There are two reasons for this. First, the anticipation of Israel was not for a suffering Messiah but a kingly Messiah. Because Jesus spoke often of the kingdom of

God, though He answered before Pilate that "my kingdom is not of this world," expectations ran high among the Jewish populace. The so-called triumphal entry is an expression of this overwhelming desire for a political and royal Messiah. Even the disciples were still awaiting the kingdom in light of their question to Him just prior to the ascension: "Lord, are you at this time going to restore the kingdom to Israel?" (Acts 1:6). Jesus of Nazareth, however, did not fulfill these expectations. And expectations die hard!

Second, and probably even more devastating for Jewish evangelism, was the way in which Jesus had died, a way expressly cursed by God. Deuteronomy 21:23 very clearly said that "anyone who is hung on a tree is under God's curse." How could the Messiah die a death particularly cursed by God? And worse, this was the very center of the gospel. Crucifixion had to be spoken of in every sermon and personal witness. As Paul himself stated: "What I received I passed on to you as of first importance: that Christ died for our sins according to the Scriptures" (1Cor. 15:3).

Though Paul might emphasize and explain in Corinthians and before a Jewish king (Acts 26:22-23) that the Messiah's death for His people's sins was predicted in the Old Testament, Peter and John's first sermons hit head-on the issue of the way in which Jesus died. At times they even seemed to go out of their way to emphasize that "the God of our fathers raised Jesus from the dead—whom you had killed by hanging him on a tree" (Acts 5:30; cf. 10:39). They obviously did not shy away from the means of Christ's death. Regardless of the religious implications of death in such a manner, it must be seen and interpreted in the light of the resurrection by the "God of our fathers," who is also the God of Deuteronomy. It was Paul in his early polemical letter to the Galatians, however, who answered the question related to Deuteronomy explicitly by appealing to the passage itself:

> All who rely on observing the law are under a curse, for it is written: "Cursed is everyone who does not continue to do everything written in the Book of the Law." . . . Christ redeemed us from the curse of the law by becoming a curse for us, for it is written: "Cursed is everyone who is hung on a tree". (Gal. 3:10, 13)

Paul thus uses the anathema of a cursed Messiah (which he himself probably used against the Christians earlier) to demonstrate the truth of substitutionary atonement. Deuteronomy is in no way set aside, but rather seen as divinely fulfilled. Man is freed from the bondage and curse he is automatically under because Christ has been cursed of God on our behalf. In fact, since Christ was sinless, He could not be cursed by God if it were not a matter extrinsic to Himself by which He was cursed and thereby could bear our curse for us. Thus Christ by bearing the curse of God in a form extrinsic to Himself liberates mankind, which is under God's curse in an intrinsic form. Paul shows how what was originally perceived as a liability was now part of the essence of the good news: "Christ redeemed us from the curse of the law by becoming a curse for us."

Proclamation and apology were of necessity often one and the same for the early evangelists to the Jewish nation. It had always been and will always be this way. On numerous occasions Christ had proclaimed His approaching death only to be ignorantly rebuffed by His disciples. The disciples on the Emmaus Road received a postresurrection apology of His death in the form of a rhetorical question: "Did not the Christ have to suffer these things and then enter his glory?" (Luke 24:26). Similarly, Paul's preaching primarily to Gentiles demanded an apology as the reaction of a Jewish audience to his speech at his arrest gives evidence: "Then the Lord said to me, 'Go; I will send you far away to the Gentiles.' The crowd listened to Paul until he said this. Then they raised their voices and shouted 'Rid the earth of him! He's not fit to live!' " (Acts 22:21-22).

Paul's most extended answer to the question of why so many Jews rejected Jesus Christ, even after erasing the original perplexity of the manner of His death, is the epistle to the Romans. In some ways, this soteriological treatise might be seen as a Christian apology to the Jewish nation, especially 2:17−4:25 and 9:1−11:36. But this was not a new question. It surfaced repeatedly during Jesus' public ministry. All four of the gospels touch upon it. In Mark, Jesus repeatedly quotes the Old Testament, particularly Isaiah, to compare Israel's treatment of the prophets to His own reception. Isaiah 6:9-10 is quoted in Mark 4:12 to explain Jewish failure to understand and accept His message. The parable of the tenants is a very pungent explanation of Israel's treatment of the prophets and of Christ (Mark 12:1-12). The result is the same as Paul later explained in Romans 9-11; God will judge the ones who have rejected the prophets and His Son and "give the vineyard to others" (Mark 12:9). Jesus' Jewish hearers readily recognized that "he had spoken the parable against them" (v. 12).

Luke expanded his account of this by identifying the "stone" that the builders rejected not only with the cornerstone of Psalm 118:22 but also with the stumbling stone of Isaiah 8:14 and the stone cut out without hands in Daniel 2:34-35 that destroys Gentile world dominion with a kingdom that will never end (Luke 20:17-18). Jewish unbelief is not a new phenomenon nor does it destroy or end the covenant promises. Moses could foresee it even before the entrance into the Promised Land (Lev. 26:14-45). Therefore, earlier in Mark 7:9, after quoting Isaiah 29:13, Jesus sarcastically stated that the Jews "have a fine way of setting aside the commands of God in order to observe [their] own traditions." Jesus *is* a stumbling block to the Jews! But it is because of their own stubbornness and willful self-righteousness—in short, their unbelief. Peter remarks that the Jews of his day "stumble because they disobey the message" (1 Pet. 2:8); Paul states that Jews were "zealous for God, but their zeal is not based on knowledge"—they attempted to establish their own righteousness rather than "submit to God's righteousness" (Rom. 10:2-3).

Romans is an extended treatment of Israel's unbelief and misunderstanding of God's program during both Old Testament times and the church age. That unbelief resulted from disobedience and is one of the foremost topics of the epistle, as is evident from Paul's familiar statement in Romans 1:16-17:

> I am not ashamed of the gospel, because it is the power of God for the salvation of everyone who believes: first for the Jew, then for the Gentile. For in the gospel a righteousness from God is revealed, a righteousness that is by faith from first to last, just as it is written: "The righteous will live by faith."

Paul does not want to be charged with trying to create a *new way* of salvation or righteousness before God. The way has always been the same—*by faith* Abraham "believed God, and it was credited to him as righteousness" (Rom. 4:3).

Salvation and righteousness are God's gifts that are acquired by the open arms of faith. *Faith is not a work.* It is simply taking God at His Word and trusting in Him. The Jews, by substituting an earned rather than a freely provided righteousness, had disregarded "the righteousness that comes from God" (Rom. 10:3). "The Gentiles . . . have obtained . . . a righteousness that is by faith; but Israel . . . has not attained it . . . . Because they pursued it . . . by works. They stumbled over the 'stumbling stone' " (Rom. 9:30-32). The faith-righteousness the Gentiles were inheriting through Christ had been spurned by Israel in favor of a works-righteousness and thus Christ (9:33), as in the gospels, is seen as a stumbling stone to unbelieving Israel. The mass rejection of Jesus as the Christ, "the end of the law so that there may be righteousness for everyone who believes" (Rom. 10:4), was not really a new thing in Israel. The majority of Israel had been rejecting God's provision of a faith-righteousness for generations in favor of their own works-righteousness. Therefore, the Jews who thought too highly of themselves (an ever-present danger for everyone), could not really "brag about [their] relationship to God" (Rom. 2:17) since they stole from God (Mal. 3:8) while they preached against stealing and committed spiritual adultery (Hos. 4:1-19) while speaking against physical adulterers (Rom. 2:18-22). Rather than an item of praise to God among the nations as Israel was supposed to be, "God's name is blasphemed among the Gentiles because of you" (Rom. 2:24). The rigorous maintenance of the sign of the covenant, circumcision, was meaningless since Israel lacked the means that were instituted for a proper relationship between God and man of which circumcision stood as a spiritual symbol. Without the reality, the symbol was valueless. Paul concludes:

> A man is not a Jew if he is only one outwardly, nor is circumcision merely outward and physical. No, a man is a Jew if he is one inwardly; and circumcision is circumcision of the heart, by the Spirit, not by the written code. Such a man's praise is not from men, but from God. (Rom. 2:28-29)

This is the true Jew, the subject of God's praise. He is not simply ethnically, but also spiritually, Jewish. A Jewish heart is as alienated from God as any Gentile's and must be regenerated by the Spirit of God. The written Word can be a dead letter. Even the custodians of the holy Scriptures (Rom. 3:1) must have *both* the Word of truth *and* the work of the Holy Spirit (John 3:5; 2 Thess. 2:13; James 1:18; 1 Pet. 1:23) to experience the new birth and inherit God's righteousness. Therefore, God is not unjust in punishing Jewish unbelief and sin any more than He is in punishing Gentile unbelief, a favorite spectator sport of ancient Jews (Rom. 3:5-6). Similarly, the lack of faith in individual Jews does not make God unfaithful to His covenant promises (Rom. 3:3-4). The Scriptures and Messiah have come through Israel, and thus being a Jew is a very great privilege. But personal salvation is still a matter of responding in faith for Jew and Gentile alike. The Jew is first, however, as the message of hope and spiritual freedom came first and exclusively to Abraham and his descendants. That God seemingly turned to the Gentiles, given the greater ratio of Gentile to Jewish Christians at the time of the writing of Romans (and probably in the Roman church), does not mean Jews should be commended for their unbelief and falsehood. To do so would be to encourage "evil that good may result"—inherently condemnable (Rom. 3:7-8).

Paul faces this issue very personally in Romans 9:1-9. He is willing to be cursed of God in place of his ethnic brothers, the people of Israel. But it is not the case that "God's word had failed" (Rom. 9:6). Rather, all those who claimed to be of Israel are not of Israel just as all the descendants of Abraham are not the children of promise. Many in Israel are like those whom Paul described in chapter 2, circumcised in flesh but not in heart. Therefore, they are not really true Jews, who are at the center of God's blessings and praise. But at the same time, there were true Jews in the first century as there always had been since Abraham, those who were circumcised in flesh *and* *heart*. Paul offers himself as an example of a believing Jew through faith-righteousness and as proof that God has not disowned His people or forgotten His covenant (Rom. 11:1-6). There is therefore an ever-present remnant of grace. "And if by grace, then it is no longer by works; if it were, grace would no longer be grace" (v. 6).

There is a final hope, however. A promise that the circle of true, believing Israel and physical, ethnic Israel will be one. Rather than this:

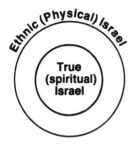 

Paul holds out the promise of this:

> I do not want you to be ignorant of this mystery, brothers, so that you may not be conceited: Israel has experienced a hardening in part until the full number of the Gentiles has come in. And so all Israel will be saved, as it is written:
>
> > "The deliverer will come from Zion;
> >   he will turn godlessness away from Jacob.
> > And this is my covenant with them
> >   when I take away their sins."
> >   (Rom. 11:25-27)

If Jews were both reachable and savable during the first century, how did the apostles go about this evangelism? For the most part the first ten chapters of Acts cover the initial outreach of the Jerusalem church to its brethren. After the Acts 13:46 statement by Paul that "since you [Jews] reject it [the gospel] and do not consider yourselves worthy of eternal life, we now turn to the Gentiles," the remainder of Acts relates to Gentile evangelism, though Paul continued his practice of beginning his ministry in the Jewish synagogue wherever one was available. An outline of the primary sermons and speeches of Acts with their attendant audiences looks like this:

> Jewish Apologetics
>   Pentecost, 2:14-39
>   Peter to Jewish populace, 3:12-26
>   Peter and John before the Sanhedrin, 4:8-12; 5:29-32

Stephen's speech, 7:2-53
Peter's sermon in Cornelius's house, 10:34-43
Paul at Antioch of Pisidia, 13:16-41
Paul before Jewish audience at his arrest, 22:1-21
Paul before the Sanhedrin, 23:1-6
Paul to Jews while under house arrest, 28:17-28
Gentile Apologetics
Paul at Lystra, 14:8-18
Paul at the Areopagus, 17:22-31
Paul before Felix, 24:10-21
Paul before Festus, 25:8-11
Apologetics with Mixed Audience
Paul before Felix with his Jewish wife, 24:24-25
Paul before Festus with King Agrippa, 26:1-29

The Cornelius episode could be classified as either Jewish or Gentile evangelism. From an ethnic perspective it was Gentile. In light of the preparation of Peter by the dream, his subsequent defense of his actions to the saints of the Jerusalem church, and the direct statements of Acts 11:1, 18 it can be seen as Gentile. Nevertheless, Cornelius was a God-fearer and thus a "spiritual" Jew. Peter's presentation is also nearly identical to his usual approach to Jews. This could perhaps be best placed in a fourth *transitional* category.

Only a representative selection of these passages can be dealt with, leaving ample opportunities for study and research on the part of the reader. Some of these passages are obviously more important and contribute to the apologetic framework to a much greater extent than others. Our concentration in this section will be on Peter's sermon at Pentecost and the early proclamation of the gospel in Jerusalem in Acts 3-5. In the final section attention will be primarily on Paul's experiences at Lystra and Athens and his final formal defense before both Festus and Agrippa, with only passing reference to Paul before Felix. We turn, then, to Acts 2:14-39.

The setting for this first presentation of the gospel of Jesus Christ after His ascension is the Jewish Feast of Weeks (Ex. 34:22; Deut. 16:9-11), or Pentecost, meaning fiftieth, as the celebration took place on the fiftieth day after the Passover. Peter, taking the leadership that had been bestowed upon him by the

Lord after his confession at Caesarea Philippi (Matt. 16:13-19), refuted the charge of drunkenness leveled at the disciples because of the tongues phenomena by pointing out that it was "only nine in the morning!" (Acts 2:15). Rather, the unusual circumstance where "each one heard them speak in his own language" (2:6) was the fulfillment of Joel's prophecy that God would "pour out [his] Spirit in those days" (2:18). It was the "last hour" or era in God's program as John states in 1 John 2:18 regarding the manifestation of the anti-Christian spirit, which was only possible after the revelation of the Christ. The long-awaited messianic age had come in Israel, and most Jews were ignorant of its arrival. Peter's sermon was the first apologetic, or explanation, of the significance and meaning of the Christ-event—even to some of those responsible for His death. After presenting his text from Joel 2:28-32, Peter began to preach. His sermon "outline" appears to have the "customary" three points:

- The Christian gospel has *positive proof* (Acts 2:22, 32)
- The Christian gospel is a *predetermined plan* (vv. 23-24)
- The Christian gospel fulfills *perfect promises* (vv. 25-36)

As we shall see, this three-pronged emphasis is the subsequent model for Jewish evangelism and apologetic by the original disciples: factual testimony, completion of God's program of redemption, and the maintenance and fulfillment of the covenants and promises to Israel. J. K. S. Reid writes of Peter's sermon: "The demolition of false interpretation, and the positive statement of the Christian faith including explanation and implication—here at this early point in Christian history the landmarks that indicate the scope of all apologetic activity have emerged with surprising clarity."[2]

Peter began from "underneath." He did not begin with the incarnation, but with what was common knowledge to a great many in his audience—the man, Jesus of Nazareth. Many of the Jerusalem Jews had seen Him personally, perhaps had seen one of His miracles or had been carried away in the excitement of His triumphal entry. Those Jews from elsewhere in the

2. Ibid., p. 16.

Roman Empire had probably been in Jerusalem the fifty days previous for Passover when Jesus was crucified and had stayed until Pentecost, or had heard all about Him and the recent commotion after they arrived. In any case, there was no denying His existence, or that He had been "accredited by God to you by miracles (*dunamis*), wonders (*teras*) and signs (*sēmeion*), which God did among you through him, as *you yourselves know*" (v. 22, italics added). There was knowable, first-hand, empirical evidence of Jesus' special relationship with God. The Jews in Peter's audience knew these things intellectually, and had seen miracles occur, even if they willfully had rejected their import.

The three words by which Peter described these miracles are very important. Two of these words, *teras* and *sēmeion*, are used in the Septuagint to describe God's intervention in Egypt through the plagues (Ex. 7:3; 10:1-2). The word for "miracle" (*dunamis*) is the word from which we get our English word dynamite. It is self-explanatory. Here are such mighty works that only the power of God is sufficient to explain them. *Teras*, or "wonders," indicates a startling and imposing amazement beyond the usual course of nature. No "wonder" that it is used in Exodus 7:3 to describe the upcoming plagues. Jesus' miracles were positive and healing, rather than judgmental, but nevertheless they were equally as unusual as the events to which the Jewish people had looked for their God-given redemption from Egypt. But now, Peter was indirectly saying a "greater than Moses is here." The most important word, however, is *sēmeion*. It is used in both chapters 7 and 10 of Exodus to indicate that the plagues *point beyond* the catastrophe in nature to the God of nature. It is the same here. Jesus' miracles pointed beyond the power and wonder of the event itself to the divine intention and ethical purpose of spiritual insight into the things of God. Peter directly stated that these miracles "God did among you through him"—and they *knew it*! This was Jesus' emphasis in John 10:37-38: "Believe the miracles, that you may learn and understand that the Father is in me, and I in the Father."

The miracles of Jesus are not the only positive proof of the truth of God's fulfillment of His messianic promises in the man Jesus of Nazareth. The climactic proof is the unique fact that separates Christianity from all other theistic religions. Jesus is not a dead man (Judaism) or an inferior prophet (Islam) but *God*! As Paul states in Romans 1:4, Jesus "was declared with power to be the Son of God by his resurrection from the dead." So here Peter provided the irrefutable truth that "God has raised this Jesus to life, and we are all witnesses of the fact" (Acts 2:32; cf. v. 24). This was the beginning both of Christ's resurrection being the central truth of Christianity and the appeal to historical facts to establish that truth. And so it must be. Without the resurrection either Judaism or Islam (or both) is correct in its respective assessments of Jesus, but there is no Christianity. The very difference between Christianity and her mother religion of Judaism is the resurrection of Jesus Christ. Either Judaism is fulfilled through the accepted substitutionary atonement of Jesus, the Christ, proved by His resurrection and the subsequent birth of Christianity at Pentecost, or Judaism is still seeking a Messiah, there is no Christianity, and we are still in our sins. But the testimony of one hundred twenty first-hand empirical witnesses, including the formerly sheepish apostles (and Peter the primary speaker), who are facing an antagonistic crowd capable of providing contradictory evidence if there had been no resurrection, would probably be accepted in any court of law as "beyond reasonable doubt."

This appeal to historical and empirical factual evidence is endemic to the New Testament apology, as we have seen in chapter 4. If we are to learn from apostolic practice, we must never shy away from the historical New Testament evidence. The theories of hallucinations, Christ's stolen body, or that everyone went to the wrong tomb, could not be offered by Peter's hearers as contrary hypotheses to the first-rate evidence of the resurrection of Jesus Christ. We are as close as this Jewish audience to this evidence through the primary historical documents of the New Testament and cannot hesitate in making it an integral facet of our twentieth-century apologetic.

An apologetic to a Jewish audience also requires an interpretation of the facts that in no way loses or restricts the absolute sovereignty of Yahweh. Peter provided such by showing that even the death of the Christ was by God's predetermined plan, for He "was handed over to you by God's set purpose and foreknowledge" (Acts 2:23). Peter later wrote that Christ "was chosen before the creation of the world, but was revealed in these last times for your sake" (1 Pet. 1:20). However, God's sovereign plan neither releases the human agents of Christ's death from their ethical responsibility nor relieves them of their guilt. "Wicked" (*anomos*, Acts 2:23) men are still held accountable to law. Some of the very men to whom Peter spoke may have helped to carry out Jesus' crucifixion.

Two things are interesting to note in passing, one directly apologetic for the first century and the other more personal but with continuing relevance. First, Peter did not shy away from mentioning the cross as the means of Jesus' execution, regardless of the stumbling stone effect this might have. Second, and more important, God's foreknowledge and predetermined purpose does not alleviate individuals of their responsiblity for sin. The men who aided in the crucifixion are "wicked" regardless of God's superintending plan. It is always the case that men are responsible for their actions, and this expression of it in regard to the most hideous crime against God incarnate absolutely substantiates it.

The Christian gospel does not break from the Old Testament but fulfills it, even David's prediction of the Messiah's resurrection (Psalm 16:8-11). As Peter pointed out, David was not talking about himself, for David's body was still in the tomb. As a prophet, David knew that his throne would have an everlasting descendant (2 Sam. 7:2-16) and thus he was speaking "of the resurrection of the Christ" (Acts 2:31). Since "God has raised this Jesus to life" (2:32), and David spoke of the physical resurrection of the Messiah, then Jesus and the Messiah are one and the same! The combination of His God-provided wonders and signs, and the substantiated resurrection, provided for no alternative but that Jesus is the Christ. Thus what the Pentecost crowd saw and heard after the Messiah's ascension to God's right hand (2:34-35) was simply the completion of God's promises of the outpouring of the Holy Spirit in the latter days. This messianic age (latter days) was inaugurated by the resurrection of Jesus and the gift of the Holy Spirit. "Therefore, let all Israel be assured of this: God has made this Jesus, whom you crucified, both Lord [*kyrios*] and Christ [*Christos*]" (2:36). In the Septuagint *kyrios* was used to translate *Adonai* very strictly, but was also "an expository equivalent for the divine name *Yahweh*."[3] Thus, there was little doubt as to Peter's intention when he used this word along with *Christos* to indicate the absolute identity of Jesus.

The response to Peter's masterful sermon is what all preachers pray for—many people were "cut to the heart" (2:37). The Holy Spirit's conviction (John 16:8-11) went to the center of their being. And, as all evangelistic/apologetic enterprises also pray for, the question came: "What shall we do?" (2:37). Peter replied succinctly, "Repent and be baptized" (2:38), that is, turn from sin, self, and Satan and be identified through baptism with God, truth, and holiness. The Holy Spirit would not only regenerate but would come in Christ's name to the new believer as the enablement of God for spiritual and holy living. That is the beginning of something new! That promise is made now not to Israel only, but to "all who are far off—for all whom the Lord our God will call" (2:39). That was a proleptic announcement, at the beginning of the Christian era to a totally Jewish audience, of the world-wide implications of the Messiah. The task of reaching out to the Gentiles would primarily fall on the shoulders of another, although from an ethnic perspective if not a religious one, Peter himself opened the door to Gentile conversion (Acts 10:23-43). Paul writes in Colossians 1:25-27 of this opened door:

> I have become its [the church's] servant by the commission God gave me to present to you the word of God in its fullness—the mystery that has been kept hidden for ages and generations, but is now disclosed to the saints. To them God has chosen to make known among the Gentiles the glorious riches of this mystery, which is Christ in you, the hope of glory.

Peter's sermon at Pentecost resulted in the conversion of three thousand souls and the establishment of the first Christian community. The disciples followed their Lord's instruction (Matt. 28:19-20) by not simply evangelizing and baptizing, but also teaching (Acts 2:42). Pentecost was obviously a very special day, so the question must be asked, Was Peter's sermon similar to the everyday witness to the populace at large and to the Jew-

---

3. Gottfried Quell, *Kurios*, *TDNT*, 3:1058.

ish authorities? In Peter's sermon in Acts 3:12-26, or the apostles' defense of their actions before the Sanhedrin in 4:8-20 and 5:29-32, we can point out the basic similarities of these apologetic presentations to the emphases in Peter's Pentecost sermon.

The immediate context of Peter's sermon in Acts 3 was the healing of a man crippled since birth. The excitement of the crowd provided an opportunity for Peter to ascribe the power of the miracle to Jesus (vv. 6, 12-13, 16), who had been glorified by the God of Abraham, Isaac, and Jacob through His resurrection after the people had "killed the author of life" (v. 15). Three aspects of this witness about Jesus are identical to Peter's sermon at Pentecost: (1) Jesus was the fulfillment of the promises to the patriarchs (vv. 13, 25) and the prophets (vv. 18, 24), (2) the Jews, not Rome, were responsible for Jesus' death (vv. 13, 15), and (3) Peter and John were immediate witnesses to God's resurrection of the man, Jesus (v. 15). In 3:20 (like 2:31-32), the Christ and Jesus are absolutely identified as being one and the same: God "may send the Christ, who has been appointed for you—even Jesus." Also as in his previous sermon, Peter emphasized that "all peoples on earth will be blessed" (3:25) through Abraham's offspring, which in the light of the following verse can only be the Messiah. Last, Peter called for the same response, repentance and a turning to, or identification with, God (vv. 19, 26). The similarities between these two sermons may be summarized:

- Jesus is the Messiah,
- Miracles help to substantiate this claim,
- The final proof of Jesus as the Messiah is that God raised Him from the dead,
- Jews of Jerusalem are responsible for His death,
- Jesus fulfills the predictions of all the prophets,
- Jesus, the Messiah, completes the promises of the covenants,
- Jesus Christ is presently in heaven with God,
- The gospel message is broader than Israel alone,
- In light of these facts, men are expected to turn from their sins and turn to God.

Because of the common thread running through these two passages, there is no question as to why Christian apologetics has emphasized Christ's miracles, fulfilled prophecy, and His resurrection. This was the early biblical norm. Though these emphases may change with Gentiles who did not have access to the Old Testament, making the argument from prophecy and covenant culturally irrelevant, the centrality of the resurrection proof is always maintained, though not as first-hand witnesses. The first four emphases enumerated above seem to form an apologetic core to the Jewish community: Jesus' identity, miracle power, crucifixion by Jewish insistence, and resurrection by God. We see these emphases, as well as the absoluteness of God's work of redemption in Jesus, when Peter and John are called before the Sanhedrin: "It is by the name of Jesus Christ of Nazareth, whom you crucified but whom God raised from the dead, that this man stands before you completely healed.... Salvation is found in no one else; for there is no other name under heaven given to men by which we must be saved" (4:10, 12).

It is interesting to note the importance of that particular apostolic miracle and the insistence on the viability of empirical evidence in the encounter with the Jewish authorities. Those authorities admitted to themselves that "everybody living in Jerusalem knows they have done an outstanding miracle, and we cannot deny it" (4:16). The miracle doubtless helped to substantiate the apostles' claims and the authorities would have given anything to be able to deny it and "shut them up." Also, when the disciples were called back and given the order to no longer speak or preach in the name of Jesus, they not only put the burden of proof back on the Sanhedrin by asking them to judge "whether it is right in God's sight to obey you rather than God" (4:19), but added, in support both of the feasibility of empirical acquisition of knowledge and the possibility of verbally communicating historical truth, "we cannot help speaking about what we have seen and heard" (4:20).

They therefore did not stop preaching in the name of Jesus and shortly found themselves back on trial before the Sanhedrin. They again claimed that Jesus was raised from the dead by God, but added that He is now at the right hand of God (5:31) and seemed to stress that He died by being hung on a tree (5:30), keeping before the learned men of the Old Testament the curse of Deuteronomy. Again they tied His work in with the Old Testament prophets in that Jesus is the Savior who grants repentance and provides forgiveness for Israel; and they were first-hand witnesses of these things. As a result, "we must obey God rather than men!" (5:29).

What may we learn from those first century practices, not only for Jewish evangelism, but for apologetics in general? Surely, we cannot eliminate or even play down the role of empirical historical evidences. If we do, our apologetic cannot claim to be a biblical apologetic. Jesus' miracles, fulfilled prophecy, and the resurrection must be central to our apologetic framework. Of course, our approach must be moderated by the individuals with whom we are dealing, as Paul instructs us by word in Colossians 4:6 and by an example in his dealings with the Gentile pagans at Athens. Nevertheless, the irrefutable biblical evidence must be appealed to directly with those who place the Bible on a pedestal, even if they do not admit it is inspired and therefore divine. This does not mean that the Bible is set aside in some kind of so-called neutral approach when dealing with either those who are ignorant of it or who reject it. The first-hand apostolic evidence cannot be appealed to without indirectly appealing to the New Testament, which the apostles helped pen, and which contains the only record of their eyewitness experiences. As we shall see when examining Paul's sermon on the Areopagus, we can *remain throroughly biblical without directly referencing or quoting the Scriptures.* Since facts must always be interpreted facts, it is the first-hand facts as well as their meaning that is presented, whether the Bible is quoted or not. Though Paul presented neither Jesus' miracles nor fulfilled prophecy to the Athenian philosophers, he had to and did end with the fact and the implications of Jesus' resurrection. Before turning to this prime example of Gentile apology, we will turn to the later, but mixed, Jewish-Gentile audience of Festus and Agrippa as a means of transition.

The Apology to the Gentiles

An argument could no doubt be made that Paul's apology before Festus and Agrippa (Acts 26:1-29) was primarily Jewish because of the prominence of the Jewish king in the hearing of Jewish accusations, and the need Festus had for Agrippa to be there so that Festus might have something to charge Paul with when he sent Paul to Rome (Acts 25:26-27). But this is a formal court of Rome, and the procurator is officially in charge while King Agrippa is simply his invited guest and possible counselor. It seems safer, therefore, to classify this as an apology before a mixed audience and leave it at that (though it is obvious that Paul addressed his apology to Agrippa and that there are similarities with his speeches to entirely Jewish audiences as recorded in Acts 13:16-41 and 22:1-21).

The date of this final apology is probably A.D. 59, based on the date that Roman coins were minted in Caesarea in commemoration of the changing of Roman procurators from Felix to Festus. Since Paul had already been imprisoned at least two years and was a holdover prisoner of Felix's administration, a very unusual situation, Festus was unsure of what charges to press against Paul when he sent him to Rome, as Paul had demanded in an earlier appearance before Festus (25:10-11). Agrippa, king of Judea and the great-grandson of Herod the Great, paid a state visit to the new procurator. Festus took advantage of this "expert" in Jewish law and custom "so that as a result of this investigation I may have something to write" to the Emperor (25:26). Paul then was brought before Festus, Agrippa, and Agrippa's sister Bernice, with Agrippa giving Paul permission to begin his *apologia*. We might outline Paul's defense speech as follows:

- Acceptance of the old promise, vv. 4-8
- Antagonism toward the new person, vv. 9-11
- Appointment with the ascended Lord, vv. 12-15
- Ambassador for the victorious Savior, vv. 16-23

Paul began by making his accusers and antagonists his character witnesses. "The Jews know of my distinct Jewishness from childhood, whether I was in Jerusalem or Antioch. I was a Pharisee's Pharisee! And now I am on trial because of my hope in God's promises." In short, Paul made his defense by making the Jewish accusations against him a rejection of their own Jewishness. It is as if Paul were saying, "My hope is the same hope as the fathers—Abraham, Isaac, and Jacob. My hope is the same hope as the twelve tribes. My hope is identical with that of the strictest Pharisee. My hope is the same as Anna, who lived in the Temple and finally saw the very hope and salvation of Israel. My hope is in the risen Jesus, the Christ." (Note the similarity with Paul's speech to the Jews at Antioch of Pisidia, Acts 13:32-36.) Paul ended the first segment of his defense with a rather disdainful question concerning the very essence of the dispute: "Why should any of you consider it incredible that God raises the dead?" (v. 8).

Paul then moved to his previous role of persecuting the Christians. He included himself with his present detractors as having been convinced "that I ought to do all that was possible to oppose the name of Jesus of Nazareth" (v. 9). He at one time had gone from city to city, synagogue to synagogue, putting Christians in prison, trying to force them to blaspheme and, on a few occasions, even supporting their execution. Thus Paul, too, had once defined Jewishness as antagonism toward Jesus of Nazareth.

What had happened that so drastically changed Paul from a persecutor of Christianity into, some twenty-five years later, perhaps its leading spokesman? It was divine intervention! Paul had an appointment with the ascended Lord, for as he had written earlier to the Galatians, God "set me apart from birth and called me by his grace" to "reveal his Son in me so that I might preach him among the Gentiles" (Gal. 1:15-16). Paul thus provided Festus and Agrippa with a personal testimony of his salvation experience, nearly identical with Luke's record of his speech to a Jewish audience at his arrest in Acts 22. Only such an encounter could explain the abrupt change from religious frenzy against the associates of Jesus to identity with them and acceptance of Jesus as both Christ and Lord.

His was a translation from the kingdom of darkness to the kingdom of light, from the legality of Jewish religiosity to the new freedom in servanthood to and witness of the risen Christ (Acts 26:16). He had exchanged authorities from the chief priests to the absolute High Priest. In place of law stood a Person. He accepted righteousness by faith rather than trying to earn it by a works-righteousness. He was now Christ's ambassador to the Gentiles, and, as he told Agrippa, "I was not disobedient to the vision from heaven" (v. 19). Though a Pharisee's Pharisee, he accepted the charge to go to the Gentiles so that they as well as the Jews might "receive forgiveness of sins and a place among those who are sanctified by faith" in Christ (v. 18). His ministry was neither entirely new nor anti-Jewish as he said "nothing beyond what the prophets and Moses said would happen" (v. 22). This is very similar to his testimony before Felix in regard to the patriarchs, prophets, and the Law: "I admit that I worship the God of our fathers, as a follower of the Way, which they call a sect. I believe everything that agrees with the Law and that is written in the Prophets, and I have the same hope in God as these men, that there will be a resurrection of both the righteous and the wicked" (24:14-15).

Nevertheless, he had been arrested because he had insisted on Jewish repentance and acceptance of Jesus as the Messiah (26:20, 23). Paul seemed to imply that the arrest was triggered by the fact that he preached the same message of repentance to Jew and Gentile alike (v. 20), even as the Old Testament predicted that the Messiah "would proclaim light to his own people and to the Gentiles" (v. 23). Not the trumped-up charges of profaning the Temple or creating a disturbance (24:12-13, 18), but his message that salvation was offered equally to Jew and Gentile alike, by and through the resurrected Jesus, was the reason for His arrest.

At this point Paul was interrupted by Festus, who charged him with insanity. Paul, however, calmly appealed to King Agrippa because "the king is familiar with these things . . . because it was not done in a corner" (26:26). Paul concluded by putting the king on the horns of a dilemma, "King Agrippa, do you believe the prophets? I know you do" (v. 27). If Agrippa answered yes, then he seemingly would agree with Paul that Jesus was both the Messiah and the fulfillment of God's Word through Moses and the prophets. If he answered no, he would lose all credence as a Jewish authority. Either answer would alienate the Jewish authorities and undercut his relationship with his Judean subjects. He answered as we might expect. In an exasperated huff, he exclaimed, "Do you think that in such a short time you can persuade me to be a Christian?" (v. 28). Agrippa was not saying that he was "almost persuaded" (KJV). Rather he was pleading for more time and at the same time giving an evasive answer for the benefit of any Jews in the audience of the court. Paul acknowledged this and replied that "short time or long—I pray God that not only you but all who are listening to me today may become what I am, except for these chains" (v. 29). Paul's evangelistic heart shows nearly as much by this answer as by his statement that he could wish himself "cursed and cut off from Christ for the sake of my brothers" (Rom. 9:3).

The primary emphasis of Paul's apology was personal testimony and what we have called life-style apologetics. Paul's statement that "I preached that they should repent and turn to God and *prove their repentance by their deeds*" (Acts 26:20, italics added) is a direct endorsement of life-style apologetics. This may be because he needed to contrast his previous activity as a Jew's Jew to his present status as cut off from the Jewish community. Thus he provided his personal testimony about the great change in his status. But keeping this context in mind, it is still a biblical affirmation of the place for personal testimony in evangelism and apologetics. At the same time, his was not a witness without facts that were verifiable by others as his appeal to Agrippa in verse 26 made clear. His reference to Christ's resurrection, indirectly in verse 8 and explicitly in verse 23, was an endorsement of the role of historical evidences. Such evidences can be verified by believer and unbeliever (Agrippa) alike. His appeal to Scripture in verses 22 and 23 was also absolutely distinctive. Paul does not bifurcate revelation and history into an either/or apologetic. But in this instance of formal defense, personal accountability and testimony were paramount.

Paul's ministry, as his testimony on his behalf makes clear in this trial, was to the Gentiles. Did he approach the Gentiles any differently than he did the Jews in the synagogues? The answer is a qualified yes. Although Paul always emphasized the resurrection and the possibility of peace with God and forgiveness of sins through the death of Christ, he did not apparently argue explicitly on the basis of Old Testament Scripture to Gentile audiences. In other words, the content of the gospel always remained the same, but the form in which it was expressed and shared must be such as to be comprehended by the listeners. As Green states, "That there was a basic homogeneity in what was preached we may agree, but there was wide variety in the way it was presented" because "evangelism is never proclamation in a vacuum; but always to people, and the message must be given in terms that make sense to them."[4] Of course, we only have one extended treatment by which to make this judgment, and therefore it must be qualified by the paucity of the evidence. Before turning to the Areopagus experience, we need to look briefly at the only other purely Gentile encounter, at Lystra.

Lystra is the contrast of Athens. While Acts 17 is an example of Christian apology to cultured Gentiles; Lystra is a model of Christian witness to uneducated Gentiles. Their speaking in the local Lycaonian language (14:11) is evidence that the episode has to do with the aboriginal peoples of the area and not the Latin-speaking upper classes. Miracle was the point of contact with these people, but given their pagan and idolatrous background, it did not have the expected effect. Rather than opening a door to proclamation, Paul and Barnabas were taken for Hermes and Zeus, much like Ovid's old tale of Jupiter and Mercury visiting two Phrygian peasants. (Jupiter and Mercury are the Latin equivalents of the Greek Zeus and Hermes. The former is the chief deity in both cases, the latter the messenger or speaker on behalf of the gods.) Richard Rackham comments that the original Lycaonians "were as yet untouched by the civilized scepticism of society; and the idea of appearances and visits of *the gods* was quite natural to them as to a genuine pagan peasantry."[5] Because the people spoke in the local language, Barnabas and Paul were ignorant of what was happening at first. Upon perceiving the intent of the priests with their bulls, the two missionaries rushed to bring a halt to the proceedings. It was at this juncture that Paul had opportunity to speak.

Paul gave no quotation of the Old Testament or reference to the Jewish patriarchs, the Mosaic Law, or the prophets. Neither were there any Messianic claims. But there was the announcement of the "good news" concerning the "living God" who had "made heaven and earth and sea and everything in them" (14:15). Although God has allowed the nations their independ-

---

4. Michael Green, *Evangelism in the Early Church*, p. 115.
5. Richard Belward Rackham, *The Acts of the Apostles*, p. 232.

ence (14:16), He has always given evidence of His existence by providing the necessary things of life. Paul thus presented a case based on natural revelation. His approach was built on creation and providence. His viewpoint was completely biblical even if there was no explicit reference to Scripture. The creation statement is very similar to Exodus 20:11, and the note of providence is found throughout the Old Testament. Although there was an attack on idolatry by calling on the Lycaonians "to turn from these worthless things to the living God" (14:15), there was no explicit enunciation of the claims of Jesus Christ or of the moral implications that exist in light of the real existence of the "living God," though the latter might be inferred from verse 16. Of course, Paul's message was curtailed shortly after this by Jews from Iconium and Antioch of Pisidia, stoned, and left for dead. Thus we cannot make many apologetic conclusions based on that episode, except to note that Paul began his argument with natural revelation and no immediate appeal to special revelation. We may safely conclude, I believe, based on what we know of Paul in other recorded missionary endeavors, that his earlier speaking (14:9) must have had more explicit mention of the life and meaning of Jesus Christ. This must have been the cause of the growing faith that Paul saw registered on the crippled man's face before he was healed and the commotion began. At Lystra, we may be seeing the beginning of the process by which the Thessalonians "turned to God from idols to serve the living and true God" (1 Thess. 1:9).

We turn now to the capital of pagan idolatry, Athens, for the purest Gentile apologetic model as well as the most analogous situation to contemporary paganism. Paul's succinct speech, or Luke's edited version, is recorded in Acts 17:22-31.

Paul had come to Athens from Thessalonica by way of Berea without Silas and Timothy. Acts 17:16 tells us he was "greatly distressed" upon seeing the city of idols. He followed his normal practice of reasoning from the Old Testament in the synagogue, but also engaged in conversation and argument in the Agora, or marketplace, immediately beneath the Areopagus, where the council of teachers and religious leaders met. It was here that he entered into debate with Epicurean and Stoic philosophers who thought he was a "babbler," or itinerant plagiarist. The word in the Greek text is *spermologos*, which literally means "seed-picker." It pictures a bird flying from place to place to get scraps of food as an itinerant teacher picks up his bits of information. The philosophers apparently understood Paul to be informing them of "foreign gods" (17:18), perhaps the gods *Healer (Iēsoun,* "Jesus") and *Restoration (anastasin,* "resurrection"), as these are the literal meanings of the Greek words Luke uses to describe Paul's activity. Those words may have sounded like personifications of two new deities to the polytheistic Greeks.[6] It demonstrates, however, that Paul preached the same gospel regardless of the sophistication of his audience (cf. 17:3, 11, 18). Paul was then either given a formal hearing to see if he was fit to be a philosopher at Athens (Acts 18:1 may indicate a forced leaving of Athens) or, more likely, he was simply being given a hearing in the usual place new doctrine is debated.

Epicureanism and Stoicism were the two predominant philosophies of the first century and are representative of the two primary philosophical orientations throughout history—naturalism and idealism. Both philosophies were antitheistic, Epicureanism being both polytheistic and naturalistic and Stoicism being pantheistic. As noted above (p. 11), neither philosophy could even conceive of the possibility of resurrection within its respective world view and thus the outburst at the conclusion of Paul's sermon. Paul did not start with the resurrection, however. Rather, he made his appeal by means of the familiar and the accepted—an altar "TO AN UNKNOWN GOD."[7] This center of universal paganism wanted to be sure that no possible god would go unworshiped by its citizens. Paul used this polytheistic practice as a bridge to gain access to his audience and so be able to introduce the living God to these "religious" people. The religiosity evidenced by the Athenians is an indication of man's inherent God-consciousness. As *homo religiosus,* man fills the vacuum in the center of his being, a vacuum meant to be filled by the Creator-God, with religious substitutes: the idols of Athens, the playthings of America, or the zeal of an avowed Marxist in Central and South America. The Christian apologist, as

6. Kenneth F. W. Prior, *The Gospel in a Pagan Society,* p. 56.
7. Considerable debate rages over whether there was one or many such altars throughout the city.

Paul did here, must always strive to meet the unbeliever practically and existentially on as common a ground as possible. The practical may be more difficult than the existential. That is, we probably will not have an altar to an unknown god or a miracle by which to gain initial entrance into, or the attention of, people's minds. But we will know that they are inherently theistic given the ontological realities of creation.

Those ontological realities that provoke a natural revelation of God that is inescapable both without and within man are what Paul appealed to in the next section of his speech. He presented an Old Testament picture of God without directly referring to the Old Testament. In this context, Paul did not use the authoritative Word of God *directly* as it was not understood yet to be *the* Word of authority by the Greeks. This does not mean that it was not the basis for what Paul said. He remained thoroughly biblical though never quoting the Scriptures as he doubtless did in Jewish synagogues where it was an absolute *and shared* authority.

Paul's argument here is in complete agreement with his exposition of natural revelation in Romans 1:18-20. Here, as there, the visible proclaims the invisible. Similarly, the creation reveals the Creator's "eternal power and divine nature" (Rom. 1:20), and therefore He cannot be limited and expected to live in manmade temples nor is He "served by human hands, as if he needed anything, because he himself gives all men life and breath and everything else" (Acts 17:25). Mankind is one! All men come from an originally created source. Men, such as the "religious" Athenians, grope in the dark in their attempt to reach out and find the God they "know" must exist. Paul pictured this, in concluding the second portion of his argument, by using a quotation attributed to Epimenides the Cretan that "in him we live and move and have our being" (v. 28). This illustrates *both* the way to use secular literature for apologetic advantage *and* demonstrates the way that man, groping in God's universe, can "feel" and vaguely approximate the truth, even though incapable of exact knowledge apart from direct revelation from God.

So far Paul would be understood as a Stoic, for Paul's theistic meaning is not what would have flashed into the pantheistic mind of the Stoic. Though Paul could and did make an entrance into numerous minds by means of the quotation "we are his offspring," his interpretation and application of that quote from the poem by Aratus of Cilicia entitled *Natural Phenomena*, left no doubt that Paul was not a Stoic. From the premise "we are his [God's] offspring," (17:28) and the hidden or unspoken premise that "men are personal creatures," Paul concluded that *God could not be an impersonal being* confined to shapes of gold, silver, or stone. God is personal! He is not impersonal nature as the Stoics thought and taught. We ourselves are the proof of God's personality. Since offspring "resemble" their parents and men are personal creatures, *God must be as equally personal as we His offspring are*! Paul used the natural revelation of God within as well as the natural revelation outside man in total compatibility with Romans 1:19-20. He has also shown us that we can legitimately argue from man to God on the basis of the ontological similarity between God and man through God's image in man. If there is no univocal dimension ontologically between God and man, then Paul's argument here was totally fallacious.

Paul moved to one final point in his argument. Men will not rightly understand God as personal because they will conform the revelation in nature to the confines of their world view, be it first-century Epicureanism or Stoicism, or twentieth-century expressions of naturalism or idealism. Therefore, God has provided more than natural revelation. He has provided the man by whom He will hold men individually responsible. He may have "overlooked" man's previous religious ignorance and groping in the dark for God, but now that the final revelation has come He (God-in-person) "commands all people everywhere to repent" (v. 30). That is an imperative! It marks a new beginning. Under the old order, there was "ignorance" (v. 30, *agnoias*, genitive singular of the participle form "not knowing," *agnoountes*, v. 23) prior to the complete revelation of God in Jesus Christ (Heb. 1:1-2). Paul's expression in Acts 14:16 concerning the freedom experienced by the various nations is identical in meaning if not vocabulary with what he said at Athens. God can "overlook" man's former ignorance of Him, even though he is "without excuse" (Rom. 1:20) in the same way He "overlooked" Israel's sin by the inadequate means of animal sacrifice prior to the final atonement in Christ (Rom. 3:25). God did not "wink" (Acts 17:30, KJV) at sin in the sense of condoning it, but paid it no attention as an example of His patience. This is similar to His actions prior to the giving of the Law (Rom. 5:13). That God is not indifferent to sin prior to the moral revelation of the Law is acutely manifested by the totality of the catastrophic Flood and the visitation of immediate judgment on Sodom and Gomorrah.

Under the new order, no one is excluded—cultured or primitive, Jew or Gentile. There is now absolutely no ambiguity possible because of the availability of knowledge of God through Christ. Since God Himself is disclosing God in the incarnation and satisfying God through propitiation, God now demands that man forsake his ignorance, repent of his deeds and inadequate religiosity, and turn to the One by whom He "will judge the world with justice" (Acts 17:31). To prove that this judgment will occur, God has provided concrete evidence by the resurrection of this Judge from the dead.

At this point Paul was interrupted by laughter (Acts 17:32, TLB). Not all laughed, however. Some wanted to hear more about this at a later date, and others—among whom were Dionysius and Damaris—believed. The responses are identical to the threefold pattern of all evangelistic and apologetic endeavor: negative rejection, neutral uncertainty but willing and perhaps even eager to hear more, and immediate acceptance.

What were Paul's emphases, then, to these cultured pagans? Certainly his presentation was biblical even if there was no appeal to fulfilled prophecy, miracles, or argumentation that Jesus is the Messiah, as we have seen at Pentecost or before Agrippa. These would have been to no avail to people ignorant of the Old Testament. Rather, as for the most part at Lystra, the appeal was to *both* the natural revelation of God in creation and providence *and* to the reality of man's nature as expressed in his religiosity, the latter being more prevalent in Athens than Lystra. That this ontological common ground cannot be totally avoided or suppressed is emphasized and brought "home" to individuals in Paul's preaching to Gentiles. It is implicitly biblical if not explicitly. All of Paul's main points are simply Old Testament theology presented without chapter and verse. Creation, monotheism, universal claims for Yahweh, God's total independence of man and limitlessness, the unity of humanity in creation and Fall, providence through the seasons of the year, provisions that provoke men to seek God, repentance, judgment, resurrection—which of these are not biblical? Paul used at Athens an apologetic that was not built on evidences of revelatory events, but nevertheless stressed the reality of God, man's moral need, provision by God for that need, and God's moral expectations and judgment. All was understood theistically and scripturally but done by logical argument built on the ontological realities, whether pagan man acknowledged them or not. It is the classic example of Christian apologetics' not forgetting its world view or epistemological roots no matter how philosophical and logical the presentation may be. The Christian must never forget that this is a theistically-interpreted world, whether Genesis 1:1 enters a discussion explicitly. *Unbelieving man can always intellectually and intuitively comprehend this approach because every man is one of these theistically-interpreted facts.*

The contrasts between Jewish and Gentile apologetic approaches by the apostles are obvious: with the Jews, the fulfillment of the Messianic promises in Jesus were emphasized as in Acts 17:2-3 in light of the common epistemological ground of the holy Scriptures; with the Gentiles the approach had to be based on the common ontological ground of the theistic fact of creation as there was no common epistemological ground. This difference may be observed today in unbelievers who have a biblical or "church" background, as opposed to those who know little or nothing of the Bible. In times past, when truth (per se) was admitted and the question was simply the identity of the truth, the direct scriptural approach was usually preferable. Today, at least for the many who question even the very notion of truth and meaning, there may very well be a need to demonstrate the necessity of truth and the meaning of individual personhood by working from the inescapable facts of natural revelation and man's intuitive consciousness of a holy God, as Paul did on the Areopagus of ancient Athens.

Finally, in terms of contemporary apologetic issues, how may we classify the apostolic practices? Surely, they were evidential. Though this is more obvious in approaches to Jewish audiences where the attempt was made to demonstrate that Jesus is the Christ, every sermon but Lystra refers explicitly in some way to the historical evidence of the resurrection. (No doubt this was also spoken of at Lystra in light of the events that preceded the healing of the cripple, as previously pointed out.) But all apologies are biblically determined also! Facts are not neutral but are to be interpreted as fulfillment of Old Testament predictions. Even when there is no explicit reference to Scripture, Paul's creation-providence arguments at Lystra or Athens are squarely within the confines of a biblical world view. Everything is theistically-interpreted. Thus, with no neutral facts there is no natural theology using such facts to argue to the reality of God as the First Cause. Likewise, there is no "easy believism." Faith is grounded in, if not caused by, historical facts. We have seen both the positive function and negative limitation of historical evidentialism in regard to Jesus' ministry itself. For just as John records Jesus saying, "Believe on the evidence of the miracles themselves" (14:11), he also writes, "Even after Jesus had done all these miraculous signs in their presence, they still would not believe" (12:37). Last, mention must be made of Paul's use of man's intuitive knowledge of God from natural revelation, particularly the intrinsic knowledge based on the personality of man in the Athenian address. Paul also made reference to what we have called life-style apologetics by arguing before Agrippa that believers should "prove their repentance by their deeds" (Acts 26:20).

On the basis of apostolic practices, therefore, we cannot easily become members of either of the two great schools of evangelical apologetics. Without doubt, the apostles were revelatory presuppositionalists in light of their use of the Old Testament and their natural revelation arguments based on the biblical doctrine of creation. But they were not afraid of facts! Not even recent facts that could be easily refuted if refutation had been possible. They built their case on the historical actualities that could only be understood in one way. Nowhere is this clearer than in the initial apologetic endeavor: Pentecost. Peter argued that the man of Nazareth had been proved to be the Christ by His miracles and the resurrection, a resurrection David predicted would be experienced by the Christ. Facts may not be neutral, but facts are used. This is the very epistemological outlook of the balanced apologetic that attempts to stand in *both* the circle of presuppositional Word *and* evidential event. It may provoke dialectical tension, but this can be borne more easily when in the presence of such excellent company.

7

CHURCH FATHERS' EXAMPLES

After examining the New Testament, the basis for all apologetic methodologies, we turn to the church Fathers to see how the apostolic examples were interpreted in the life of the early church. Though the church Fathers are obviously not normative for us as are the apostles, much can be learned from how the church handled the first sustained Jewish and pagan attacks against the new faith. We will first look at two of the so-called Apostolic Fathers from the turn of the first century, Ignatius and Polycarp—though Polycarp's long life took him into the third quarter of the century (martyred about A.D. 156). From there, we will focus our attention on the anonymous second century apologetic tract to "Diognetus." The group of Fathers in the middle of the second century—Justin Martyr, Aristides, Athenagoras, Theophilus, Tatian—are usually called the Apologists. We will look briefly at two of these, Martyr and Athenagoras. We will also study Irenaeus, who is from the later Polemicist period.

Reading the Fathers is often like reading an early version of the *Apostles' Creed*. They never tired of quoting Scripture, as if an appropriate quotation will put an end to all argument. This is particularly true for the Apostolic Fathers, as we shall see

with Ignatius and Polycarp. Similarly, they never tired of writing of the virgin birth, Christ's miracles, the vicarious death,
and the resurrection. The authority of Scripture was never
questioned. It is quite possible to trace the growing authority of
the New Testament and its eventual equality with the Old Testament through the writings of the Fathers. It is frequently
remarked that much of the Old Testament and nearly all of the
New Testament can be reproduced from their writings. In fact,
the Fathers are one of the sources for New Testement textual
criticism. Though their arguments at times may need more
staying power, the early Fathers knew how to use the authority
of Scripture.

All of the writings of the Apostolic Fathers and the Apologists
were accomplished in the setting of a rapidly growing church,
as Christianity continued to grow along the primary trade
routes. The authors were mostly Gentiles, indicative of the
transfer of influence within the church from Jew to Gentile.
Throughout the second century, the theological formulation of
Christian doctrine was taking shape. What from our perspective may seem to be heretical teaching is evidence of the hard
work of original exegesis and theological statement. The church
was at the same time gaining a catholic consciousness in that
local churches were seeing beyond themselves to unity with
similar groups of believers throughout the Roman Empire.
That eventually dictated greater organization. The churches in
the larger cities were becoming influential over surrounding
areas, frequently because of the administrative abilities of their
pastors who began to exercise oversight of the smaller parishes.
The role and authority of the pastor, or bishop, was thus
enlarged and was frequently spoken of in the writings of the
earlier Fathers. The *kērygma* (proclamation) of the New Testament was also becoming the second-century's rule of faith as a
doctrinal summation of tradition, frequently by means of baptismal confessions. This era was nearly as formative for Christianity as was the first century, and therefore a brief review of
their apologetic interests and attempts seems necessary, ending
with Irenaeus prior to A.D. 200. Many Fathers will not be
touched, including significant apologists of the early third century, such as Clement of Alexandria, Origen, and Tertullian. We
begin with Ignatius and Polycarp.

THE APOSTOLIC FATHERS

Ignatius,[1] bishop of Syria, was martyred during the reign of Trajan (A.D. 98-117), probably between 110 and 115. His letters were written to the various churches along the way as he traveled overland, under Roman guard, from Syria to Rome. Thus we have seven letters—to the Smyrnaeans, Ephesians, Trallians, Magnesians, Philadelphians, Romans, and to Polycarp, the original collector of the letters. Each of the letters gives greetings and pastoral advice, but three primary interests seem to predominate: approaching martyrdom, unity of the church through the authority of the bishop, and apologetic attacks on Judaizers and Docetists.[2]

Though our interest is primarily the latter two facets, insights into the man cannot be totally passed over. Like Kierkegaard, suffering equals discipleship except that for Ignatius, suffering really means martyrdom. Throughout his letters he desires to "get to God," which, in the Smyrnaean letter, translates to "near the sword means near God. To be with wild beasts means to be with God" (Smyrnaean 4:2). Even more morbid, in his letter to the Romans, Ignatius writes, "What a thrill I shall have from the wild beasts that are ready for me! I hope they will make short work of me. I shall coax them on to eat me up at once and not to hold off, as sometimes happens, through fear. Forgive me—I know what is good for me" (Romans 5:2-3*a*). What are we to make of this? Although Ignatius was apparently mentally balanced given his very normal behavior in every other area as well as his keen spiritual insights and firm Christian conviction, his unseemly desire for martyrdom cannot be condoned. It doubtless has had an ill effect on many individuals throughout church history.

Another pervasive theme found in all of Ignatius's letters is

---

1. For Ignatius, as for nearly all the church Fathers, the exact dates of his life are impossible to discern. The practice used thus far of putting the dates of the men mentioned in the text within parentheses will not be done for the Fathers.
2. These three emphases can be clearly seen in reading Ignatius's letters, but they were originally suggested to me by Cyril C. Richardson, ed. and trans., *Early Christian Fathers*, 1:75-77. Although the original writings of the Fathers will be noted within the text in the traditional manner for each Father, Richardson's book has usually been the means of access to their writings.

that only persistent obedience to the church authorities can preserve the unity and doctrine of the church. This can be understood in some degree due to the early date and thus the fact that the New Testament was not universally accepted as the authoritative norm for church doctrine, and many in the churches were semieducated at best. However, Ignatius still seems to go too far when he writes "that we should regard the bishop as the Lord himself" (Eph. 6:1), or the cryptic "pay attention to the bishop so that God will pay attention to you" (Polycarp 6:1). The rise of the monoepiscopate is easily seen throughout Ignatius. He instructs Polycarp to "not let anything be done without your consent" (Polycarp 4:1). The prayer of the bishop was superior to anyone else's prayer (Eph. 5:2). The priestly growth that eventually supplanted the one mediatorship of Jesus Christ (1 Tim. 2:5) had an early seedbed. The bishop's power would soon be absolute if to be subject to God meant one must "avoid resisting the bishop" (Eph. 5:3).

The emergence of the monoepiscopate was not all bad. It was a means to avoid divisions and doctrinal deviations. Many of the pastors at A.D. 100 probably had known one or two apostles for a few years. Thus the bishop had an authority that appeared to be nearly apostolic. Tradition was quickly being established from which apostolic succession would eventually develop and assert itself, especially in light of early writers like Ignatius who seemed to endorse it. How else might generations to come understand the following? Smyrnaen 8 reads:

> Flee from schism as the source of mischief. You should all *follow the bishop as Jesus Christ did the Father*. Follow, too, the presbytery as you would the apostles; and respect the deacons as you would God's law. Nobody must do anything that has to do with the Church without the bishop's approval. You should regard the Eucharist as valid which is celebrated either by the bishop or by someone he authorizes. Where the bishop is present, there let the congregation gather, just as where Jesus Christ is, there is the Catholic Church. Without the bishop's supervision, no baptisms or love feasts are permitted. On the other hand, *whatever he approves pleases God as well*. In that way everything you do will be on the safe side and valid (italics added).

Within the context of the early second century, with no universal authority yet apparent in the church, Ignatius's intentions are impeccable. His reference to the bishop at this juncture basically had the idea of oversight (*episcopos*, "bishop," is made up of two Greek words meaning to "oversee" or administer) of a local congregation—a pastor. It had not evolved to what is normally thought to be the role of a bishop in episcopal church polity, neither does "Catholic Church" portend more at this time than the growing universality of the Christian church. But at the same time, to make the analogy that Christians following the bishop are like Christ doing the will of the Father is a bit much. The bishop is already the "vicar of Christ" on earth if "whatever he approves pleases God." Not much imagination need be added to Ignatius to develop a very integrated and authoritarian structure of church administration. Unparalleled church growth demanded consideration of church structure simultaneously with the perceived need of human authority to protect the Christian community from heresy and needless divisions. The two went hand-in-hand historically, if not biblically.

Ignatius had two primary heresies to refute: a legalism of works-righteousness and a denial of the humanity of Jesus Christ. Neither of these was a new threat. Paul had battled the one probably fifty years previous in Galatia, and the other John had more recently refuted in his first letter. Ignatius contrasted Christianity and Judaism in the eighth and ninth chapters of the Magnesian letter by arguing that "the prophets themselves lived Christ Jesus' way" as He is God's "Word issuing from the silence." Thus "if we still go on observing Judaism we admit we never received grace" (Magnesian 8:1). "It is monstrous to talk Jesus Christ and to live like a Jew" (Magnesian 10:3).

The Christ-event was all-important, then, and Ignatius rightly refuted Docetism (from *dokeō*, "to seem") in many of his letters. He knew that if Jesus Christ only "seemed" to be human, but was not actually human and historical, man would still be living *without grace*. Thus he wanted to caution the Magnesians lest they fall for "stupid ideas" and not be "thoroughly convinced of the birth, Passion, and resurrection, which occurred while Pontius Pilate was governor" (Magnesian 11:1). Christ's Passion, in particular, was a physical and historical actuality, not a "sham" (Smyrnaen 1:1–2:1). Another warning against Docetic teaching is found in Trallians 9:1–10:1: "Be deaf, then, to any talk that ignores Jesus Christ, of David's lineage, of Mary; who was really born, ate, and drank; was really persecuted under Pontius Pilate; was really crucified and died, in the sight of heaven and earth and the underworld. He was really raised from the dead, for his Father raised him, just as his Father will raise us, who believe on him, through Christ Jesus, apart from whom we have no genuine life. And if, as some atheists (I mean unbelievers) say his suffering was a sham (it's really *they* who are a sham!) why, then, am I a prisoner? Why do I want to fight with wild beasts? In that case I shall die to no purpose. Yes, and I am maligning the Lord too!" (original italics).

There is no doubt that historical and empirical evidence was important for Ignatius. The centrality of the life of Christ was paramount. But we do not learn much about the role of natural revelation or life-style apologetics, unless a Christian should be willing, if not equally eager with Ignatius, to suffer martyrdom. Nevertheless, we do get the pulse-beat of the Christian church during the first decade of the second century from Ignatius, and Polycarp would extend this to mid-century.

We know more of Polycarp's death that we do his life, though it too is shrouded in mystery and some myth as the *Martyrdom of Saint Polycarp* demonstrates. Polycarp's reply to the proconsul's encouragement to deny the faith upon his arrest was, "Eighty-six years I have served him, and he never did me any wrong. How can I blaspheme my King who saved me" (*Martyrdom* 9:3). Whether this means he was eighty-six years old at his martyrdom, or perhaps even ten or more years older, we are not sure. He certainly spanned the era of missionary growth to the era of establishment and also therefore more systematic persecution. Irenaeus provided a picture of Polycarp *and* the reason for the respect and authority of the early pastors that gave rise to the monoepiscopate when he wrote of the apostolic tradition that had come down to himself and "is one and the same life-giving faith which has been preserved in the Church from the apostles to the present, and is handed on in truth":

Polycarp, who not only was taught by apostles, and associated with many who had seen Christ, but was installed by apostles for Asia, as bishop in the church in Smyrna—I saw him myself in my

early youth—survived for a long time, and departed this life in a
ripe old age by a glorious and magnificent martyrdom. He always
taught what he learned from the apostles, which the church continues to hand on, and which are the only truths. (*Against Heresies*
3.3.4)

Polycarp, whose martyrdom is usually thought to have
occurred in A.D. 156, was the last link with the apostles if what
Irenaeus says is correct, and we have no reason to believe otherwise. The venerable respect paid to Polycarp, and the source
of the insistence of Ignatius to "regard the bishop as the Lord
himself," can both be understood if Polycarp and other bishops
at the time of Ignatius's writing were direct links to the apostles
who had spoken authoritatively for the Lord by means of Spir-
it-breathed inspiration. It is in this context that Polycarp's apologetic practices must be discussed.

Polycarp's writing is simple and direct, unphilosophical and
nonspeculative. Though he apparently did not believe himself
to be well-versed in the Old Testament (*Letters to the Philippians* 12:1), he was very familar with the New Testament, frequently interjecting it with no intention of a verbatim quotation. He quoted the sayings of Jesus freely and was well
acquainted with Acts and the Pauline corpus as well as making
frequent reference to 1 Clement and allusions to the Ignatian
letters. In brief, he authoritatively quoted what would eventually become the majority of the New Testament books.

Only three apologetic insights can be gleaned from Polycarp:
there is a body of definite orthodox teaching to be defended,
apostolic authority continues, and heresy is to be condemned.
The seventh chapter of his *Letter to the Philippians* provides a
statement of orthodox beliefs, which are negatively phrased to
label those who do not accept such beliefs as antichrists. It also
provides a feeling for his personal intensity and passionate
devotion to the New Testament in his frequent paraphrasing of
it:

For "whosoever does not confess that Jesus Christ has come in the
flesh is antichrist"; and whosoever does not confess the testimony
of the cross "is of the devil"; and whosoever perverts the sayings
of the Lord to suit his own lusts and says there is neither resurrec-

tion nor judgment — such a one is the first-born of Satan. Let us, therefore, forsake the vanity of the crowd and their false teachings and turn back to the word delivered to us from the beginning, "watching unto prayer" and continuing steadfast in fasting, beseeching fervently the all-seeing God "to lead us not into temptation," even as the Lord said, "The spirit indeed is willing, but the flesh is weak." (*Letter to the Philippians* 7:1-2)

Polycarp's doctrine was apostolic and his disdain for heresy is obvious. It is reported that he once answered Marcion, the heretic who had two gods (the evil creator-god of the Old Testament and the good god and father of Jesus Christ), with "I know you; I know the first-born of Satan" (*Martyrdom* 23:3). Polycarp is perhaps the best example among the church Fathers of treating heresy with disdain and contempt. Apostolic authority was final. He did not, however, claim such for himself (regardless of early apostolic ties), and there is no reference to the authority of the bishop in Polycarp. Rather he wrote that "neither I nor anyone like me can follow the wisdom of the blessed and glorious Paul, who, when he was present among you face to face with the generation of his time, taught you accurately and firmly 'the word of truth' " (*Letter to the Philippians* 3:2). There is no apostolic succession claimed, then, by one who might have done so, though it was implied by Ignatius earlier and explicitly stated by Irenaeus later. Polycarp was content to refute heresy and defend the gospel by the unique authority of the apostolic literature that was then in the process of being recognized as the New Testament.

AN ANONYMOUS APOLOGY

Diognetus is not the name of a second-century Christian apologist, but the pseudonym for the addressee of a very cogently written apologetic tract. The author is unknown, though much scholarly endeavor has tried to identify him as either Quadratus, an apologist of Asia Minor who presented an apology to the emperor Hadrian (117-138), or Aristides, who also wrote an apology to either Hadrian or Antoninus Pius (138-161). Other suggestions have been Theophilus of Antioch or Hippolytus. It is unlikely that the debate will ever be satisfactorily ended. This is partially because the letter is never quoted, which gives credence to the idea that it was addressed to an emperor and thus was not in general circulation. It is assumed here to be written by either Quadratus or Aristides and written to either Hadrian or Antoninus Pius.

The *Letter to Diognetus* must be termed life-style apologetics. It is primarily Johannine in tone, but Pauline thought is not absent from it. It is quite classical in style and tightly organized. It is set in the context of a philosophy of history that emphasizes the divine initiative in history, and therefore contrasts Christianity as a supernatural factor in human relationships with the man-made religions of Gentiles and the current practice of Judaism. It opens with a threefold statement as to what Diognetus supposedly wants to know about Christianity and uses this as the basic outline:

> You want to know, for instance,
>
> 1. what God they believe in and how they worship him, while at the same time they disregard the world and look down on death, and how it is that they do not treat the divinities of the Greeks as gods at all, although on the other hand they do not follow the superstition of the Jews.
>
> 2. You would also like to know the source of the loving affection that they have for each other.
>
> 3. You wonder, too, why this new race or way of life has appeared on earth now and not earlier. (*Diognetus* 1:1)

The idols of the Greeks are dismissed as stupidity after examining what they are made of: stone, which is walked on; bronze, like cooking utensils; pottery, of which vessels for the "most ignoble purpose" are made; wood, which rots; iron, which rusts; or last, silver, which must be guarded so it will not be stolen. How can such lifeless things be gods? They are the product of talented craftsmen. Their material could have taken different form, and might yet. This is why pagans hate Christians so: because they intuitively know the Christians are right in denying that such things are gods.

Christians separate from Jewish worship because, while the Jews "adore the one God of all things and honor him as Lord," they also "worship more or less in the same manner" as the

Greeks, "offering gifts to God just as if he needed them" (*Diognetus* 3:3). The Greeks "think that they are offering something to objects which in reality cannot appropriate the honor," and Jews "imagine that they are giving something to him who has need of nothing" (*Diognetus* 3:5). Jewish legalism in regard to food, the Sabbath day, circumcision, and fast days and new moons is rejected outright as being "ridiculous, and not worth arguing about" (*Diognetus* 4:1).

Polemics over, Diognetus is instructed on the two remaining questions. Christianity is absolutely distinguished from all other religions and philosophies because Christianity is supernatural, not human. He states that "this doctrine of theirs [Christians] has not been discovered by the ingenuity or deep thought of inquisitive men, nor do they put forward a merely human teaching, as some people do" (5:3). The activity of God in Christ is also addressed in chapter 7, but in the remainder of chapter 5 and all of chapter 6 of Diognetus some of the most memorable expressions of what Christian living is are recorded. "To put it simply, what the soul is in the body, that Christians are in the world." The soul is dispersed throughout the body as the Christians are in the world, and in rather Platonic tones, the "soul dwells in the body, but does not belong to the body, and Christians dwell in the world, but do not belong to the world." Although this smacks of Platonic and not biblical ontology, there is a healthy personal separation from the world here because of the lordship of Christ. Christian life-style is indisputable evidence of this new revelation that creates such love between Christian brothers and distinctive public morality. In beautiful dialectic contrast, the author delineates this life-style in 5:5-11:

> They live in their own countries, but only as aliens. They have a share in everything as citizens and endure everything as foreigners. Every foreign land is their fatherland, and yet for them every fatherland is a foreign land. They marry, like everyone else, and they beget children, but they do not cast out their offspring. They share their board with each other, but not their marriage bed. It is true that they are "in the flesh." They busy themselves on earth, but their citizenship is in heaven. They obey the established laws, but in their own lives they go far beyond what the laws require. They love all men, and by all men are persecuted.

The cause of this life-style change is the direct intervention of God in human history. God sent the very Designer and Maker of the universe—Christ. But He did not send Him to rule by tyranny, fear, and terror, as might be presumed by the human mind.

> He sent him out of kindness and gentleness, like a king sending his son who is himself a king. He sent him as God; he sent him as man to men. He willed to save men by persuasion, not by compulsion, for compulsion is not God's way of working. In sending him, God called men, but did not pursue them; he sent him in love, not in judgment. Yet he will indeed send him someday as our Judge, and who shall stand when he appears. (*Diognetus* 7:3-6)

Here is complete affirmation of the deity and humanity of Jesus Christ. Here, as in chapter 10, man is not seen as a totally determined creature, but one capable of intelligent choice based on persuasive evidence. In 10:2 it states that God gave men and women "reason and intelligence, and to them alone he entrusted the capacity for looking upward to him, since he formed them after his own image." It was to them that "he sent his only-begotten Son, and to them that he promised the Kingdom in heaven which he will give to those who love him" (*Diognetus* 10:2). This is the source of the deep-seated joy that enables Christians to have love both to those within and to those outside the Christian community. The ability to know and love the true and living God is the well-spring of the Christian life-style that is so different from the pagan way of life.

Diognetus thus endorses two of our previous emphases: the importance of Christian life for effective apologetics and man's mental capacity to comprehend God's revelation in both word and historical event. Though our second-century apologist can answer no better than we why the revelation of the God-man occurred when it did, it nevertheless did occur and was every bit as historical as the birth or death of the emperor to whom he is writing. There is no natural theology here, in fact no direct appeal even to natural revelation, for in light of the format he has set up by his initial rhetorical questions, special revelation is paramount. Knowledge of God is possible, but it is initiated by God and not man. God is now among men. Wild animals and other means of persecution cannot stamp out God's program. That is why, despite Rome's attempts to eliminate it, Christianity is increasing. Such growth and persistence, in the face of such antagonistic force, does not "come from a human power," but is "a mighty act of God," providing "proofs of his presence" (*Diognetus* 7:7-9).

THE APOLOGISTS

From the unknown author of *Diognetus* we turn to the most influential apologist of mid-century—Justin Martyr. Justin is the best known to us because his writings are more numerous and more complete than those of any other Father before A.D. 160. His chief works are three: *First Apology, Second Apology,* and *Dialogue with Trypho.* It is the latter work, in which Martyr demonstrated an apology to an inquiring Jew very similar to the New Testament witness to Jews, that we learn the most about the man himself. Prior to meeting an old man on a lonely seacoast where Justin had retired to contemplate Plato's philosophy, Justin had passed through the various schools of the day, much like Augustine would some two hundred years later. At the conclusion of his discussion with this unnamed man, who refuted the claim that the philosophers had any knowledge of God and turned Justin's attention to the Hebrew prophets, Justin would testify:

> When he had spoken these and many other things, which there is no time for mentioning at present, he went away, bidding me attend to them; and I have not seen him since. But straightway a flame was kindled in my soul; and a love of the prophets, and of those men who are friends of Christ, possessed me; and whilst revolving his words in my mind, I found this philosophy alone to be safe and profitable. Thus, and for this reason, I am a philosopher. (*Dialogue* 8)

Justin never gave up being a philosopher. The *Dialogue* begins with Justin's being hailed by Trypho and other students because he was a philosopher and they desired their questions to be answered. Platonism remained with Justin and perverted his theology and historical perspective to some extent. For example, creation was viewed as God's giving form to unformed matter (*First Apology* 10.59). Justin also claimed that Plato was basically correct because he took some of his ideas from Moses (*First Apology* 44.59). Philosopher or not, Justin did not write in the classical manner of another philosopher-apologist, Athenagoras, whose writings we shall look at next. Rather, he attempted to lead the inquirer into the church rather than simply defending Christian beliefs from attack. Because of this, Justin's works contain a wealth of information concerning the early church, but are not tightly developed logically in the manner of the *Letter to Diognetus* or Athenagoras's *A Plea Regarding Christians*, making them more difficult to analyze for their apologetic framework.

Our narrow interest means we must center on the two primary facets of Justin's methodology: reason and fulfilled prophecy. Justin apparently settled in Rome and supported himself by lecturing in philosophy, but he was also a teacher-evangelist and gave instruction in the Christian faith, the one true philosophy, to any who desired it.[3] Reason was the center of philosophy and also of Christianity. It is Justin who developed the logos doctrine for Christian apologetics as a means of relating philosophy and Christianity. By the fact that reason (*logos spermatikos*) is in all men and unites men to God, Christians who know God through the *logos*, Christ, are of all men the most rational. He states this thesis frequently, but perhaps its most definitive statement is in chapter 46 of the *First Apology*:

> We have been taught that Christ is the First-begotten of God and have previously testified that he is the Reason of which every race of man partakes. Those who *lived in accordance with Reason are Christians*, even though they were called godless, such as, among the Greeks, Socrates, and Heraclitus and others like them . . . . So also those who lived without Reason were ungracious and enemies to Christ, and murderers of those who lived by Reason. But *those who lived by Reason, and those who so live now, are Christians*, fearless and unperturbed (italics added).

3. Michael Green, *Evangelism in the Early Church*, p. 204.

And in chapter 13 of the *Second Apology* he explains why the ancient philosophies and Christianity are not totally alike:

> Each man spoke well in proportion to the share he had of the spermatic word [*logos spermatikos*], seeing what was related to it. But they who contradict themselves on the more important points appear not to have possessed the heavenly wisdom, and the knowledge which cannot be spoken against. Whatever things were rightly said among all men, are the property of us Christians.

Justin no doubt had good intentions, but he went too far. Although all men are made in the image of God and therefore have the capacity to reason, that does not mean that all who have lived by Greek philosophy (reason) were or are Christians. He conceded too much to paganism. And vice versa, even though Christians know Christ (*logos*, "reason"), this does not mean that all that was rightly known in the past belonged to Christians, but simply that men using their abilities have known a *little* about God's thoughts and interpretations of the universe. In the *Second Apology* quotation above, Martyr did at least recognize the shortcomings of natural reason in regard to completely knowing the truth.

Revelation, then, is still the key to knowing God for Justin. Chapters 30-53 of the *First Apology* explain how the prophets speak through the inspiration of the Holy Spirit. The predictions of the prophets in no way, however, imply fateful destiny that destroys man's moral choice possibilities and therefore eliminates his moral responsibility before a holy God (*First Apology* 43). Neither did these men speak or write their own words, but only "by the divine Word that moved them" (*First Apology* 36). According to Justin, it was Christ, the preincarnate *logos*, or Word, who taught the prophets. Therefore, to say "the Scripture says" is the same as saying "the *logos* says," which may be understood as "Reason" philosophically or "Christ" theologically.

The constant contrast of philosophy and Christianity makes Justin Martyr a very important apologist, but also one we must examine with a critical eye. That is particularly the case when we note his comparisons of paganism and Christianity,[4] which is a questionable means of apology, and perhaps even a more questionable theory, capable of causing more problems than it resolves:

> In saying that the Word, who is the first offspring of God, was born for us without sexual union, as Jesus Christ our Teacher, and that he was crucificd and died and after rising again ascended into heaven we *introduce nothing new beyond* [what you say of] those whom you call sons of Zeus. (*First Apology* 21, italics added)

Did pagans read this, as Justin presumed, in the context of demon-inspired myths? If not, which is probable, the very uniqueness of the Christian revelation is undermined. Though there may be a kernel of truth to such demonic activity, it does not seem the way to approach the pagan world. In his attempt to provide common ground between himself and the pagan world by these comparisons, and by calling previous pagans *Christians* because they followed Reason (*logos*), it would seem that Justin may have "pulled the carpet" out from under his own feet, blocking any future attempt to demonstrate the uniqueness of Christianity and its difference from all other perspectives.

This does not mean that Justin is of no assistance for constructing a viable twentieth-century apologetic framework. Certainly, within limits, his emphasis on reason's being in all men is correct, as well as the fact that man can get a segment of truth because he is God's creature living in God's universe. Though Justin does not quote the Scriptures authoritatively because of his projected readers' ignorance of them—much like Paul in Athens—he does not set them aside for he realizes they are the

---

4. In chapter 41 of the *First Apology*, Justin quoted Psalm 96:5 to indicate that "all the gods of the nations are images of demons." Therefore, he wrote later that "those who hand on the myths invented by the poets offer no demonstration to the youngsters who learn them—indeed I [am prepared to] show that they were told at the instigation of the wicked demons to deceive and lead astray the human race. For when they heard it predicted through the prophets that Christ was to come, and that impious men would be punished by fire, they put forward a number of so-called sons of Zeus, thinking that they could thus make men suppose that what was said about Christ was a mere tale of wonders like the stories told by the poets" (*First Apology* 54).

final criterion of truth. The role of fulfilled prophecy in his apologetics (both the *First Apology* and the *Dialogue with Trypho* have extended treatment of these fulfillments) demonstrates his adherence to *both* the importance of historical event *and* the necessity of the predictive or interpreted Word. Fulfilled prophecy doubtless played an important role in Justin's apologetic argument because of the role it played in his own conversion. Justin seemingly accepted deductive reasoning, but also empiricism as a legitimate means of the acquisition of knowledge. Natural revelation obviously plays a part through its manifestation in the reasoning processes of every man made in God's image. Our final assessment would thus be more positive toward what we perceive to be his epistemological orientation than toward his actual attempt at apology.

Athenagoras was a Greek philosopher who, in contrast to Justin, was converted simply by reading the Scriptures. Though he is passed over by the later Fathers, his *Plea* is perhaps the best organized of all the early apologies, though it is not actually a speech before the emperor. It was most likely written in A.D. 177, since it was addressed to the Emperors Marcus Aurelius Antoninus and his son, Lucius Aurelius Commodus, during an apparent time of peace in the Empire. Since the two of them reigned together from 176-180 (but only the first year was free of war), it seems safe that Athenagoras penned his *Plea* in 177.

Athenagoras wrote two works that we know of: *A Plea for Christians* and *On the Resurrection*. Our attention here is only on the former, which is a classic apology. We know little of the man himself other than that he was an Athenian by birth and a philosopher by vocation. He addresses his *Plea* to the emperors as philosophers. His apology is tightly reasoned. The intent is to show that the three primary criminal charges against Christianity—atheism, incest, and cannibalism—are false, and that Christians are really persecuted only because of their name (*Plea*, chapter 1).

Athenagoras's main goal of refuting the charge of atheism takes up twenty-six of the thirty-two chapters given over to the three charges. Christians were thought to be atheists because they denied the traditional pagan gods, refused sacrifice, and refuted the usual association of gods with race and soil, an impossible association since Christianity transcended ethnic and geographical boundaries. Athenagoras made frequent use of Justin's word *logos* to refer to Christian truth, which, as in *Diognetus*, was not man-made (*Plea*, chapter 11), but revelation from God. He wrote that the philosophers, contrary to the Christians,

> proceeded by conjecture. They were driven each by his own soul and through a sympathy with the divine spirit to see if it were possible to find out and to comprehend the truth. They were able, indeed, to get some notions of reality, but not to find it, since they did not deign to learn about God from God, but each one from himself.

Christians, on the contrary, as "witnesses of what we think and believe have prophets who have spoken by the divine Spirit about God and the things of God" (*Plea*, chapter 7).

Athenagoras did not totally reject the ideas of the philosophers, since he knew they were based upon facts of natural revelation. Plato, for instance, had some true insights concerning God. This was the case, he realized, since men are driven by their own souls and by a sympathy with the divine Spirit because they are God's creatures and made in His image. His assertions are very similar to Calvin's in regard to man's intuitive knowledge of God. Like Calvin, Athenagoras believed that men receive only "some notions" and cannot find reality until they are willing "to learn about God from God" by special revelation. Special revelation refers to both the prophets and the apostles, Old Testament as well as New Testament (*Plea*, chapter 9). In this same chapter, referring to Moses, Isaiah, and Jeremiah as being above human reason, is the most famous statement in *A Plea Regarding Christians*. Speaking of divine inspiration of the human authors of holy Scripture, Athenagoras wrote, "The Spirit used them just as a flute player blows on a flute." It should be noted that by being "above" human reason, Athenagoras did not mean that the revelation was irrational, only that its source was *beyond* human reason alone. Elsewhere he writes that philosophers occasionally concentrate so much on "the forms of matter, they *miss the God who is known only by reason*" (*Plea*, chapter 22, see also chapter 23, italics added).

Dependent then on the special revelation of God, while not denying the possibility of at least God-consciousness to all men through creation and natural revelation, Athenagoras had two more positive arguments to present against the charge of atheism before he attacked the pagan deities who were simply human creations. These two were the doctrine of the Trinity and the distinctiveness of Christian morality. He wrote, "Who, then, would not be astonished to hear those called atheists, who admit God the Father, God the Son, and the Holy Spirit, and who teach their unity in power and their distinction in rank" (*Plea*, chapter 10). That is a remarkable statement at this early date. The Christological controversies were still to come in church history, but Athenagoras used the doctrine of the Trinity to refute the charge of atheism in the eighth decade of the second century!

More important for our concern with apologetic methodology is his use of the Christian life as evidence for the truth of Christianity and the reality of God. He contrasted the philosophical promise of happiness with the reality of those who do love their enemies and bless those who curse them as well as praying for those who persecute them (Matt. 5:44-45). Among the Christians, contrary to the actual back-biting and desire to work harm on others that persisted among the philosophers given to "skill in oratory rather than proof by deeds," were unlettered people and others who,

> though unable to express in words the advantages for our teaching, demonstrate by acts the value of their principles. For they do not rehearse speeches, but evidence good deeds. When struck, they do not strike back; when robbed, they do not sue; to those who ask, they give, and they love their neighbors as themselves. (*Plea* chapter 11)

Athenagoras's argument was not only based on the uniqueness of the Christian life as an indication of the truth of Christianity and its special revelation, but also on his own version of the moral argument for God. Though not arguing for a Lawgiver because there was an inherent moral law in every man's breast, he did argue that Christians would not live so morally if they were not sure of divine judgment. He writes in chapter 12:

If we did not think that God ruled over the human race, would we live in such purity. The idea is impossible. But since we are persuaded that we must give an account of all our life here to God who made us and the world, we adopt a temperate, generous, and despised way of life. For we think that, even if we lose our lives, we shall receive from the great Judge for a gentle, generous, and modest life.

Though this argument may be demeaning to Christians as individuals, it is realistic! Man without the new birth cannot live as he describes. And not only can they not so live, there is no reason to so live for, as Athenagoras well knew, one of the most popular philosophies of the era (if not to the Stoic emperor) was "eat, drink, and be merry for tomorrow we die" — and death was nothing. That moral argument might be even more telling to an ethicist like Marcus Aurelius who strove for moral goodness but also knew how impossible it was.

The remainder of the apology attempted to show the meaninglessness and inadequacies of pagan idolatry in a considerably more extended fashion than the *Letter to Diognetus*. Those who accused Christians of atheism because they did not acknowledge "the same gods that they believe in are not agreed among themselves about the gods" (*Plea*, chapter 14). Two other powerful charges brought against idolatry by Athenagoras were that idols are man-made and thus the gods "need the aid of man and of art to come into existence" (*Plea*, chapter 17) and that the gods' immorality was frequently worse than man's. This latter argument stood the gods in stark contrast to the Christians who, as supposed atheists, lived lives greatly more ethical and moral than the gods they were accused of not accepting. Actually those pagan gods were simply men deified (*Plea*, chapter 28). For certainly, as Athenagoras wrote, "wrath, lust, passion, and procreation are not appropriate to God" (*Plea*, chapter 21). Those gods were depicted as evil, and occasionally exhibited real power though they did not exist because, on the testimony of philosophers (e.g., Justin Martyr), those gods represented demons (*Plea*, chapter 23). Christians, he concluded, were in a sense the only non-atheists.

The other charges against the Christians were rebutted in short order. Incest charges came from the great love evidenced in the Christian community and its spiritual warmth and emphasis on brotherhood. He pointed out that if non-Christians were going to be consistent in hating "indiscriminate intercourse as a frightful thing, they should have hated Zeus" (*Plea* chapter 32). Nevertheless, Christians were not guilty as charged as intercourse was only between married couples "for the purpose of having children" (*Plea* chapter 33). "A second marriage is a veiled adultery" (*Plea* 33). Thus some particular Christian attitudes toward sex and marriage have ancient roots.

The charge of cannibalism was easily refuted by a detailed explanation of the Lord's Supper and by argument that if Christians so abhorred murder that they avoided the gladiator spectaculars, understood abortion as murder, and believed in the resurrection of the body, certainly they could not be murderers, and thus would not be cannibals.

Athenagoras's polemics are perhaps more valuable than his apologetic framework, though we have more interest in the latter. He demonstrated how to meet our enemies directly. Though our battles are different today, we must have the same fortitude. Likewise, we find added support for our understanding of the function of natural revelation in mankind that points to an indispensable need for special revelation long before John Calvin, or even Saint Augustine. Though he made little direct appeal to historical evidences such as fulfilled prophecy or Jesus' miracles, Athenagoras still insisted on the centrality and finality of God's revelation in Jesus Christ, raised from the dead, and one day to be the Judge of every man. Basically, he had copied Paul's approach with cultured and philosophical Gentiles at Athens.

A POLEMICIST

Irenaeus is the latest of our six church Fathers. He was pastor for many years in Lyons, France, and was extremely influential throughout the Roman province of Gaul. He came on the scene about A.D. 177 as bishop during the time of severe persecution in Gaul. He was a native of Smyrna and heard Polycarp during his youth (*Against Heresies* 3.3.4.), giving him a second-hand tie to the apostles.

Against Heresies is a massive work. Parts one and two are primarily against the Gnostic systems of Valentinus and Basilides, two men slightly older than Irenaeus. Part four is given over to the refutation of Marcion by defense of the unity of the Old and New Testaments. These polemics are important to patristic scholars who are interested in the detail of second-century heretical teaching, but are not of prime importance for our purposes. Irenaeus was not writing for posterity, but was a pastor interested in defending his flock against false teaching. His work is really the best source for comprehending the teaching of Gnosticism or the Marcionites.

In a manner reminiscent of Polycarp, Irenaeus at times treated his opponents with disdain. His primary means of rebuttal was Scripture and tradition, the latter being the public proclamation of the truth in the churches established by the apostles. Irenaeus made no clear distinction between written and oral testimony. He recognized the supreme authority of the apostles. He quoted all of the books that would be canonized as the New Testament except Philemon, 3 John, and Jude. He referred to them in an individually—not collectively—authoritative manner and accused the Gnostics of using the Scriptures "as if they were not correct, not of authority" (*Against Heresies* 3.2.1). But he also referred to the oral tradition (*paradosis*, literally, "handing down") over forty times and clearly implied that the truth was "handed down" by both Scripture and the church and therefore both must be and were used against the heretics. Irenaeus was doubtless moved to this position of public tradition as a tactic to refute the Gnostic private and secret tradition. Tradition was not a formal authority as was Scripture, but nevertheless it was authoritative as a living contact with the "rule of truth" in the church. That treatment of tradition planted the doctrine of apostolic succession, quiet since Ignatius, quite firmly in the church. For example, Irenaeus singled out the practices of the Ephesian church as "a true witness of the tradition of the apostles" (*Against Heresies* 3.3.4). Tradition was confirmed by Scripture, however, and really was identical in content.[5]

The "rule of truth" was used against the Gnostics. Irenaeus asserted in one place that the rule of truth was received

---

5. J. N. D. Kelly, *Early Christian Doctrines*, p. 39.

through baptism (*Against Heresies* 1.9.4). It was more than the baptismal confession, however, it was the truth necessary for salvation, the truth traditionally preached in the churches, perhaps best described as a "condensed summary, fluid in its wording but fixed in content, setting out the key-points of the Christian revelation in the form of a rule."[6] That rule of truth was what the Gnostics perverted. It was in reality the fruit of proper hermeneutics. It absolutely refuted the fanciful use of Scripture to support a theory that was for all practical purposes independent of the Bible. Thus those who had the rule of truth in their spiritual possession could readily recognize the perverted misuse of Scripture and apostolic tradition. Gnosticism was not Christian, nor was it a higher knowledge, but inventive imagination.

Parts 3 and 5 of *Against Heresies* are, like Justin Martyr, a treasury of early church information while also containing some important theological insights. In Part 5, for instance, Irenaeus put forth a "recapitulation doctrine of the atonement," meaning that "the enemy would not have been justly conquered unless it had been a man [made] of woman who conquered him. For it was by a woman that he had power over man from the beginning, setting himself up in opposition to man" (*Against Heresies* 5.21.1). Irenaeus was also an early proponent of a literal millennium (*Against Heresies* 5.32.1-35). He considered the role of the Holy Spirit in testifying to the Word of God—both written and incarnate—and His work in the conversion and sanctification of our hearts as very important apologetically. J. N. D. Kelly, quoting at length from an unavailable Irenaeus source, writes:

> As for the Spirit, it was He "through Whom the prophets prophesied, and the fathers learned the things of God, and the righteous were led into the way of righteousness, and Who at the end of the age was poured out in a new way...renewing man unto God." The Spirit's role is indeed essential for "without the Spirit it is impossible to behold the Word of God . . . . since the knowledge of the Father is the Son, and the knowledge of the Son of God can only be obtained through the Spirit; and a the life of God."[7]

6. Ibid., p. 37.
7. Ibid., p. 107.

Irenaeus thus put primary emphasis upon the Word and Spirit. The argument of fulfilled prophecy was not prevalent in Irenaeus, but this would seem to be more a function of what he argued against with the Gnostics than a rejection of such. Empirical evidence was obviously important, with the great emphasis placed on the apostles, as well as the very possibility of oral tradition itself. Natural revelation was likewise an apologetic tool as a by-product of creation. Special revelation in Christ and Scripture was paramount, however, as in all of the preceeding five church Fathers. The life-style of Christians, particularly the apostles, was quite conspicuous, especially their testimony in the face of martyrdom, to indicate the reality and truth of Christianity (*Against Heresies* 3.3.3).

Each of the church Fathers was concerned with the immediate problems at hand: Polycarp treated heresy with contempt, Ignatius specifically battled Docetism, and Irenaeus fought Gnosticism; particular charges against the Christians were met by Athenagoras, and by the writer of *Diognetus* through lifestyle apologetics; and Justin attempted to contrast Christianity with Greek philosophy. They are instructive for apologetic example, if not as helpful as Augustine, Aquinas, Calvin, Pascal, or Kierkegaard for apologetic methodology. For that, perhaps the little *Letter to Diognetus* is as valuable as any second century apology.

8

BOTH / AND: A BALANCED APOLOGETIC

The framework of the balanced apologetic should be obvious by now. The frequent juxtaposition of the two primary Christian apologetic frameworks of evidentialism and presuppositionalism throughout the book makes it clear that an apologist cannot be only the one or the other, as we have been told for so long in evangelical circles. This debate has been the expression in theological dress of the philosophical dispute between a priori and a posteriori theories of knowlege—a debate over rationalistic or empirical methodologies. The conclusions reached by those philosophers who attempted to keep these methodologies mutually exclusive during the seventeenth and eighteenth centuries, for example Spinoza and Hume, should have been sufficient for Christian thinkers to have done otherwise. But it was not!

Christian thinkers had more than the philosophical catastrophes of monism and skepticism to alert them to the impossibility of believing that these methodologies of knowledge could be kept completely separate. The Christian doctrine of creation and its implications of *two* unequal, but nevertheless real, *realities* certainly pointed to the impossibility of monism, which is the usual consequence of an a priori rationalistic theory of knowledge. However, an empirical orientation that normally leads to a transcendent denial of naturalism is equally incompatible with the Christian doctrine of revelation. These two fundamental Christian teachings make a mutually exclusive methodology, as usually expressed by the adherents of evidentialism and presuppositionalism, absolutely impossible. A Christian methodology, based on the ontological implications of creation and the epistemological assumptions of special revelation, demands an eclectic apologetic framework that does justice to *both* the a priori person of God *and* the a posteriori interpreted work of God in creation and revelation.

There is no need to reproduce the chapters on ontology, epistemology, and theology in this final chapter. But it must be remembered that these are the primary expositional chapters for a Both/And apologetic framework. From an ontological perspective, the fact that there are two realities—the infinite, self-existing God and the finite, dependent creation, including man—means that both realities must determine our apologetic framework. Because the dependent creation is defined by God, nothing exists that is not related to and interpreted by God. Therefore the debate between evidentialists and presuppositionalists over self-interpreting facts or God-interpreted facts is artificial, since both sides accept and believe that this is a God-created world with a God-sanctioned history.

The presuppositionalist is correct, as he begins a priori from the ontological perspective of creation, in having everything ultimately related to and interpreted by God's will and Word. The evidentialist is equally correct as he begins in an a posteriori fashion with the actual facts and argues epistemologically that the facts rightly interpreted have only one possible meaning, and in that sense carry their meaning with them in a self-interpreting manner. This is exactly what John Calvin realized when, in the very beginning of his *Institutes*, he wrote that our wisdom "consists of two parts: the knowledge of God and of ourselves. But as these are connected together by many ties, it is *not easy to determine which of the two precedes, and gives birth to the other*" (1.1.1, italics added). Presuppositionalists want to begin with God, evidentialists with ourselves; the balanced apologist says start with *both* God *and* ourselves simultaneously, as these cannot be broken apart. That apologist is then rejected by the other two orientations as holding a theoretically uncomfortable position, though they admit that without God there is no man, and given man, "we cannot clearly and properly know God unless the knowledge of ourselves be added" (*Institutes* 1.15.1).

The study of God shows that the relationship between God and ourselves is not arbitrary; neither is the interpreted meaning of that relationship relative or variable. Though God is absolutely free and independent and nothing in its own right can limit or determine God's actions but His own nature, *God has limited Himself by the fact of creation* and thus always abides by His original decision to have something else exist in its own right. The acme of terrestial creation, man, is free but is never independent of God. The Christian apologist must *actually* begin with the epistemological realities before man, realizing, however, that these realities as well as man himself are ontologically and ultimately understood only as God-ordained creation or as products of His sanctioned history. From this theistic viewpoint, man is never autonomous but neither is he ever meaningless. Given this fact of creation, the Both/And apologist can never speak correctly or truthfully of God in total neglect of God's creative and/or revelatory handiwork.

This does not commit a Both/And apologetic to the usual methodology of natural theology, which begins only with natural reality and argues to the reality of God. As we have just emphasized, God and creation cannot be so dichotomized. Natural revelation is concomitant with the fact of creation and is therefore a priori and cannot be identified with natural theology, which is the derivative of an a posteriori argument from the fact of existence to the cause of such existence. The a priori natural revelation means that man cannot escape that which is "naturally engraven on the human heart" (*Institutes* 1.4.4). That knowledge of God is innate and is thus prior to and independent of all empirical experience. That is what we earlier identified as the intuitive knowledge of God through which men "occasionally feel the truth" that "they are desirous not to know" because of their sin and present separation from God (*Institutes* 1.3.2).

This ontological nature of man made in God's image and living in God's universe, then, not only necessitates a natural revelation outside of man by which the visible things point to the invisible God, but also a natural revelation within man through his intuitive God-consciousness. The ontological nature of man provides him not only with the moral law written on his heart and his artistic and mental creativities, but also with the substructure of logic to differentiate *this* from *that* empirically. Man is also provided with the possibility of meaningful linguistic communication between God and himself and among men. Man could not comprehend God's special and propositional revelation without God's endowment of logic. Both natural and special revelation come only to the creature who has the prerequisite abilities to logically differentiate *this* from *that* by being made in God's image.

Some may feel, as some have thought of Augustine, that there is not sufficient distinction made between the essence of God and the essence of man due to this emphasis on the ontological similarity between man and God, brought about by man having been made in God's likeness and image. We have twice argued for a real and univocal knowledge of God obtained by means of biblical revelation and based on the ontological foundation of man made in God's image. This, however, does not deny the absolute qualitative difference between God and man because of God's infinity and man's finiteness. This can be most easily illustrated by means of the concept of "existence" as it relates to God and man. Although both exist, there is an absolute and qualitative difference between the existence of One who is self-existent and totally unconditioned and we who are contingent and completely dependent on God for existence and on our physical environment and bodily state for physical existence. This does not mean, however, that man has absolutely no idea of what it means for God "to be," only that we cannot know self-existence. But, as we have quoted Hodge previously, "knowledge in Him does not cease to be knowledge because it is omniscience,"[1] so existence does not cease to be existence because it is self-existence. This infinite-finite difference is also seen in regard to God's nature, which is absolute perfection and thus immutable, and our created nature that did change at the Fall and can be changed again through the new birth. Immuta-

1. Charles Hodge, *Systematic Theology*, 1:338.

bility is held out for us when we are eventually conformed to the image of Christ in eternity future.

God does not ask us to "be self-existent because I am self-existent" but rather "be holy because I am holy." To created beings the first command would be contradictory, and thus we obviously have no ontological foundation to univocally comprehend self-existence, only existence that is adequate to know that God is. But as creatures created originally in God's image as righteous personality with the requirements of the law engraven inherently on our moral psyche and the resultant conscience, we do have an ontological foundation to univocally comprehend the imperative to "be holy because I am holy." We thus have a true, if far from exhaustive, knowledge of what it means when the Scriptures speak of God's love, truth, personality, life, and so on, because God has selected to reveal Himself by means of those personal attributes that are also attributable to man by means of God's image, and which we ourselves self-consciously and intuitively know. Man made in God's image is the ontological foundation for *revelatory univocacy* that *provides the only real and true knowledge of God.*

This ontological univocacy between the infinite God and finite man made in God's image has one more very important significance—the incarnation. If man and God are so absolutely different in kind that we can have no idea of what God is like in Himself, then the incarnation would be absolutely impossible, or as Kierkegaard stated it, Absolute Paradox. The second person of the Godhead, however, *did become man*, demonstrating once and for all the epistemological significance of man's ontological essence in the image of God for God "has spoken to us by his Son" (Heb. 1:2).

Jesus Christ is the culmination of special revelation by being both God and man, and, like all supernatural revelation, both historical event and divine Word. As the ontological nature of man created in God's image provides the source and basis for the logical capabilities in man as well as the intuitive knowledge of God, special revelation in history demonstrates the reality and viability of sense experience in the acquisition of knowledge. Because God has created, He also acts in the realm of nature on behalf of His people and before all men. These acts, be they the Old or New Testament record, are events *capable of universal perception if only very particular and special interpretation.* This can be easily illustrated by the handwriting on the wall, which king and court could see, but only Daniel could interpret (Dan. 5:5-8, 17-28). This is of course true for the plagues in Egypt, as we have seen, and the miracles performed by Jesus during His incarnation. Christ's miracles were frequently misinterpreted or consciously denied their only possible implication by the viewers and hearers, but were recorded and given their only possible interpretation throughout the entire New Testament.

It is the empirical evidence of historical revelation that must be the content of our apology. God has done something in history. God has entered personally into history by means of the incarnation. God is in history now as evidenced by transformed lives and the ongoing care of and provision for His people. Those are the material facts that must be formally presented in a noncontradictory manner because truth is *both* formal validity *and* material facts. That is the evidence that Pascal said was neither absolutely convincing, given the inherent probable nature of inductive investigation, nor unreasonable in itself. Thus we are provided with "both evidence and obscurity to enlighten some and confuse others" (*Pensees* No. 564). There is then sufficient evidence for faith, but also insufficient for absolute proof, and so a loophole is provided for unbelief to continue.

The evidence, however, can only be truly interpreted one way—as many in Pharaoh's court knew and many in the first-century Sanhedrin realized. Nevertheless, logic and reasoning processes are not identical. Of course all men have the same logic as all men have the same image, but all men are not theonomous. In fact, the great majority of men, it being the evidence of man's greatness perverted and therefore the curse of his wretchedness, are autonomous. "In his pride the wicked does not seek him [God]; in all his thoughts there is no room for God" (Ps. 10:4). This is why man does not read correctly the abundant evidence of God's reality and saving provision in Jesus Christ. All facts are God-interpreted facts, especially the supernatural facts of special revelation in history, but man believes facts are humanistically and secularly interpreted. If he does not so interpret the facts, he must bow to the infinite-personal God as Creator and Savior, losing his autonomy and self-deluded godness. In his actual godlessness and wickednsss, then, man suppresses and/or interprets in a nontheistic framework the obvious evidence of God's reality and care. The Fall thus affects the reasoning process if not the ability to reason as God's unique creature. Man no longer wills to will God's will. He is in a wretched and abnormal state compared to his initial splendor. Man's will is "bent" away from God. His self-law framework means that man will not and thus cannot interpret this world of God's revelation in a properly theistic manner.

Nevertheless, special revelation is objective and historical. It is there for man to see if he would. The events are recorded and definitively interpreted so that, as John writes, "you may believe that Jesus is the Christ, the Son of God" (John 20:31). These revelatory events/miraculous signs are for both the enemies and the people of God. Deuteronomy 34:11-12 states that the works of God through Moses were done for *both* unbelieving Egyptians *and* God's people, Israel: "[Moses] did all those miraculous signs and wonders the LORD sent him to do in Egypt—to Pharaoh and to all his officials and to his whole land. For no one has ever shown the mighty power or performed the awesome deeds that Moses did in the sight of all Israel."·

In light of hard, cold, objective facts that point rather distinctively to the truth of God in history and God in Christ, what do Christians mean by faith? If John tells us that he is writing so that we "may believe," and it frequently says in both the Old Testament (e.g., Pharaoh) and the New Testment that people who are obviously unbelievers "know" what is implied by the miraculous signs/revelatory events, how are such called unbelievers? And what then do we mean by believers? This is the same problem, perhaps in slightly different dress, that we termed the question of reason and faith in chapter 5. It is the question of the relationship between objective evidences and the conviction and regenerating work of the Holy Spirit.

> When he [the Holy Spirit] comes, he will convict the world of guilt in regard to sin and righteousness and judgment: in regard to sin, because men do not believe in me; in regard to righteousness, because I am going to the Father, where you can see me no long-

er; and in regard to judgment, because the prince of this world now stands condemned. (John 16:8-11)

The Holy Spirit certainly is pictured here as using objective facts in regard to the saving work of Christ, His ascension and glorification, and the climactic if not yet final judgment of Satan. This is parallel to the orderly and logical presentation of the gospel that we have seen in Acts. Certainly such conviction does not come to one who neither hears, nor at least personally reads, the message of the gospel (Rom. 10:12-15). But this being the case, there must then be a rational understanding of the preached or read Word for the possibility of the Holy Spirit's conviction. Unless such conviction *always* brings conversion, which is doubtful, it means that some individuals have a *rational* comprehension of the gospel in continuing unbelief.

What then is the relationship between this rational comprehension and *saving* faith? Obviously, rational comprehension is not enough, even if prerequisite to Spirit-wrought conviction and regeneration. That is the truth that is reiterated throughout the Scriptures, be it Moses, Isaiah, or Jesus, who tells his disciples who have empirically witnessed the miracles, the crucifixion, and the evidence of the resurrection that He must open "their minds so they could understand the Scriptures" (Luke 24:45; see also Deut. 29:2-4; Isa. 6:9-11). It is the conflicting difficulty of accepting evidence as true but not as personally, existentially, and transcendentally significant. It is the problem of theonomy versus autonomy we have already touched upon in this chapter. It is a problem of the will and affection since men have "loved darkness instead of light because their deeds were evil" (John 3:19) and not a problem of the gospel's inductive evidentiality for either the believer or unbeliever. The gospel does not become either true or rational only after regeneration and acceptance. This may be the subjectivistic orientation of much of contemporary religious thought, but *it is not biblical*! Reread Acts 2, 17, and 26 to note that the apostles, whether to a Jewish or Gentile audience, *always* gave a logical, factual, and existential (personal and decision oriented) presentation of the gospel truth. This is why Augustine wrote, "We must refuse so to believe as not to receive or seek a reason for our belief, since we could not believe at all if we did not have rational souls" (*Letter* 120).

Faith, then, refers to *both* the objective factual evidence, which can only be inductively probable and is the object of belief, *and* the subjective response of the person who reaches out in a personal trusting decision to the personal God. The latter is what Pharaoh did not, would not, and could not do. Unsaved individuals may have credence or rational belief, but are not willing to forsake autonomy for theonomy by placing their whole being in the hands of God through Christ. Faith as belief must be rational, for it is the intellectual comprehension of the propositional Word, but this comprehension is not enough, given the experience of the demons (James 2:19). One must *both* comprehend the message intellectually *and* "throw one's entire being out upon the Lord" (existentially). This is not possible without the work of the Holy Spirit in creating a new will and love by means of the "message of reconciliation" (2 Cor. 5:19) provided by the gracious gift and work of Christ.

Knowledge alone never satisfies the *whole* man because it is impersonal. Philosophy leads to disillusionment because it divests man from everything that makes him a unique personal individual. We only know another person's uniqueness when he communicates in the context of fellowship. That is what is meant by 1 John 1:7. Personal relationship and love does not displace knowledge but makes it meaningful. Biblical faith is thus *both* objective, rational comprehension of God's redemptive activity in special revelation, *and* personal and subjective appropriation to the very core and essence of one's being because God is personal.

This is not seen only in biblical practice, but also in explicit biblical statement. Hebrews 11:1 defines faith:

> Now faith is being sure of what we hope for and certain of what we do not see.

The word for "sure" ("assurance," NASB) is the Greek word *hypostasis*, which literally means "substance" or "foundation," but here means apprehension of reality by the individual. Vincent comments that "it is that to which the unseen objects of hope become real and substantial. *Assurance* gives the true idea. It is the firm grasp of faith on unseen facts."[2] It thus denotes the subjective certitude provided by the regenerating work and personal indwelling of the Holy Spirit of God. The other word, *elegchos*, "certain" ("evidence," NASB), pertains to the factual basis of evidence and conviction upon which the subjective certitude is originally grounded by the convicting work of God's Spirit.

On this subject of the dependence of spiritual faith on rational evidence, B. B. Warfield wrote:

> One might as well say that photography is independent of light, because no light can make an impression unless the plate is prepared to receive it. The Holy Spirit does not work a blind, an ungrounded faith in the heart. What is supplied by his creative energy in working faith is not a ready-made faith, rooted in nothing, and clinging without reason to its object; nor yet new grounds of belief in the object present; but just a *new ability of the heart to respond to the grounds of faith, sufficient in themselves, already present to the understanding.* We believe in Christ because it is rational to believe in him not though it be irrational . . . . That is to say, for the birth of faith in the soul, it is *just as essential* that grounds of faith should be present in the mind as that the Giver of faith should act creatively upon the heart (italics added).[3]

This Reformed presuppositional position differs little from the following Lutheran evidentialist statement by John Warwick Montgomery (note p. 111 that the leading contemporary presuppositionalist, Cornelius Van Til, endorses Warfield's insistence on the unbelievers' intellectual comprehension of the gospel):

> Absolute proof of the truth of Christ's claims is available only in personal relationship with Him; but contemporary man has every right to expect us to offer solid reasons for making such a total commitment. The apologetic task is justified not as a rational substitute for faith, but as a ground for faith; not as a replacement for the Spirit's working, but as a means by which the objective truth

2. Marvin Vincent, *Word Studies in the New Testament*, 4:510.
3. B. B. Warfield, introduction to *Apologetics*, by F. R. Beattie, 1:25.

of God's Word can be made clear so that men will heed it as the vehicle of the Spirit who convicts the world through its message.[4]

That is *fides* (a believing *that*) rather than *fiducia* (a believing *in*). Spirit-induced biblical faith is seen here, then, as *both* belief (*fides*) and trust (*fiducia*), *both* objective *and* subjective, *both* rationally propositional *and* existentially personal. Carl F. H. Henry wrote in *Christianity Today* about the gospel ministry and preaching in this decade that "the gospel is a message to be communicated and understood before it can be accepted or rejected."[5]

The apologist-preacher's task, therefore, is to provide the cognitive content by which the unbeliever can intellectually comprehend the claims of the gospel. This is the first step in the Spirit's preliminary work of conviction that prayerfully will bring about the Holy Spirit's crowning work of "unbending" the will and enabling the new creation in Christ to exercise full and complete personal trust in Jesus as Lord. The purest evidentialist who believes evidence piled on evidence will convert the soul is in error. The Kuyper-like Calvinist who believes man cannot comprehend anything of the gospel prior to regeneration is either wrong, or we stop preaching. There is a difference between intellectual comprehension and spiritual understanding that is personal and life-changing. "The man without the Spirit does not accept the things that come from the Spirit of God, for they are foolishness to him, and he cannot understand them because they are spiritually discerned" (1 Cor. 2:14; note also the sequence for both unbelief and belief in Acts 28:24-27).

Spiritual discernment comes subsequent to the regeneration that changes our autonomous disposition to one of trusting obedience in our Creator and Savior. In this sense, regeneration precedes the full-fledged faith of belief/trust (*fides/fiducia*), but it does not precede *fides* or credence alone. Pascal put this well when he wrote of those who did not have saving faith, "We can give it only by reasoning, waiting for God to give them spiritual

---

4. John Warwick Montgomery, *Faith Founded on Fact*, p. 40.
5. Carl F. H. Henry, "An Agenda for the 1980's," *Christianity Today* 24 (4 January 1980): 27.

insight; without which faith is only human, and useless for salvation" (*Pensees* No. 282). Faith, as Francis Schaeffer says, is simply "raising empty hands in accepting the gift" of God's grace.[6] That raising of our hands is not works but merely our acceptance of God's provision. On the basis of a rational comprehension and the Holy Spirit's conviction, one desires "to turn" or be converted, but cannot until God brings about a new birth with a new orientation toward holiness, trusting obedience, and freedom from sinful autonomy and egotistic selfishness. This divine-human cooperative, if we may call it such, was distinctively stated by Augustus H. Strong:

> The Scriptures recognize the voluntary activity of the human soul in the change as distinctively as they recognize the causative agency of God. While God turns men to himself (Ps. 85:4; Song. 1:4; Jer. 31:18; Lam. 5:21), men are exhorted to turn themselves to God (Prov. 1:23; Is. 31:6; 59:20; Ez. 14:6; 18:32; 33:9, 11; Joel 2:12-14). While God is represented as the author of the new heart and the new spirit (Ps. 51:10; Ez. 11:19; 36:26), men are commanded to make for themselves a new heart and a new spirit (Ez. 18:31; 2 Cor. 7:1; cf. Phil. 2:12, 13; Eph. 5:14). This twofold method of representation can be explained only when we remember that man's powers may be interpenetrated and quickened by the divine, not only without destroying man's freedom, but with the result of making man for the first time truly free. Since the relation between the divine and the human activity is not one of chronological succession, man is never to wait for God's working. If he is ever regenerated, it must be in and through a movement of his own will, in which he turns to God as unconstrainedly and with as little consciousness of God's operation upon him, as if no such operation of God were involved in the change. And in preaching, we are to press upon men the claims of God and their duty of immediate submission to Christ, with the certainty that they who do so submit will subsequently recognize this new and holy activity of their own wills as due to a working within them of divine power.[7]

The final facet of a Both/And apologetic is the new birth lifestyle that reinforces one's testimony of being "born again." Like

---

6. Francis Schaeffer, *Death in the City*, p. 87.
7. Augustus H. Strong, *Systematic Theology*, pp. 829-30.

revelation, new creation must be *both* word *and* event. Verbal testimony without a Christian life will force the onlooking unbeliever to conclude that Christianity is not true, though it is the "supposed" Christian that is lying either by his testimony or his life. A rather distinctive Christian life-style need not necessarily be attributed to Jesus Christ by the God-denying and autonomous individual but may perhaps be interpreted simply as a "do-gooder." Life and word must go hand-in-hand.

Jesus realized the difficulty of this in the midst of Satan's domain and therefore particularly prayed for His disciples in John 17 because "they are still in the world" (v. 11). Though His disciples had been taken "out of the world" (v. 6) and were very distinct from the world as evidenced by Christ's prayer (v. 9), they nevertheless were being very definitely sent *into* the world even as Christ was sent into the same world by the Father (v. 18). However, they went as new creatures in Christ, as His ambassadors, with *the* message of reconciliation. They went with the Word of truth (see v. 17) and were thereby set apart from the world in the midst of the world. That is, they were *in* the world but not *of* the world. Theirs was a new Master, the Lord of Glory rather than the prince of the power of the air, the God of truth rather than the father of lies. Therefore, the world "hated" them as the possessors of God's truth, and Jesus prayed that they may be protected "from the evil one" (v. 15). But, as the possessor of God's truth through His Word, *they themselves were to be God's truth*—His contemporary Christian evidences—as the *truth possessed them*. As this happened, they became, as Jesus prayed (vv. 21, 23), *one*! That is, not simply a oneness of community but a *oneness of righteous personality*.

Truth is always unity of word and deed, of testimony and life-style. Man was created righteous, and the goal of justification by faith (faith-righteousness) is that we might eventually be in fact what we are declared to be in Christ—righteous! That is not, as many have erroneously thought, a works-righteousness but the assured results of a faith-righteousness that sets apart or "sanctifies" (v. 17) by means of God's Word of truth. Righteous personhood will yet be provided to those who will be "conformed to the likeness" of the Second Adam (Rom. 5:12-21; 8:29). Though this process is being carried out, Christ prayed that our verbal testimony and our spiritual actuality might be one (John 17:21, 23). That is, if there is no spiritual facade, but only genuine Christlikeness permeating our restored and now righteous personhood, then our "outer reality" and our "inner reality" will be one, much like the visible Christ was absolutely one with the invisible Father in essence and will. This is irrefutable Christian evidence. No unbeliever can dispute, even if he does not believe, my testimony of why "I am as I am" because of the substitutionary and victorious work of Christ *for* me and the creative and cleansing work of the Holy Spirit *in* me. Christ therefore prayed that each believer "may be one, Father, just as you are in me and I am in you. May they also be in us *so that the world may believe that you have sent me*"(17:21, italics added). Our lives, like Christ's miracles, are to provoke the possibility of belief. In verse 23, Jesus repeated this prayer by asking that they may "be brought to complete unity to *let the world know that you sent me* and have loved them even as you have loved me" (italics added).

Three additional aspects concerning the Christian life-style should be noted: first, Christ's prayer was not limited in scope to first-century disciples. His prayer was for every Christian throughout the history of the church, for Christ prayed "for those who will believe in me through their message" (v. 20). Thus whether it was the first-century oral proclamation of the apostles, or whether the majority of saints have come to new life through their written proclamation in the New Testament, Christ prayed for an effective evidential life-style.

Second, this type of life-style was certainly evident in the first and second century. Green notes:

> The truth of their claims must have been assessed to a very large degree by the consistency of their lives with what they professed. That is why the emphasis on the link between mission and holiness of life is given such prominence both in the New Testament and the second century literature . . . . This connection between belief and behaviour runs right through Christian literature. The two cannot be separated without disastrous results, among them the end of effective evangelism. That is why the New Testament writers are so intolerant both of doctrine and moral defections among their converts.[8]

8. Michael Green, *Evangelism in the Early Church*, pp. 178-79.

The great effect that the new *life* has on the new *life-style* can clearly be seen in the changes that took place in the life of the man who would soon be called the apostle Paul:

> This encounter with Christ touched Paul at every level of his being. *His mind* was informed and illuminated. Jesus was not, as he had thought, accursed, but was the Lord. *His conscience* was reached: he faced up to the fact that he had been kicking against the pricks. *His emotions* were stirred as he saw the implications of his rebellion against Christ. But this was a mere incidental on the way to his will, Christ's real goal. *His will* was bent in trusting surrender to Jesus who had called him, and who was henceforth to be Lord of his life. And in consequence *his life* was transformed: in direction, immediately, and in achievement as time went on.[9]

Third, and last, man innately desires to be genuine. Various psychoses reveal the extremes of a split personality, but all men outside of the possibility of genuine oneness in Christ have the *inclination* to disunity. This is not surprising since they belong to the father of lies, and thus verbal testimony will not be one with actual reality. Some may be outwardly very wicked but with a hope to turn over a new leaf, though they often would not admit this to anyone, perhaps not even themselves; much more frequently others may appear to be morally good but with evil imaginations (see Matt. 5:28). Jesus called the Pharisees and other hypocrites "whitewashed tombs, which look beautiful on the outside but on the inside are full of dead men's bones and everything unclean" (Matt. 23:27). That is why believers, as the exhibitors of truth and the essential oneness of the outer and inner man, are hated by the world. Jesus therefore must pray for their protection from the evil one who yearns to destroy the actualization of such personal oneness in and through Christ (John 17:14-15). Questions as to the genuineness and source of our spiritual and personal oneness should open many doors to witness that the Christ has been sent. Though Jesus prayed that both our outer man and inner man may be one and thus keep us from hyprocrisy, He also realized that the options are only either/or—oneness or duality. If we Christians live a life of duality where our word and deed are not one, can we expect that the

9. Ibid., p. 161.

unbeliever will care whether the Christ has come or not? Is there no existential difference between those who believe He has come and those who do not believe in Jesus, the Christ?

One task remains to be done. The Both/And apologist must be able to answer the same seven questions that were put to the apologists of chapter 5. Before we do that, however, we need a diagram to picture at one glance what it is the Both/And apologist is attempting to do, and why it is inherently uncomfortable. It will always seem safer and more consistent to emphasize one or the other of the ontological, epistemological, and theological concerns rather than attempting to balance them dialectically. The attempt to be both an a priorist and an a posteriorist is inherently uncomfortable to a purist of either methodology. But it must be done, regardless of inconsistencies as perceived by either school of thought. Physical reality demands both of the scientist, and the ontological structure demands such an epistemology whether one is a Christian apologist or not. Christian revelation that is both historic event and the spoken Word of God demands the same of the Christian theologian-apologist. The Both/And apologist, however, rejects the extremes of the purists of either school. Inductive arguments of natural theology really assume what they wish to prove, as their proof leaves much to be desired either formally or materially, while the rigors of the deductive ontological argument for God's logical necessity seemingly commits the existential fallacy. The apparently fideistic orientation of some a priori presuppositionalists is as vehemently rejected as are the rationalistic tendencies of some a posteriori evidentialists. Thus our ontological, epistemological, and theological Both/And (nonexhaustive) diagram looks like this:

ONTOLOGICAL

BEING PER SE

BOTH	AND
GOD	CREATION
INFINITE	FINITE
PERMANENCE	CHANGE
UNITY	PLURALITY
ABSOLUTENESS	RELATIVITY
PURPOSE	SPONTANEITY
NECESSARY	CONTINGENT
GRACE	NATURE

BEING OF MAN

BOTH	AND
SPIRIT	BODY
GREATLY DIGNIFIED	WRETCHEDLY DEPRAVED
IDEALLY THEONOMOUS	ACTUALLY AUTONOMOUS
INHERENTLY DEPENDENT	SINFULLY INDEPENDENT
LOVING	CRUEL
CREATIVE	DESTRUCTIVE

EPISTEMOLOGICAL

BOTH	AND
A PRIORI	A POSTERIORI
DEDUCTIVE	INDUCTIVE
RATIONAL	EMPIRICAL
UNIVERSAL	PARTICULAR
CERTAINTY	PROBABILITY
INTERNAL RELATIONS	EXTERNAL RELATIONS
CONSISTENCY	COHERENCE
OBJECTIVE	SUBJECTIVE
LOGIC	INTUITION
KNOWLEDGE	MYSTERY

THEOLOGICAL

BOTH		AND
THREE	God	ONE
TRANSCENDENT	God	IMMANENT
INWARD	General Revelation	OUTWARD
EVENT	Special Revelation	WORD
DIVINE	Christ	HUMAN
HISTORIC	Christ	CONTEMPORANEOUS
HOLY SPIRIT	Inspiration	MAN
SOVEREIGNTY	Ethics	FREEDOM
PROVISION	Salvation	RESPONSE
BELIEF	Faith	TRUST
ALREADY	Last Things	NOT YET

Some of those dialectical contrasts may be best understood as antinomies since they seem irreconcilable although they are undeniable. An antinomy is "an observed relation between two statements of fact" which is "forced upon us by the facts themselves.... We do not invent [them], and we cannot explain [them]. Nor is there any way to get rid of [them], save by falsifying the very facts that led us to [them]."[10] Packer illustrates this from the realm of modern physics where "it is not apparent

10. J. I. Packer, *Evangelism and the Sovereignty of God*, p. 21.

how light can be both waves and particles, but the evidence is there, and so neither view can be ruled out in favour of the other. Neither, however, can be reduced to the other or explained in terms of the other; the two seemingly incompatible positions must be held together, and both must be treated as true."[11]

Packer goes on to apply this to one of our own antinomies, God's sovereignty and human responsibility. It is equally applicable to many, if not all, of the ontological foundations, epistomological determinations, and biblical theological necessities of *Both/And: A Balanced Apologetic*.

To conclude, that balanced apologetic can be summarized with the help of our seven questions.

1. What is the role of philosophy in Christian theology and apologetics?

   Philosophy and theology are interdependent for the Christian thinker. Philosophy and theology are concentric circles as the former attempts to work out in detail and systematize a Christian world view based on and within the parameters of divine revelation and theological doctrine. However, from the perspective of intellectual problems and cultural implications of the Christian faith, philosophy functions differently than theology, albeit never independent of God and His revelation. In regard to theological prolegomena, philosophy is the handmaiden of theology in dealing with the ontological and epistemological assumptions of the theologian, but it is never capable of constructing a viable natural theology apart from special revelation.

2. How are reason and faith related?

   These are neither identical nor opposites. Faith as belief and trust is both objective and subjective. As belief, faith is rational and dependent on reason for a logical presentation of the evidence. Like the disciples who were first told by the women of the resurrection, we cannot believe if what we are to believe seems "like nonsense" (Luke 24:11). And like John, we do need to "see" rationally if we are to believe (John 20:8). Spiritual understanding is more than rational comprehension, however, and thus with Blaise Pascal we must wait

---

11. Ibid., p. 19.

for God, by means of the Holy Spirit, to give "spiritual insight, without which faith is only human, and useless for salvation" (*Pensees* No. 282).

3. Of what significance is the doctrine of sin for Christian apologetics?

Man is totally depraved and can do nothing on his own to either know God or gain God's favor. Although total depravity does not mean man is no longer man made in God's image, it does mean that his God-given abilities are perverted and unconsciously and consciously used wrongly to maintain what man perceives to be his own independence and divinity. Thus the evidence of God's reality and His redemptive activity and care for man is plainly visible in both creation and supernatural revelation, but man's willful refusal to accept God's gracious provision is a product of both his sin nature and his actual sinfulness.

4. Do the theistic proofs have worth for convincing the unbeliever?

Because of the persuasiveness of natural revelation, particularly in man's intuitive knowledge of God through his own ontological makeup, there is a built-in receptivity to the claims of natural theology. However, the arguments are not only logically invalid, the Christian apologist must disclaim God's special revelation in order to claim the Thomistic path of natural theology. Though for some minds it may raise healthy questions by which the Christian apologist may gain entrance, it more frequently is evidence of man's controlling God at the end of a series of arguments and thus *God* is more an abstraction of irreligion than the personal, loving, God of the Bible.

5. To what extent may a believer and unbeliever form a shared point of contact on common ground?

There is common ontological ground on three fronts: creation, God's image in man, and historical revelation. Because believer and unbeliever alike live in God's universe and are made in His image, the ultimate structure of being is identical. The Christian apologist must appeal to this inherent "feel" for the transcendent and personal that can only be met and fulfilled by the living, personal, triune God. Similarly, believer and unbeliever have the same history, including the culmination of God's special revelation—the incarnate and resurrected Jesus of Nazareth, the Christ. *However*, man's willful and autonomous sinfulness will not permit him to see and interpret these realities and facts in the only possible way they can be truly interpreted. Thus there is no epistemological common ground until an individual is enabled by the Holy Spirit to accept revelation as revelation. Until then, common ground between the believer and unbeliever may be implicit given creation and history, but it is never explicit.

6. Are historical Christian evidences important, or even possible, as evidence for the unbeliever?

They must be or what Jesus claims concerning His works (John 10:37-38), and what John writes (John 20:30-31) cannot be correct! This is the historical reality that cannot be reasonably denied. This is the means by which the Holy Spirit convicts of sin, righteousness, and judgment (John 16:8-11). But, at the same time, eyes covered with scales (Acts 9:18) and blinded by Satan (2 Cor. 4:4) will not correctly discern these facts without the indispensable work of the Holy Spirit. This does not permit us to omit such evidences, because "the Holy Spirit does not work a blind . . . ungrounded faith in the heart."[12]

7. What degree of certainty is there in the truthfulness of Christianity?

All historical evidence is only probable, and that is all we can ask of Christianity from the standpoint of objective and rational evidence. Regardless of the high degree of probability that is indicated, inductive, historical evidence is not susceptible to deductive proof. But neither is any other reality, and if it were, there would be no need of trust in the person of God beyond the evidence. This does not mean the believer is left with *only* probability. There is absolute personal *subjective* certitude by means of the witness of the Holy Spirit that enables us to see scriptural revelation as God's special revelation, and through indwelling the believer "the Spirit himself testifies with our spirit that we are God's children"

12. Warfield, 1:25.

(Rom. 8:16). Thus the heart (man's very being) does have "reasons, which reason does not know" (*Pensees* No. 277).

GLOSSARY

Absolute—That which is unconditioned, uncaused, and not limited by anything outside of itself.

Agnosticism—The theory that it is impossible to obtain knowledge about anything, especially God.

Analogy—The resemblance in some particulars of things otherwise unlike; a mode of speaking about God first advocated by Aquinas that is supposedly midway between equivocal and univocal use of language; basis of the a posteriori theistic arguments.

Analysis—The separation of a whole into its component parts; a particular form of philosophical reasoning; deductive; logically necessary. Antonym: *Synthesis*.

Animism—The primitive belief that all living things or natural objects are inhabited by a spirit.

Apologetics—The establishment of the truthfulness of a world view; Christian apologetics attempts to enable believers to understand the implications of their faith to a fuller extent, philosophically and theologically construct the biblical framework of the Christian world-and-life view, and point out the inconsistencies and inadequacies of alternative perspectives.

A posteriori—A method of thinking that goes from particulars to universals; a posteriori knowledge is based on the evidence of sense experience; such knowledge is only probable. Synonym: *Inductive*; antonym: *A priori*.

A priori—A method of thinking that goes from universals to particulars; a priori knowledge is based on the innate capacities and knowledge of the human mind, logic, the image of God in man, and general and (from an interpretive standpoint) special revelation; such knowledge is necessary and universal and thus certainly true. Synonym: *Deductive*; antonym: *A posteriori*.

Axiom—A basic principle that cannot be deduced from other principles, but is the starting point from which other statements are deduced.

Behaviorism—A psychological theory that equates consciousness and identity of an organism with its behavior; ultimately naturalistic.

Being—An entity or object that exists or has existence; Christianity distinguishes between conditioned and created being and unconditioned and eternal Being.

Cartesian—The philosophical emphasis of Descartes (1596-1650).

Category—A fundamental principle that is implied or presupposed for all experience, e.g., the category of *space* must be assumed before one can think of material objects.

Cause—In science, the antecedent of a given event; usually called empirical. In philosophy, the ultimate power that produces the *being* of anything; such cause is, therefore, metaphysical.

Coherence—An epistemological view that believes that that which is systematic and internally consistent as well as externally adequate to the facts is the truth.

Concept—A universal object or category of the mind; independent of sensation.

Cosmological argument—An argument that is empirical because it is based on observation of nature, but attempts to derive some universal generalizations (such as *God exists*).

Deduction—The type of argument or inference whereby the conclusion is claimed to *necessarily* follow from the premise.

Deism—The theory that God is only transcendent and not immanent in His creation.

Determinism—The theory that the universe is so constructed that everything occurs as the inevitable consequence of antecedent causes.

Dialectic—(1)The process of considering pros and cons in an effort to arrive at a decision as to what is true or is to be done (Plato). (2)The view that the history of the world is the result of the tendency of an idea to develop into another more complete idea that incorporates both the partial truth of the original idea and the partial truth contained in the denial of the original idea (Hegel, Marx).

Dualism—The view that there exist two ultimate principles neither of which can be reduced or explained in terms of the other. In metaphysics, the view that reality is made up of two opposing forces such as body and spirit. In epistemology, dualism refers to the mental idea and the object known.

Empiricism—The epistemological theory that contends that the only source of knowledge is experience; experience is usually limited to sensation.

Epistemology—The branch of philosophy that seeks to discover the sources and limits of human knowledge; "how we know that we know."

Equivocal—Using the same word with two different meanings in the same argument or presentation.

Essence—That which makes an object what it is in itself; the nature rather than the existence of anything.

Ethics—The branch of philosophy and religion that attempts to set or discover norms by which people ought to live.

Existence—The state of actual being instead of simply possible being; that which can have a definite place in space and time.

Existential fallacy—The mistaken logical assumption that there is at least one particular member of a universal category; for example, the actual existence of a necessary being, or the ontological argument.

Existentialism—The belief that the universe is basically irrational and that man is responsible for inserting meaning into his individual existence. Philosophical expressions are usually atheistic and pessimistic. Theological existentialists stress man's absolute dependence on God and the subjective and noncognitive facets of religious experience.

Faith—Belief founded on the basis of rational evidence; trust and dependence in another.

Fallacy—An error in reasoning that makes it impossible to establish the conclusion in question on the given premise; a logical mistake that makes deductive arguments invalid.

Fideism—The exclusive reliance upon irrational faith (belief without evidence) with a consequent disparagement of rational assessment of philosophical and religious truth (Kierkegaard); in another sense, all perspectives are fideistic as they must start somewhere, that is, presuppositions (Augustine, Pascal).

God—This is traditionally defined as the supreme and ultimate Being who is the ground and cause of all existence. Contemporary philosophy often uses the term to mean simply the religious object, be it defined as personal, impersonal, or imaginative.

Humanism—The world view that conceives of humanity as the supreme factor in reality.

Idea—(1)A universal or eternally real object (Plato). (2)A synonym for God or the Absolute (Hegel). (3)In psychology, a perception in consciousness of an object.

Idealism—The theory that reality is of the nature of mind or consciousness. There are many types, but objective (or one mind, usually pantheistic) idealism and subjective (many minds, God being the supreme one) idealism are its primary manifestations in the history of thought.

Immanent—That which dwells in or is present with. Example: an immanent God is present in the world.

Indeterminism—The theory that the universe is constituted in such a way that some events are not the inevitable consequence of antecedent events.

Induction—The process of arriving at generalizations (universals) by an observation of facts (particulars).

Inference—A proposition that follows logically from other statements; an implication.

Infinite—That which is without limit; unending.

Innate—That which is inborn; arising from the mind rather than from experience.

Intuition—An act whereby the mind discerns nonempirical qualities and groups a priori truths; a direct or immediate perception.

Judgment—The activity of the mind in describing or interpreting reality.

Knowledge—A statement that can be affirmed both by empirical facts and valid logic.

Logic—A study of the principles by which one may distinguish correct from incorrect reasoning.

Materialism—The metaphysical theory that views reality as only matter and its determinations, cf. *Naturalism.*

Metaphysics—The study of the nature and structure of being (reality). Synonym: *Ontology.*

Monism—The theory that one principle or nature will explain the plurality in the world. Primary monisms are idealism and materialism.

Mysticism—The belief that direct knowledge of God may be obtained by the human spirit separate from both empirical experience and propositional revelation; such knowledge is incommunicable.

Naturalism—The theory that physical nature, however defined, is a sufficient explanation of everything. Thus, the whole of reality consists of objects and events occurring in space and time and thus all interpretation is historically continuous.

Naturalistic fallacy—The mistake of defining the "good" or "ought" in terms of natural qualities; the attempt to derive normative statements from probable ones; deriving the "ought" from the "is."

Natural law—A fundamental principle of right or justice that human reason can supposedly discern, usually by intuition.

Natural theology—The attempt to know (prove) God by studying nature and relying on human reason; a posteriori and empirical in methodology.

Necessary—In logic, any statement whose denial would involve a contradiction. In ontology, the quality of a being that has the cause of its existence within itself.

Neo-orthodox—A twentieth-century theological movement that denies the supernatural quality of the Bible because God cannot communicate verbally with man.

Nihilism—Literally "nothing"; a view that nothing is worth living for and thus human existence is meaningless.

Nominalism—The view that universals exist only in language and are thus only *names* and not *realities*.

Noumena—The object as it is in itself, independent of thought (Kant).

Objective—That which relates to objects in reality that are supposedly the same for all experiences.

Omnipotence—Having infinite power.

Omniscience—Having infinite knowledge.

Ontological argument—The classic argument that attempts to prove God by demonstrating that the denial of the proposition "God exists" is self-contradictory. The argument that the essence of God demands His existence, i.e., God exists by definition; originated by Anselm though overtones of such in Augustine; a priori.

Ontology—The study of the structure of being; metaphysics.

Panentheism—The teaching that everything exists in God but God is greater than the totality of reality; usually associated with process theology (Whitehead).

Panpsychism—The view all reality consists of mind (spirit) of various levels of consciousness (Leibniz, Hegel).

Pantheism—The theory that identifies the totality of the universe with God.

Paradox—An apparently self-contradictory assertion that is neverthe-less made on the ground that to eliminate the apparent contradic-tion would involve denying some truth.

Percept—That which is "before the mind" through perception; sense data.

Perception—The process of understanding or viewing the world through the senses.

Phenomenon—The object as it appears to the senses.

Phenomenalism—The view that the reality of a material object con-sists only in its being perceived by some perceiver.

Philosophy of religion—That which seeks to explain the universality and necessity of religious experience, the validity of religious knowledge, and the problem of evil.

Pluralism—The idea that reality is not reducible to one or two ultimate substances; contrasts with dualism and monism.

Positivism—The idea that philosophy is science; all knowledge is thus empirical; no metaphysical knowledge is possible.

Pragmatism—The idea that truth is determined by the practical conse-quences of ideas; Deweyism.

Presupposition—Initial assumption(s) upon which all thought is based; difficult to become aware of or prove because they stand prior to proof and become the criteria of possibility, e.g., theistic or nontheistic world view.

Proposition—That which is affirmed or denied by a declarative sen-tence. Propositions have the quality of being either true or false.

Propositional revelation—Scripture is the written Word of God and thus has conceptual form and cognitive content that can be stated in propositions that are either true or false.

Rationalism—The theory that reason is the source of knowledge inde-pendent of sense perceptions; a priori.

Realism—That which refers epistemologically to the fact that the object known is independent of the knowing mind. Metaphysically it denotes that universals exist external to our minds as opposed to nominalism; also, any belief that reality is extramental.

Reality—Everything that is; contrasted with appearance.

Reason—(1)The final or ultimate cause as opposed to antecedent or secondary causes; (2) the capacity to know things without reliance on sense experience; (3) ability to make inferences and discover explanations.

Relativism—The view that one's understanding is always limited to one's situation; particularly applicable to ethics.

Revelation—(1)General revelation is given to man by nature and one's selfhood through creation. It demonstrates God's existence and holy majesty. (2) Special revelation is given to man as sinner through God's intervention in history. It uncovers His person and will and reveals redemptive acts for man's salvation, culminating in the incarnation of Jesus Christ.

Scientism—The elevation of science to the position of being the sole source of knowledge on any subject; positivism.

Scholasticism—The name given to medieval philosophy and theology.

Self-evident—The quality of a proposition that can be seen to be true merely by considering the proposition itself, and thus need not be proved either by deduction or induction; tautology.

Sense data—The immediate, uninterpreted objects of sense experience.

Skepticism—The view that something cannot be known; may be total, or restricted to ethics, metaphysics, religion, etc.

Solipsism—The belief that "myself alone" exists. All objects and persons around me are *only* my ideas. Probably no philosopher ever held to such a view, but many have been told that it is the logical conclusion of their philosophy.

Subjective—This is used to denote what exists only in consciousness but is not true of objects beyond consciousness.

Substance—The primary nature of the real; that which possesses attributes, properties, qualities, etc.; essence.

Summum bonum—Literally "highest good"; that which is most worthy of being sought for its own sake; in Christianity, God.

Supernatural—That which is beyond and above the natural order of the universe; belief that God is outside the universe and in control of it.

Syllogism—The logical form that has two premises in which the conclusion necessarily follows if valid; deduction.

Synthesis—The combination of parts or elements so as to form a whole; particular form of philosophical reasoning; inductive; probability. Antonym: *Analysis*.

System—A comprehensive set of coherent and interdependent propositions by which one attempts to understand reality; may be either philosophical or theological, or both.

Tautology—An analytic proposition that is necessarily true; self-evident; a formal statement containing no information.

Teleological—Pertaining to ends, goals, purposes; the view that reality is being guided by an Ultimate for definite purposes.

Teleological argument—The argument that the coordination of means/ends in natural phenomena suggests an intelligent designer; analogical and empirical methodology; one of the classic a posteriori "proofs" of God.

Theism—The belief in a personal God that is other (transcendent) than all created beings but nevertheless is in and with (immanent) all creation; world view that reality can only be understood if a Supreme Being is presupposed.

Theodicy—An attempt to show that the occurrence of evil in the world is consistent with belief in a God who is perfect in knowledge, power, and goodness.

Theology—The study of God within a given religion; in Christianity, the systematization of cognitive propositions that are only known through God's self-revelation; the sum of biblical teaching.

Transcendent—(1)Literally "other than," " beyond," "outside of"; example—a transcendent God is other than the world; (2) beyond the categories of human experience (Kant); (3) beyond the world of space and time. Antonymn: *Immanence*.

Truth—This is variously defined according to one's world view: generally, that which corresponds with reality as it is; for theism, that which corresponds to the mind of God.

Universal—That which is common to all members of a class.

Univocal—Having the same basic meaning in all instances of the use of a word. Antonym: *Equivocal*.

Valid—In logic, the term that indicates that the conclusion is in keeping with the premises; a conclusion may be formally valid but not materially true.

Value—That which is intrinsically worthy rather than simply desired or preferred.

Verifiability—Testability; for example, a theory is verifiable if it is possible to set up experiments the results of which prove the theory.

Vitalism—The view that some creative principle is operating within nature.

Via negativa—A mode of speaking of God wherein one attempts to say not what God is but what He is *not*. The practice was popular in medieval times.

Voluntarism—The metaphysical theory that identifies cosmic energy with will (Schopenhauer).

Weltanschauung—World view; the system of belief held by each man that enables him to live and act in the world and that explains how the various parts of the universe fit together.

BIBLIOGRAPHY

BOOKS

Albright, William F. *From the Stone Age to Christianity.* 2d ed. New York: Anchor Books, 1957.

Anselm. *Proslogium, in Medieval Philosophy.* Edited by Herman Shapiro. New York: Random House, 1964.

Aquinas, Thomas. *Summa Contra Gentiles,* in *Basic Writings of Saint Thomas Aquinas.* Edited by Anton Pegis. New York: Random House, 1945.

_____. *Summa Theologica,* in *Great Books of the Western World.* Vols. 28-29. Edited by Robert Maynard Hutchins. Chicago: Encyclopedia Britannica, 1952.

Athenagoras. *A Plea Regarding Christians,* in *Early Christian Fathers.* Edited and translated by Cyril C. Richardson. Philadelphia: Westminster, 1953.

Augustine. *City of God.* Translated by Marcus Dods. New York: Modern Library, 1950.

_____. *Confessions.* Trans. J. G. Pilkington. New York: Liveright Publishing, 1943.

_____. *Enchiridion.* Edited by Henry Paolucci. Chicago: Henry Regnery, 1961.

_____. *Free Choice of the Will.* Translated by Anna S. Benjamin and L. H. Hackstaff. New York: Bobbs-Merrill, 1964.

_____. *On the Predestination of the Saints,* in *Basic Writings of Saint Augustine.* Edited by Whitney J. Oates. Grand Rapids: Baker, 1980.

Ayer, Alfred J. *Language, Truth and Logic.* New York: Dover, 1952.

Bancroft, Emery. *Christian Theology.* Edited by Ronald B. Mayers. Grand Rapids: Zondervan, 1976.

Barnes, Harry Elmer. *A History of Historical Writing.* 2d rev. ed. New York: Dover, 1963.

Blackstone, W. *The Problem of Religious Knowledge.* Englewood Cliffs, N. J.: Prentice-Hall, 1963.

Blamires, Harry. *The Christian Mind.* Ann Arbor, Mich.: Servant, 1978.

_____. *The Secular Heresy.* Ann Arbor, Mich.: Servant, 1980.

Bonhoeffer, Dietrich. *Letters and Papers from Prison.* Enl. ed. Edited by Eberhard Bethge. New York: Macmillan, 1971.

Bray, John S. *Theodore Beza's Doctrine of Predestination.* Nieuwkoop, The Netherlands: B. DeGraaf, 1975.

Brown, Colin. *Philosophy and the Christian Faith.* Downers Grove, Ill.: InterVarsity, 1969.

Bruce, F. F. *Jesus and Christian Origins Outside the New Testament.* Grand Rapids: Eerdmans, 1974.

————. *The Defense of the Gospel in the New Testament.* Rev. ed. Grand Rapids: Eerdmans, 1977.

Buber, Martin. *I and Thou.* Translated by Walter Kaufman. New York: Scribner's, 1970.

Cairns, David. *The Image of God in Man.* London: SCM, 1953.

Calvin, John. *Institutes of the Christian Religion.* 2 vols. Translated by Henry Beveridge. Grand Rapids: Eerdmans, 1964.

————. *Calvin's Commentaries, The Penteteuch.* Grand Rapids: AP&A n.d.

————. *Calvin's Commentaries, Joshua and the Psalms.* Grand Rapids: AP&A, n.d.

————. *Calvin's Commentaries, Isaiah.* Grand Rapids: AP&A, n.d.

————. *Hebrews and the First and Second Epistle of St. Peter.* Translated by William B. Johnson. Grand Rapids: Eerdmans, 1963.

Carnell, Edward J. *An Introduction to Christian Apologetics.* Grand Rapids: Eerdmans, 1950.

————. *A Philosophy of the Christian Religion.* Grand Rapids: Eerdmans, 1952.

Charlesworth, M. J. *Philosophy of Religion: The Historic Approaches.* New York: Herder and Herder, 1972.

Clark, Gordon. *A Christian View of Men and Things.* Grand Rapids: Eerdmans, 1952.

————. *Religion, Reason and Revelation.* Philadelphia: Presbyterian and Reformed, 1961.

————. *Historiography: Secular and Religious.* Grand Rapids: Baker, 1971.

Corduan, Winfried. *Handmaid to Theology.* Grand Rapids: Baker, 1981.

Cullmann, Oscar. *Christ and Time.* Translated by Floyd V. Filson. Philadelphia: Westminster, 1964.

Dewey, John. *Reconstruction in Philosophy.* Boston: Beacon Press, 1948.

Diamond, Malcolm. *Contemporary Philosophy and Religious Thought.* New York: McGraw-Hill, 1974.

Dooyeweerd, Herman. *New Critique of Theoretical Thought.* Translated by David H. Freeman, et. al. Philadelphia: Presbyterian and Reformed, 1953.

_____. *In The Twilight of Western Thought.* Philadelphia: Presbyterian and Reformed, 1960.

Dulles, Avery. *A History of Apologetics.* New York: Corpus Books, 1971.

Eliade, Mircea. *The Sacred and the Profane.* New York: Harcourt Brace Jovanovich, 1959.

Farrar, Austin. *Finite and Infinite.* Westminster: Dacre, 1943.

Ferre, Frederick. *Language, Logic and God.* New York: Harper & Row, 1969.

Feuerbach, Ludwig. *The Essence of Christianity.* Translated by George Eliot. New York: Harper Torchbooks, 1957.

Finegan, Jack. *Light from the Ancient Past.* Princeton, N. J.: Princeton U. Press, 1946.

Flew, Antony, and MacIntyre, Alasdair. *New Essays in Philosophical Theology.* New York: Macmillan, 1964.

Garstang, John. *Joshua Judges.* London: Constable, 1931.

Geehan, E. R., ed. *Jerusalem and Athens.* Nutley, N. J. Presbyterian and Reformed, 1977.

Geisler, Norman. *Philosophy of Religion.* Grand Rapids: Zondervan, 1974.

_____. *Christian Apologetics.* Grand Rapids: Baker, 1976.

Gerstner, John. *Reasons for Faith.* New York: Harper & Row, 1960.

Gilkey, Langdon. *Naming the Whirlwind.* New York: Bobbs-Merrill, 1969.

Gill, Jerry H. *The Possibility of Religious Knowledge.* Grand Rapids: Eerdmans, 1971.

_____. *On Knowing God.* Philadelphia: Westminster, 1981.

Gilson, Etienne. *Elements of a Christian Philosophy.* Garden City, N. Y.: Doubleday, 1960.

Gottschalk, Louis. *Understanding History.* New York: Alfred A. Knopf, 1963.

Gray, Wood. *Historian's Handbook.* Boston: Houghton Mifflin, 1956.

Green, Michael. *Evangelism in the Early Church.* Grand Rapids: Eerdmans, 1970.

Hackett, Stuart. *The Resurrection of Theism.* Chicago: Moody, 1957.

Halsey, Jim S. *For a Time Such as This.* Philadelphia: Presbyterian and Reformed, 1976.

Hamilton, Floyd. *The Basis of Christian Faith.* Rev. ed. New York: Harper & Row, 1964.

Hanna, Mark M. *Crucial Questions in Apologetics.* Grand Rapids: Baker, 1981.

Harvey, Van A. *The Historian and the Believer*. New York: Macmillan, 1965.

Heiss, Robert. *Hegel, Kierkegaard, Marx*. Translated by E. B. Garside. New York: Dell, 1975.

Henry, Carl F. H. *God, Revelation and Authority*. 6 vols. Waco, Tex.: Word, 1976-83.

Hick, John. *Arguments for the Existence of God*. New York: Seabury, 1971.

Hick, John H., and McGill, Arthur C., eds. *The Many-Faced Argument*. New York: Macmillan, 1967.

Hodge, Charles. *Systematic Theology*. 3 vols. Grand Rapids: Eerdmans, 1981.

Hollander, Lee, ed. *Selections from the Writings of Kierkegaard*. New York: Anchor Books, 1960.

Holmes, Arthur. *Christian Philosophy in the Twentieth Century*. Nutley, N. J.: Craig Press, 1969.

————. *Faith Seeks Understanding*. Grand Rapids: Eerdmans, 1971.

————. *All Truth Is God's Truth*. Grand Rapids: Eerdmans, 1977.

Hooykaas, R. *Religion and the Rise of Modern Science*. Grand Rapids: Eerdmans, 1972.

Hume, David. *Dialogues Concerning Natural Religion*, in *The Empiricists*. Garden City, New York: Doubleday & Company, n.d.

Ignatius. *Letters of Ignatius: Ephesians, Magnesians, Trallians, Romans, Philadelphians, Smyrnaens, Polycarp in Early Christian Fathers*. Edited and translated by Cyril C. Richardson. Philadelphia: Westminster, 1953.

Irenaeus. *Against Heresies*, in *The Ante-Nicene Fathers*. Vol. 1. Edited by Alexander Roberts and James Donaldson. Grand Rapids: Eerdmans, 1975.

James, William. *Pragmatism*. Cleveland: World Publishing, 1955.

Kähler, Martin. *The So-Called Historical Jesus and the Historic Biblical Christ*. Translated by Carl E. Braaten. Philadelphia: Fortress, 1964.

Kalsbeek, L. *Contours of a Christian Philosophy*. Toronto: Wedge Publishing, 1975.

Kant, Immanuel. *Religion Within the Limits of Religion Alone*. Translated by Theodore M. Greene and Hoyt H. Hudson. New York: Harper Torchbooks, 1960.

Katz, Steven T., ed. *Mysticism and Philosophical Analysis*. New York: Oxford U. Press, 1978.

Keil, C. F. and F. Delitzsch. *Commentary on the Old Testament*. 10 vols. Translated by James Martin, et. al. Grand Rapids: Eerdmans, 1973 reprint.

Kelly, J. P. D. *Early Christian Doctrines*. 2d ed. New York: Harper & Row, 1960.

Kierkegaard, Sören. *Attack upon "Christendom."* Translated by Walter Lowrie. Princeton, N. J.: Princeton U. Press, 1944.

_____. *Concluding Unscientific Postscipt*. Translated by David F. Swenson and Walter Lowrie. Princeton, N. J.: Princeton U. Press, 1941.

_____. *Either/Or*. 2 vols. Translated by Walter Lowrie. New York: Anchor Books, 1959.

_____. *Fear and Trembling* and *The Sickness unto Death*. Translated by Walter Lowrie. New York: Anchor Books, 1954.

_____. *Journals and Papers*. Edited and Translated by Howard V. Hong and Edna H. Hong. Bloomington, Ind.: Indiana U. Press, 1967.

_____. *On Authority and Revelation*. Translated by Walter Lowrie. Princeton, N. J.: Princeton U. Press, 1955.

_____. *Philosophical Fragments*. Translated by David F. Swenson. Princeton, N. J.: Princeton U. Press, 1936.

Kittel, Gerhard and Friedrich, Gerhard, eds. *Theological Dictionary of the New Testament*. Translated by Geoffrey Bromiley. 10 vols. Grand Rapids: Eerdmans, 1964.

Letter to Diognetus, in *Early Christian Fathers*. Edited and translated by Cyril C. Richardson. Philadelphia: Westminster, 1953.

Lewis, C. S. *Mere Christianity*. New York: Macmillan, 1943.

_____. *Miracles*. New York: Macmillan, 1947.

_____. *Abolition of Man*. New York: Macmillan, 1961.

Lewis, Gordon R. *Testing Christianity's Truth Claims*. Chicago: Moody, 1976.

Liddell, Henry George, and Scott, Robert. *A Greek-English Lexicon*. 9th ed. Revised by Henry Stuart Jones. Oxford: Clarendon Press, 1961.

Lightfoot, J. B. *Saint Paul's Epistles to the Colossians and to Philemon*. Grand Rapids: Zondervan, 1959.

Linton, Irwin H. *A Lawyer Examines the Bible*. Grand Rapids: Baker, 1943.

Locke, John. *The Reasonableness of Christianity*. Edited by I. T. Ramsey. Stanford, Cal.: Stanford U. Press, 1958.

Machen, J. Gresham. *The Origin of Paul's Religion*. Grand Rapids: Eerdmans, 1965.

Marshall, I. Howard. *Luke: Historian and Theologian*. Grand Rapids: Zondervan, 1971.

_____. *I Believe in the Historical Jesus*. Grand Rapids: Eerdmans, 1977.

Martyr, Justin. *First Apology in Early Christian Fathers.* Edited by Cyril C. Richardson. Philadelphia: Westminster, 1953.

————. *Second Apology,* in *The Ante-Nicene Fathers.* Vol. 1. Edited by Alexander Roberts and James Donaldson. Grand Rapids: Eerdmans, 1975.

————. *Dialogue with Trypho,* in *The Ante-Nicene Fathers.* Vol. 1. Edited by Alexander Roberts and James Donaldson. Grand Rapids: Eerdmans, 1975.

Mascall, E. L. *Existence and Analogy.* New York: Longmans, Green and Co., 1949.

Matthews, Victor. *Growth in Grace.* Grand Rapids: Zondervan, 1970.

Mayers, Ronald. *Religious Ministry in a Transcendentless Culture.* Wash., D. C.: University Press of America, 1980.

McDowell, Josh. *Evidence That Demands A Verdict.* San Bernardino, Cal.: Here's Life, 1972.

Meadows, Denise. *A Short History of the Catholic Church.* New York: All Saints Press, 1960.

Mitchell, Basil. *The Justification of Religious Belief.* New York: Seabury, 1973.

Montgomery, John Warwick. *The Shape of the Past.* Ann Arbor, Mich.: Edwards Brothers, 1962.

————. *Faith Founded on Fact.* New York: Nelson, 1978.

————. *History and Christianity.* Downers Grove, Ill.: InterVarsity, 1964.

————, ed. *Christianity For The Tough-Minded.* Minneapolis: Bethany Fellowship, 1973.

Morison, Frank. *Who Moved the Stone?* Downers Grove, Ill.: InterVarsity, n.d.

Morris, Thomas. *Francis Schaeffer's Apologetics: A Critique.* Chicago: Moody, 1976.

Mourant, John A., ed. *Saint Augustine: Selected Readings and Commentaries.* University Park, Penn.: Pennsylvania State U. Press, 1964.

Murray, John. *The Epistle to the Romans.* 2 vols. London: Marshall, Morgan and Scott, 1960.

Nash, Ronald, ed. *The Philosophy of Gordon Clark.* Philadelphia: Presbyterian and Reformed, 1968.

Notaro, Thom. *Van Til and the Use of Evidence.* Phillipsburg, N. J.: Presbyterian and Reformed, 1980.

Nielsen, Kai. *Contemporary Critiques of Religion.* New York: Herder and Herder, 1971.

Oates, Whitney J. *Basic Writings of Saint Augustine.* 2 vols. Grand Rapids: Baker, 1980.

Orr, James. *The Christian View of God and the World.* Grand Rapids: Kregel, 1989.

Otto, Rudolf. *The Idea of the Holy.* Translated by John W. Harvey. New York: Oxford U. Press, 1958.

Packer, J. I. *Evangelism and the Sovereignty of God.* Downers Grove, Ill.: InterVarsity, 1961.

Parrinder, Geoffrey. *Mysticism in the World Religions.* New York: Oxford U. Press, 1976.

Pascal, Blaise. *The Thoughts of Blaise Pascal.* Edited by Brunschvicg. Garden City, N. Y.: Doubleday, n.d.

Pegis, Anton. *Basic Writings of Saint Thomas Aquinas.* 2 vols. New York: Random House, 1945.

Peirce, Charles. *Philosophical Writings of Peirce.* Edited by Justus Buchler. New York: Dover Publications, 1955.

Penelhum, Terence. *Problems of Religious Knowledge.* New York: Herder and Herder, 1971.

_____. *Religion and Rationality.* New York: Random House, 1971.

Pinnock, Clark. *Set Forth Your Case.* Chicago: Moody, 1971.

Plantinga, Alvin. *The Ontological Argument.* New York: Anchor Books, 1965.

Polycarp. *Letter to the Philippians* in *Early Christian Fathers.* Edited and translated by Cyril C. Richardson. Philadelphia: Westminster, 1953.

Prior, Kenneth F. W. *The Gospel in a Pagan Society.* Downers Grove, Ill.: InterVarsity, 1975.

Rackham, Richard Belward. *The Acts of the Apostles.* Grand Rapids: Baker, 1964.

Ramm, Bernard. *Protestant Christian Evidences.* Chicago: Moody, 1953.

_____. *Varieties of Christian Apologetics.* Grand Rapids: Baker, 1961.

_____. *The God Who Makes A Difference.* Waco, Tex.: Word, 1972.

Ramsey, Ian. *Religious Language.* New York: Macmillan, 1963.

Ramsey, William M. *St. Paul, The Traveler and Roman Citizen.* Grand Rapids: Baker, 1965.

Reichenbach, Bruce. *The Cosmological Argument: A Reassessment.* Springfield, Ill.: Charles C. Thomas, 1972.

Reid, J. K. S. *Christian Apologetics.* Grand Rapids: Eerdmans, 1969.

Reymond, Robert L. *The Justification of Knowledge.* Philadelphia: Presbyterian and Reformed, 1976.

Richardson, Alan. *History Sacred and Profane.* London: SCM Press, 1964.

Richardson, Cyril C., ed. and trans. *Early Christian Fathers.* Philadelphia: Westminster, 1953.

Roberts, Alexander, and Donaldson, James, eds. *The Ante-Nicene Fathers*. Vol. 1. Grand Rapids: Eerdmans, 1975.

Rogers, Jack, ed. *Biblical Authority*. Waco, Tex.: Word, 1977.

Rowe, William L., and Wainwright, William J., eds. *Philosophy of Religion: Selected Writings*. New York: Harcourt Brace Jovanovich, 1973.

Schaeffer, Francis. *Escape from Reason*. Downers Grove, Ill.: InterVarsity, 1968.

————. *The God Who Is There*. Downers Grove, Ill.: InterVarsity, 1968.

————. *Death in the City*. Downers Grove, Ill.: InterVarsity, 1969.

————. *He Is There and He Is Not Silent*. Wheaton, Ill.: Tyndale, 1972.

Schleiermacher, Friedrich. *On Religion: Speeches to Its Cultural Despisers*. Translated by John Oman. New York: Harper Torchbooks, 1958.

Sherwin-White, A. N. *Roman Society and Roman Law in the New Testament*. Grand Rapids: Baker, 1978.

Smith, T. V., ed. *From Thales to Plato*. Chicago: U. of Chicago Press, 1956.

Smith, Wilbur M. *Therefore Stand*. Grand Rapids: Kregel, 1981.

Spier, J. M. *An Introduction to Christian Philosophy*. Translated by David H. Freeman. Nutley, N. J.: Craig Press, 1966.

Strong, Augustus H. *Systematic Theology*. 3 vols. in 1. Westwood, N. J.: Revell, 1962.

Tillich, Paul. *The Protestant Era*. Abridged ed. Translated by James Luther Adams. Chicago: U. of Chicago Press, 1948.

————. *Biblical Religion and the Search for Ultimate Reality*. Chicago: U. of Chicago Press, 1955.

————. *Dynamics of Faith*. New York: Harper Torchbooks, 1957.

Trueblood, D. Elton. *Philosophy of Religion*. Grand Rapids: Baker, n.d.

Underhill, Evelyn. *Mysticism*. New York: New American Library, 1955.

Unger, Merrill F. *Archaeology and the Old Testament*. Grand Rapids: Zondervan, 1954.

Van Til, Cornelius. *A Christian Theory of Knowledge*. Philadelphia: Presbyterian and Reformed, 1969.

————. *Defense of the Faith*. Rev. ed. Philadelphia: Presbyterian and Reformed, 1972.

————. *Jerusalem and Athens*. Edited by E. R. Geehan. Nutley, N. J.: Presbyterian and Reformed, 1977.

Vincent, Marvin. *Word Pictures in the New Testament*. 4 vols. Grand Rapids: Eerdmans, 1946.

von Hugel, Friedrich. *Essays and Addresses on the Philosophy of Religion*. New York: E. P. Dutton, 1921.

Vos, Howard. *Can I Trust My Bible?* Chicago: Moody, 1963.

Warfield, Benjamin B. *Calvin and Augustine.* Philadelphia: Presbyterian and Reformed, 1974.

Way of Martyrdom of Saint Polycarp, in *Early Church Fathers.* Edited and translated by Cyril C. Richardson. Philadelphia: Westminster, 1953.

Webster's New Twentieth Century Dictionary of the English Language. Unabridged. 2d ed. New York: Simon and Schuster, 1980.

Whitehead, Alfred North. *Science and the Modern World.* New York: Macmillan, 1953.

Williamson, Peter, and Perrotta, Kevin, eds. *Christianity Confronts Modernity.* Ann Arbor, Mich.: Servant, 1981.

Zaehner, Robert C. *Mysticisms, Sacred and Profane.* New York: Oxford U. Press, 1961.

ARTICLES

Augustine. *Letter 120 in Introduction to the Philosophy of Saint Augustine: Selected Readings and Commentaries.* Edited by John A. Mourant. University Park, Pa.: Pennsylvania State U. Press, 1964, pp. 47-53.

_____. *Sermon 43,* in *Introduction to the Philosophy of Saint Augustine: Selected Readings and Commentaries.* Edited by John A. Mourant. University Park, Pa.: Pennsylvania State U. Press, 1964, pp. 39-44.

_____. *Sermon 126,* in *Introduction to the Philosophy of Saint Augustine: Selected Readings and Commentaries.* Edited by John A. Mourant. University Park, Pa.: Pennsylvania State U. Press, 1964, 45-47.

Clark, Gordon. "The Axiom of Revelation." *The Philosophy of Gordon H. Clark.* Edited by Ronald H. Nash. Philadelphia: Presbyterian and Reformed, 1968, pp. 57-92.

_____. "Veridicalism Versus Presuppositionalism: A Review Article." *Journal of the Evangelical Theological Society* 24:2 (June 1981), pp. 163-71.

Dahms, John V. "How Reliable Is Logic?" *Journal of the Evangelical Theological Society* 21:4 (December 1978), pp. 369-80.

_____. "A Trinitarian Epistemology Defended: A Rejoinder to Norman Geisler." *Journal of the Evangelical Theological Society* 22:2 (June 1979), pp. 133-48.

Edwards, Paul. "The Cosmological Argument." *Philosophy of Religion: Selected Writings*. Edited by William L. Rowe and William J. Wainwright. New York: Harcourt Brace Jovanovich, 1973, pp. 136-48.

Ferre, Frederick. Editor's Introduction to *Natural Theology: Selections*, by William Paley. Indianapolis: Bobbs-Merrill, 1963, pp. xi-xxxii.

Geisler, Norman. " 'Avoid...Contradictions' (1 Timothy 6:20): A Reply to John Dahms." *Journal of the Evangelical Theological Society* 22:1 (March 1979), pp. 55-65.

————. "Avoid *All* Contradictions: A Surrejoinder to John Dahms." *Journal of the Evangelical Theological Society* 22:2 (June 1979), pp. 149-59.

Henry, Carl. F. H. "An Agenda for the 1980's." *Christianity Today* 24: 26-28.

Hick, John. "Necessary Being." *Philosophy of Religion: Selected Writings*. Edited by William L. Rowe and William J. Wainwright. New York: Harcourt Brace Jovanovich, 1973, pp. 14-27.

Mayers, Ronald. "Both/And: The Uncomfortable Apologetic." *Journal of the Evangelical Theological Society* 23, no. 3 (September 1980): pp. 231-41.

Peirce, Charles Sanders. "How to Make Our Ideas Clear." *Philosophical Writings of Peirce*. Edited by Justus Buchler. New York: Dover Publications, 1955, pp. 23-41.

Rogers, Jack. "The Church Doctrine of Biblical Authority." *Biblical Authority*. Edited by Jack Rogers. Waco, Tex.: Word, 1977, pp. 15-46.

Stace, Walter T. "The Nature of Mysticism." *Philosophy of Religion: Selected Readings*. Edited by William L. Rowe and William J. Wainwright. New York: Harcourt Brace Jovanovich, 1973, pp. 264-79.

Warfield, B. B. "Introductory Note" in *Apologetics*, by F. R. Beattie. Richmond: Presbyterian Committee on Publishing, 1903, pp. 19-32.

UNPUBLISHED MATERIAL

Spencer, Stephen. *"A Comparison and Evaluation of the Old Princeton and Amsterdam Apologetic"*. Th.M. Thesis, Grand Rapids Baptist Seminary, 1980.

Van Til, Cornelius. *"Apologetics"*. Class syllabus, Westminster Theological Seminary.

SUBJECT INDEX

PERSON INDEX

SCRIPTURE INDEX